The

Whole Life Nutrition
Cookbook

The

Whole Life Nutrition
Cookbook

Whole Foods Recipes for Personal and Planetary Health

Alissa Segersten

Tom Malterre, MS, CN

Second Edition

WHOLE LIFE PRESS

Fourteenth Printing, July 2013

Whole Life Press
Phone: **360-676-2297**
Fax: **360-671-5372**
Email: **orders@wholelifepress.com**

ISBN: **0-9798859-0-6**

ISBN-13: **978-0-9798859-0-7**

Library of Congress Control Number: **2007935036**

Cover Design: Jessica Renner, Studiohatch **www.studiohatch.com**

Cover Photographs by Alissa Segersten

Recipes from top left to bottom right:

Mexican Pink Bean Burritos, *page 261*
Creamy Cauliflower Soup, *page 162*
Raw Chocolate Hazelnut Brownies, *page 330*
Buckwheat Pancakes, *page 108*

DISCLAIMER: This book is not intended to treat or diagnose any health condition. Please seek professional help regarding any health conditions. The authors are not responsible for any adverse food or health reactions from any of the information and recipes contained herein.

This book is dedicated to
our four children,
Lily, Grace,
Sam, and Ben

and to my mother
who filled my childhood
with healthy, nourishing meals.
ALISSA

This book is dedicated to
all of our clients.

May you find
nourishment, heallng, and hope
within these pages.
TOM

Table of Contents

Acknowledgements

*F*irst, I would like to thank my family for their encouragement to create this book; my two daughters for being my recipe testers day in and day out; my parents for encouraging me to start this book in the first place and then for their continued support throughout this entire project; and of course, Tom, for his depth of knowledge on the subject of food and health which continually inspires me to create new and delicious recipes for the benefit of all.

Many thanks to all of my recipe testers. If it wasn't for you the recipes in this book would not be what they are today. I am also especially grateful to my dad and to my dear friend, Roberta Stefurak, for their tireless efforts in editing this book, your skills are much appreciated; and to my dear friend, April Brown, for testing so many of the recipes in this book and encouraging me throughout the whole process. I would also like to acknowledge my friend Jenna Boudreau, who inspired me to create many of the gluten-free recipes in this book. A very special thanks to those of you who contributed so many hours of childcare for our children. This second edition wouldn't be here if it wasn't for you! Thank you to my two Bastyr University cooking instructors, Cynthia Lair and Mary Shaw, who have inspired me to be where I am today. And a special thanks to Mary Shaw for permitting me to use some of her delicious recipes in this book.

ALISSA

I would like to acknowledge, first and foremost, that this book is mostly Ali's creation. Without her countless hours spent in the kitchen and behind the computer, this invaluable resource of healing recipes and information would not have come to fruition. Your cooking has nourished my body, and your companionship, my soul. Thank you.

For the nutrition information I contributed, I would like to thank my clients. Your need to find relief from your ailments has inspired me to relentlessly search the scientific literature for articles demonstrating the power of food as medicine. I am also especially thankful to my parents for their wisdom, love, and constant encouragement; and to my children, for giving me hope and a desire to better the lives of generations to come.

TOM

Forward

*P*roviding our clients and readers with many fabulous, well-tested, whole foods recipes is the overall goal of this book. As we began writing, we realized that adding basic information about food and health was necessary. With a wealth of information and research available, narrowing down the material into a simple, usable form was a unique challenge. We made a diligent effort to keep the information short, simple, and to the point.

The delicious, satisfying, and healing recipes offered in this book revolve around eating a plant-based diet. Cultures all over the world have eaten plant-based diets for centuries. This wise pattern of eating is based on foods such as fruits, vegetables, whole grains, beans, nuts, and seeds. Animal-based foods are eaten in smaller amounts, if at all. Eating a diet rich in plant foods promotes optimal health and has been found to be protective against many different diseases. This way of eating also protects and sustains our planet for future generations to enjoy.

In addition to eating an antioxidant-rich, plant-based diet, the current research reveals that eliminating any potential food allergens is equally beneficial to promoting optimal health. However, we should not forget that some of the longest lived, healthiest, happiest people were the ones who shared the most laughter, love, and deep connection with others at the dinner table and throughout their lives.

It is our wish that this book will inspire you to make healthy food choices for yourself and your family. We sincerely hope you might incorporate the wisdom and recipes offered here into your daily lives.

May you live in health, happiness, and joy!

Alissa Segersten
Tom Malterre
Whole Life Nutrition
Bellingham, Washington
October 22, 2006

"Let thy food be thy medicine and thy medicine be thy food"

-Hippocrates

INTRODUCTION

Welcome

*"When health is absent, wisdom cannot reveal itself,
art cannot manifest, strength cannot fight, wealth becomes useless, and
intelligence cannot be applied."*

~ Herophilus 300 BC

The diet that humans have evolved with over the last tens of thousands of years has changed drastically within the last several decades. With that change has come rising rates of obesity, childhood and adult cancers, heart disease, diabetes, chronic pain, and more. There is overwhelming evidence now that our food choices drastically affect our state of health. Humans are not meant to have high cholesterol, high blood pressure, high blood sugar, chronic pain, or other common health problems. These health conditions are primarily a result of dietary, environmental, and lifestyle factors.

Food is powerful medicine. It is energy and information. Every molecule that exists in our body was created from the food we eat, the water we drink, and the air we breathe; we quite literally are what we eat. *Whole foods*, or foods in their natural unrefined forms, offer us the vitamins, minerals, and antioxidants we need to prevent and treat most diseases while creating a state of balance and health within us. Whole grains, beans, nuts, seeds, vegetables, and fruits provide thousands of important phytochemicals that work with our bodies to maintain and build optimal health. Science is just beginning to unveil many of these compounds as researchers expect to discover over 40,000 new phytochemicals over the next decade. Eating food is so much more than a way to fill our bellies. Food affects our quality of life, how we look, how we feel, how much we weigh, how much energy we have, how we age, and how healthy we are.

The goal of this book is to provide you with a source for fabulous tasting recipes using nutritious whole foods that promote optimal health. *The Whole Life Nutrition Cookbook* was created under the premise that **food can be both healing and taste delicious**. Food is pleasure and eating is something we do all day, every day, for our entire lives. Why not create a daily diet that heals our bodies and is absolutely satisfying to all of our senses? As we partake in the joy of eating nutritious organic food, we share this joy with others and together we build a healthier community, country, and planet.

You will find an array of delicious healthful recipes in this book, **all of which are gluten-free**, with various options for using dairy and eggs in some recipes. You will also find useful information about the basics of a whole foods diet, stocking your whole foods pantry, ideas for a quick nutritious breakfast, cooking beans and whole grains, selecting and storing fresh produce, adding more vegetables to your diet, and nutritious snack ideas.

Some of the recipes in this book may be healthier versions of traditional favorites and some may be very new to you. If you feel overwhelmed and don't know where to begin, then simply begin by making a few of the recipes that look familiar to you. As your cooking repertoire builds, so will your confidence and soon you will want to try other recipes. Lasting dietary change takes time. You don't need to do it all at once. Remember that nourishing ourselves is a process and that making small changes can be enough to begin with.

How to Use This Book

"Health is a state of complete physical, mental, and social well-being, and not merely the absence of disease or infirmity."

~Constitution of the World Health Organization

*T*his book has something for everyone—from cleansing green smoothie recipes to decadent desserts. Every lifestyle can benefit from using this book. Most recipes can be adapted to fit individual needs and tastes. For example, if you have a soy sensitivity, you can still use most recipes containing soy if you adapt them. Use sea salt in place of tamari, and meat, vegetables, or beans in place of tofu or tempeh. Dairy is optional in some recipes, and corn can easily be left out of most. For those of you with blood sugar imbalances, you can use agave nectar or stevia in place of other sweeteners. See the sweetener substitution chart on *page 56*. We hope you have fun and get creative with this book.

The Whole Life Nutrition Cookbook is divided into five sections. Each section provides you with information that will guide you in making decisions on food choices to nourish your body, mind, and soul. In the back of the book we have provided a handy recipe reference guide to assist you in quickly finding recipes.

The last chapter of this section, the *Introduction*, contains information on food sensitivities, specifically to gluten, dairy, and eggs. Lists of common symptoms and diseases associated with each sensitivity are given. Case studies from Tom's private counseling practice will help you relate personally with these sensitivities.

The next section, *Eating Whole Foods* (Chapters 4 through 8), will truly help you to understand the importance of healthy food choices. Starting with Chapter 4, The Basics of a Whole Foods Diet, invaluable information is included on what whole foods are and why it is important to every cell in your body to eat a whole foods diet. For example, did you know that whole grains are an excellent source of antioxidants? Or that beans help to lower cholesterol? Then in Chapter 5, you will read information on organic food and a list of the top twelve most contaminated fruits and vegetables in the United States. This will help you to understand the importance of buying organic for both you and your family. Chapter 6 discusses the relationship between your diet and global warming and easy steps you can take to reduce the climate impact of your diet. Chapter 7 has a list of tips for making the change to a whole foods diet. Chapter 8 contains a sample menu plan, which is free of gluten, dairy, and eggs.

In the next section, *Your Whole Foods Kitchen*, you will find useful information to prepare yourself and your kitchen for eating more whole foods. If you find you are not familiar with some of the ingredients used in this book, then it might be helpful to read through Chapter 9 on stocking your whole foods pantry. Here you will find descriptions of each food item and where you would use them. Chapter 10 provides a list of useful cooking equipment to have on hand. If you are not familiar with cooking techniques, then it may be helpful to refer to Chapter 11 for definitions of each.

The Recipes include everything from breakfast to soups and salads, whole grains, vegetarian meals, meats and fish. The section ends with nutritious desserts, plus much more and is the heart and soul if this cookbook. Those who have the first edition state that they "live by" this cookbook and that "every recipe that they have tried is outstanding and their favorite!"

And finally, in the *Appendix*, you will find Hidden Sources of Gluten, a 28-Day Elimination and Detoxification Diet, and a schedule for Introducing Solid Foods to Infants, as well as measurement equivalents, allergy substitution charts, and other useful resources.

What's up with Gluten, Dairy, and Eggs?

"A journey of a thousand miles must begin with a single step"

~ Lao Tzu

Current research suggests that food allergies and sensitivities are far more common than we might have imagined. Gluten, dairy, and eggs are some of the most common foods that people can be sensitive to. The majority of clients that we see are sensitive to at least one of these food groups. Upon providing them with options that are gluten, dairy, and egg free, their lives change. The following conditions can be associated with a sensitivity to gluten, dairy, or eggs:

- Acid Reflux
- Constipation
- Diarrhea
- Chronic Headaches
- Migraines
- Sinus Problems
- Arthritis
- Eczema
- Asthma
- Irritable Bowel Disease
- Chronic Fatigue
- Hypothyroidism
- ADD / ADHD
- Type 1 Diabetes
- Gallbladder Problems
- Osteoporosis
- Dementia
- Multiple Sclerosis

What is a Food Sensitivity?

A food sensitivity can occur when the immune system considers a protein from food as being a potential threat to the body. As a response, the immune cells secrete chemicals called *inflammatory cytokines*. These chemicals are signaling molecules that alert other cells of the body of the perceived foreign invader—the food you just ate. This starts a cascade of events, which can lead to inflammation and disease in the body. The term "food sensitivity" literally means that your body is sensitive to eating a particular food. We are all biochemically unique. It seems logical that we would all respond differently to the biological chemicals in food. As world renowned nutritional biochemist Dr. Jeffrey Bland often says, "The food of one can be the poison of another."

Top 6 Food Sensitivities:

1. **Gluten**
2. **Dairy**
3. **Yeast**
4. **Eggs**
5. **Corn**
6. **Soy**

*Note: The following success stories were written by Tom regarding clients he has assisted through his nutritional counseling practice.

Case Study:

In December of 2006, Sally came into my office with a laundry list of symptoms. She had been diagnosed with asthma, acid reflux and other digestive imbalances, chronic fatigue, and a host of psychiatric disorders, including atypical bipolar disorder, anxiety, and depression. Due to Sally's chronic fatigue, she could only function for about 5 to 6 hours per day. After bouncing around from specialist to specialist for 10 years, Sally was referred to my office by her neurologist. It appeared obvious from her symptom list that she was reacting to gluten and potentially a few other food proteins. After three sessions, Sally (and her husband) reluctantly agreed to try an elimination diet (page 381) to identify possible foods that could be making her symptoms worse. On day 12 of the diet, Sally's chronic fatigue all but disappeared. Her digestive symptoms calmed, the asthma vanished, and her mood stabilized. After nine months of dietary changes, Sally is healthier than ever and experiences 15 hours of abundant energy per day as long as she avoids gluten, dairy, eggs, yeast, and soy. In addition to cooking many of the recipes from this book as daily staples, Sally also added a number of cultured and fermented foods to her diet, including kombucha, cultured vegetables, and homemade gluten-free sour dough bread. The only complaint she has now is that she needs to spend money on new clothes as she continues lose weight.

Gluten

Gluten is a protein that is found in **wheat**, **spelt**, **kamut**, **barley**, **rye**, and **sometimes oats** (oats are most often contaminated with gluten). The immune system in people who are either celiac positive or gluten sensitive perceives gluten as a foreign invader. This leads to an activation of the immune cells in the intestines when exposed to gluten. These immune cells release chemicals that can lead to the destruction of the surface, or villi, of the intestines. When the intestinal villi are damaged, there is an inability to absorb nutrients from food. This often leads to malnutrition conditions including anemia and osteoporosis. Celiac disease is a genetic condition that can be triggered by pregnancy, childbirth, viral infections, severe emotional stress, or even after a surgery.

Although many organizations say the prevalence of celiac disease is anywhere between 1 in 100 to 1 in 300, the clinical presentation is much more common. Dr. Kenneth Fine, a renowned gastroenterologist, is finding that a gluten sensitivity might be found in greater than 1 in 3 people. From our own clients, we have seen that most cases of chronic diarrhea, arthritis, chronic fatigue, and irritable bowel disease are associated with a gluten sensitivity. When our clients transition to eating foods free of gluten, most of these conditions either disappear entirely or improve considerably.

Symptoms associated with a gluten sensitivity and celiac disease:

- Gas
- Recurring abdominal bloating and pain
- Chronic diarrhea
- Nausea with or without vomiting
- Acid reflux
- Weight loss / Weight gain
- Fatigue
- Unexplained anemia
- Bone or joint pain
- Osteoporosis / Osteopenia
- Behavioral changes
- Tingling numbness in the legs (from nerve damage)
- Muscle cramps
- Seizures
- Missed menstrual periods (from malnutrition)
- Infertility / Recurrent miscarriage
- Delayed growth
- Failure to thrive in infants
- Pale sores inside the mouth, called aphthous ulcers
- Tooth discoloration or loss of enamel

- Itchy skin rash called dermatitis herpetiformis

Source: NIH Publication No. 06-4269, 2005

Gluten is found EVERYWHERE in our food supply. Baking powder can contain gluten. So can pasta, cottage cheese, soy sauce, beer, and marshmallows. In addition, non-food sources of gluten include the adhesives on stamps and envelopes. View *page 378* for a list of hidden food sources that contain gluten, or go to **www.celiac.com** and view their "Safe and Forbidden" food lists. Adhering to a gluten-free diet can be challenging. We would estimate that over 90% of our clients who attempt a gluten-free diet still consume a small source of gluten without ever knowing it. It often requires a thorough diet diary evaluation to find all the potential pitfall foods. Once these foods are replaced in a gluten sensitive individual, changes in health are often seen immediately.

Case Study:

Marian, a 58 year old busy school teacher from California, called with constant arthritis pain. She had been experiencing this pain for over 8 years and had heard that dietary changes may be able to help. Her other conditions also included carpal tunnel syndrome, trigger finger, frequent loose stools, and fatigue. Marian needed to have energy to keep up with her students. After our initial phone consultation I suspected that her symptoms indicated a potential sensitivity to gluten-containing foods. I recommended Marian try a gluten elimination diet for two weeks. After her initial two week dietary change, her symptoms and pain diminished substantially, bowel movements normalized, and she experienced increased energy. I gave Marian many of our gluten-free recipes, supplements to help heal her intestines, and continued with our phone consultations. She is now following a gluten-free diet, is living pain free, and says she feels 20 years younger.

We invite you to explore this topic further with your local health care practitioner and Gluten Intolerance Group, **www.gluten.net**. If you are interested in getting tested for a gluten sensitivity, we recommend you visit **www.enterolab.com** and view their "Gluten Sensitivity and Gene Panel Complete" test. For our clients, this test, along with an elimination diet, has proven to be the most accurate diagnostic tool for this condition. Saliva tests, blood tests, and even biopsies have not always uncovered a gluten sensitivity. For more information on celiac disease and gluten sensitivities, please visit **www.celiac.com** or **www.celiac.nih.gov**.

Dairy

For many years, cow's milk has been advertised as the elixir of health. Whether it was for strong bones, or big muscles, most of us were told to drink up. In formula, and in bottles, some of us started drinking it at birth. Because cow's milk was designed for an entirely different species of animal, a large portion of the population has an adverse reaction when consuming it. Beyond the majority of the world's population that are lactose (milk sugar) intolerant, many people also have various reactions to the proteins in cow's milk. There are at least 30 antigenic primary proteins in milk. Casein is the most commonly used milk protein in the food industry; lactalbumin, lactoglobulin, bovine albumin, and gamma globulin are other protein groups within milk. Milk proteins are listed on food labels with a variety of names such as milk solids, skim milk powder, casein, caseinates, whey, and albumin.

The feeding of cow's milk formula has been well documented to contribute to cases of eczema, colic, diarrhea, and sinus conditions in infants. When breastfeeding mothers consume dairy products, their exclusively breast-fed children may test positive to having a cow's milk protein immune reaction. Later in life, a cow's milk sensitivity can contribute to sinus conditions, asthma, eczema, headaches, arthritis, acid reflux, constipation, and other bowel problems.

Common symptoms associated with a dairy sensitivity include:

- Gas
- Abdominal bloating and pain
- Diarrhea
- Constipation
- Gastrointestinal bleeding
- Anemia
- Nausea and vomiting
- Acid Reflux
- Chronic Headaches / Migraines
- Joint pain / Arthritis
- Rhinitis
- Ear infections
- Hay fever
- Asthma
- Eczema
- Depression and mood swings
- ADHD
- Bed wetting in children

In our own practice, we have seen that by eliminating or reducing dairy products, many health conditions resolve on their own—without the use of medications. When milk antigens get through the gut mucosa intact, they may be responsible for a host of delayed immune responses which do not depend on IgE antibodies. These delayed immune responses depend on IgA and IgG antibodies and do not show up on skin prick tests. To get a test to determine if you react to dairy, look for a doctor who offers an updated ELISA blood allergy test. Visit **www.usbioteklabs.com** to learn more about this type of test and view the different blood panels available. We advise you to discuss this further with your health care provider.

Case Study:

Katie, a 2 year old girl, and her mother, Joan, came in to see me regarding Katie's asthma. Her doctor's skin prick test had identified Katie as having multiple airborne allergies, including dust, mold, and pollen. Katie also displayed behavioral problems, dark circles under her eyes, and reoccurring sinus infections. After a few visits to the emergency room, Katie's family did everything they could to eliminate the airborne allergens in their home including removing all of their carpeting and replacing it with hardwood flooring, repainting the walls, and covering all mattresses and pillows with hypoallergenic covers. After doing all of this, Katie's symptoms did not change. Katie's mother then decided to see me. I mentioned to Joan that Katie's symptoms might be associated with a dairy sensitivity. Joan was apprehensive to take cheese out of Katie's diet, considering it was her favorite food. After a few more consultations and a health food store tour, Joan felt confident that she had enough dairy-free food options for her daughter. After the second week of eating dairy-free, Katie's sinuses began to drain, and, more importantly to Joan, Katie's mood was better than it had been in the last six months. Joan now controls Katie's asthma attacks through dietary changes alone, and is grateful to have a happy, healthy daughter.

Eggs

Eggs have long been known to be one of the most common allergens in children. Current recommendations say that eggs should not be introduced into a child's diet until the age of 24 months. We have noticed that people with conditions such as eczema and migraines often improve with an egg-free diet. The four proteins in eggs that cause much of the problems are ovomucoid, ovalbumin, ovotransfferin, and lysozyme. Eggs can be an ingredient in many processed foods including glazes on pastries, ice cream, some margarines, noodles, processed meats, sauces, candy, a wide variety of ready-made foods, custards, and breads. Egg proteins can also hide in lotions, shampoos, vaccines, and in some medications. Always read labels to determine if a product contains eggs. Eggs listed on the label may appear as albumin, globulin, livetin, lysozyme, or lecithin. In addition, many people who react to hen's eggs will also react to eggs of another species, including duck and turkey.

Common symptoms associated with an egg sensitivity include:

- Abdominal bloating and pain
- Diarrhea
- Constipation
- Nausea and vomiting
- Chronic Headaches
- Migraines
- Rhinitis
- Asthma
- Dermatitis
- Eczema
- Hives
- Itching of the mouth and tongue
- Wheezing

Case Study:

Christy, a 48 year old business woman, came in to my office with chronic migraines and chronic back pain. I suspected a food sensitivity and advised her to see her doctor to get an updated ELISA blood allergy test. The test results showed positive IgG and IgE antibodies for eggs and dairy. Ali then provided cooking classes, recipes, and meal planning. After three weeks of eliminating all dairy and egg products, Christy's chronic migraines disappeared. Christy then had laboratory tests done for both vitamin D deficiency and gluten sensitivity, which both showed imbalances. She then went on a gluten-free diet and supplemented with vitamin D, and is now free of her back pain as well.

Jim, an 81 year old man from Seattle, came to see me to discuss possible dietary alternatives to help with his arthritis pain. Jim had been living with rheumatoid arthritis for 31 years and rated his pain as 7 out of 10 on the pain scale. He could not garden or walk without severe pain and was on heavy arthritic medication. I advised Jim to eliminate dairy products and decrease all animal products and refined foods. Ali gave private cooking lessons, teaching how to prepare healthy, dairy-free meals using whole foods. Jim then stopped eating all red meat, poultry, dairy, wheat, eggs, and greatly reduced his sugar and fat consumption. He and his wife went through their pantry and discarded things with trans fats, such as his favorite Ritz Crackers and soda crackers, and other items with ingredients that they couldn't pronounce. It was a traumatic experience for both of them because of the complete change in cooking style required. After about 3 months of transitioning to a dairy-free diet, with no animal products and more fruits and vegetables, Jim's pain substantially decreased to 4 out of 10 on the pain scale. Within the next few weeks his pain level went to zero. Jim is now living pain-free and enjoys gardening, taking yoga classes, dancing, and dining on delicious dairy-free whole foods.

EATING WHOLE FOODS

The Basics of a Whole Foods Diet

"The doctor of the future will give no medicine, but will instruct his patient in the care of the human frame, in diet and in the cause and prevention of disease."

~Thomas Edison

Eating a diet consisting largely of fresh, unrefined, whole plant foods every day is like consuming an arsenal of medicine with no negative side effects. Whole foods contain all of the vitamins, minerals, antioxidants, and phytochemicals we need to prevent and reverse disease and aging.

At the same time, all people are different and some do not react well to certain foods. New research has found that a whole foods, oligo-antigenic diet provides the body with all of the necessary building blocks for disease-free living and life-long health. An oligo-antigenic diet is one in which steps are taken to avoid or minimize foods that might cause a food allergy or intolerance. By eating a diet that does not irritate the immune system at every meal, people can avoid a major contributor to disease processes. An ideal diet would consist of allergen-free whole foods that are organic and locally grown.

What is a Whole Food?

Whole foods are foods that are as close to their whole or natural state as possible. If you can imagine the food growing then it is a whole food. Examples of whole foods include whole grains, dried beans, fresh vegetables and fruits, nuts and seeds, and fresh wild salmon. Whole foods have not been processed in any way which would disturb their nutrition or flavor. They are therefore free of all processing additives, such as chemical preservatives, food dyes, flavorings, solvents, and many others.

Whole foods have not had any parts removed from them. These foods retain all of the nutrients to properly digest and metabolize themselves. For example, white flour is only part of the whole wheat berry, the nutrient-rich germ and bran parts have been removed. White rice is also missing its germ and bran, and cornstarch is only part of the whole corn kernel.

By choosing whole foods, you keep things out of your body that can contribute to many health problems. For example, the flavor enhancer, MSG, is found in many foods, including processed "health foods." It can be found in yeast extract, calcium caseinate, hydrolyzed vegetable protein, and other foods. It may be difficult to have every aspect of your diet be a whole food. Small amounts of foods that are still close to their whole form can be used such as extra virgin olive oil and natural sweeteners without compromising your health.

What does a Whole Foods Diet look like?

A whole foods diet is a balanced way of eating that promotes life-long health. This way of eating emphasizes an abundance of fresh organic raw and cooked VEGETABLES, fresh organic raw and cooked GREENS, fresh organic seasonal FRUIT, WHOLE GRAINS, BEANS, and plenty of purified WATER. Nuts and seeds, unrefined oils, natural sweeteners, and sea vegetables enhance the meals with flavor and nutrition. If animal products are included at all, they appear less frequently and in lower quantities than is standard in the American diet.

Whatever combination of foods you choose, remember to emphasize *whole*, *fresh*, *organic*, *local*, and *seasonal* ingredients to the best of your ability. A whole foods diet, combined with plenty of sunshine, deep breathing, and exercise in fresh air is your key to unlocking your unbounded health and vitality.

The Whole Life Healthy Eating Guide

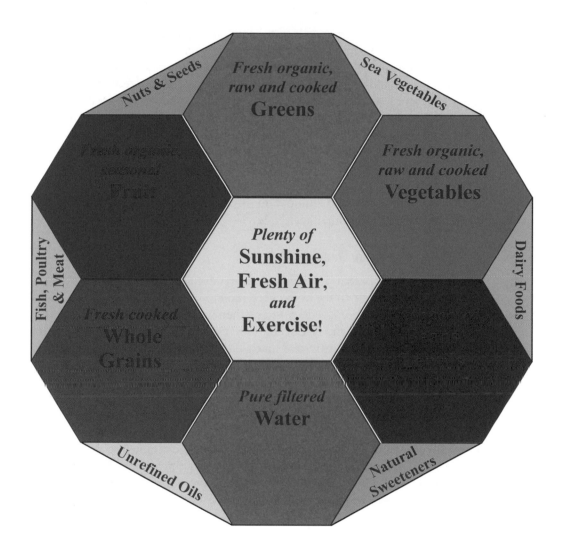

Nuts & Seeds

Sea Vegetables

Fresh organic,
raw and cooked
Greens

Fresh organic,
seasonal
Fruit

Fresh organic,
raw and cooked
Vegetables

Fish, Poultry
& Meat

Dairy Foods

Plenty of
**Sunshine,
Fresh Air,**
and
Exercise!

Fresh cooked
**Whole
Grains**

Pure filtered
Water

Unrefined Oils

Natural
Sweeteners

© 2006 Alissa Segersten & Tom Malterre MS, CN

7 Good Reasons to Eat Whole Foods:

1. **To Promote Intestinal Function**

   There are more micro-organisms in the human intestinal tract than there are known stars in the universe. Certain species of bacteria help us digest our food, repair our intestinal cells, and even calm our immune systems. Foods such as raw cultured vegetables, raw sauerkraut, unpasteurized miso, and kombucha are sources of these beneficial bacteria. Many plant foods, such as apricots, asparagus, burdock root, Jerusalem artichokes, and onions provide compounds that feed these bacteria, allowing them to flourish. In addition, whole plant foods, such as beans and whole grains, provide soluble fibers that regulate bowel function, bind to cholesterol and toxins, and slow the release of sugars into our bloodstream. As the prime spot for both the absorption of nutrients and elimination of wastes, taking care of your intestines is a key to optimal health.

2. **To Decrease Cellular Damage**

   Whole foods offer potent phtyochemicals to counteract the negative effects that free radicals have on the body. Free radicals are unstable molecules that are toxic to our cells because they attack them at the molecular level causing destruction, mutations, and cell death. Free radical damage can contribute to cancer, heart disease, arthritis, and many other diseases. Phytochemicals are naturally occurring compounds in plants. "Phyto" is the Greek word for plant. These plant chemicals have been formed by nature and work with the body to fight disease. Phytochemicals, which give plants their color, flavor, and natural disease resistance, are very powerful in preventing and treating cancer. Diet has been found to be one of the most important lifestyle factors in the development of chronic disease and has been estimated to account for up to 80% of cancers of the large bowel, breast, and prostate. Phytochemicals work within the body to prevent cell mutation while keeping cells reproducing normally. Common phytochemicals include carotenoids, flavonoids, phytosterols, isoflavones, and phenols. Phytochemicals work synergistically with other nutrients found in foods, so supplementing with these chemicals does not produce the same effect as eating them in their whole form, in *whole foods*.

3. **To Decrease Systemic Inflammation**

   Low amounts of inflammation are needed to run a healthy body. Problems arise when you take in large amounts of animal products, refined sugar, refined vegetable oils, and refined carbohydrates. These foods promote the conversion of fats, namely arachidonic acid, into pro-inflammatory compounds. Either directly or indirectly, these foods also have the ability to trigger the gene expression of hundreds of inflammatory chemicals. This can lead to an increase in pain, swelling, and cellular damage. When you are in a state of chronic inflammation, cholesterol can collect in your arteries causing damaging plaque to build up, fat is deposited in the abdominal region around your organs, and cancerous cells may replicate unchecked. An increase in inflammatory chemicals has been associated with most chronic diseases including arthritis, heart disease, diabetes, high blood pressure, osteoporosis, and various cancers. When you consume an anti-inflammatory diet, or one that comes mainly from unrefined plant foods, your body produces chemicals that cause mild, rather than excessive inflammatory reactions, which are conducive to health.

Foods and compounds that trigger and increase inflammation:

- Refined polyunsaturated oils such as sunflower, safflower, and corn
- Red meat
- Grilled and processed meats
- Refined carbohydrates and sugars
- Dairy products, especially highly processed
- Chemical additives and preservatives
- Pesticides and herbicides
- Foods to which you are allergic or sensitive to

Foods that decrease inflammation:

- Ginger, turmeric, and other spices
- Green tea, nettles, and other herbs
- Omega 3 fatty acids from wild salmon, flax, walnuts, leafy greens, and purified fish oil
- Foods rich in antioxidants such as fresh organic fruits, vegetables, and unrefined, gluten-free whole grains

4. To Support Optimum Organ Function

Whole foods work synergistically to support the entire human body. Because whole foods have not undergone any processing, they retain all of their nutrients and fibers. These components slow the release of sugar into the bloodstream as well as optimize insulin signaling, thereby allowing for normal functioning of the pancreas. Whole foods contain all of the nutrients that are needed to support your liver. Your liver is an important organ in detoxification. Supporting your liver helps to maintain a healthy weight, keeps inflammation in check, and slows down the development of many chronic diseases. Brain function also is well supported by eating whole foods. A 2006 article from *Neurology* found that eating fresh vegetables, particularly dark leafy greens, helps to keep the brain young, improves memory, and slows the mental decline that is sometimes associated with growing old by 40%. When it comes to cardiovascular health, a diet rich in beans, whole grains, raw nuts, and plenty of fruits and vegetables has comparable benefits to many cardiovascular medications.

5. To Assist with Hormonal Balance

In order to produce and metabolize hormones, our bodies need the proper ingredients to do so. Estrogen, testosterone, and even the active form of Vitamin D come from cholesterol. If our liver is functioning well, we produce all the necessary cholesterol-based hormones and still have normal cholesterol levels. The consumption of whole grains, fruits, vegetables, nuts, and beans assist with normalizing cholesterol levels in our bodies. Did you know that our liver also breaks down and transforms hormones when we are done with them? Let's look at estrogen for example. The liver has three choices when transforming the different forms of estrogen. It can transform estrogen into a helpful molecule, a harmful molecule, or a really harmful molecule. When we have certain foods in our diet, such as cruciferous vegetables (cabbage, broccoli, cauliflower, Brussels sprouts), flax seeds, soy, kudzu, green leafy vegetables, and beans, we have a tendency to transform estrogen into the beneficial form which protects our bodies. This is particularly important for women at risk with estrogen-positive cancers of the breast.

6. To Regulate the Immune System

Over 50% of your immune cells are located in your intestines with over 70% of the body's antibodies being produced there! By eating plants rich in fibers and phytochemicals that feed beneficial bacteria, you ensure a calm environment for the first stage of your immune system. According to an article in the journal *Cell* in 2004, our intestines actually sense when certain bacteria are present. When an abundance of beneficial bacteria are present, we have a tendency to have mild immune reactions throughout our bodies. If the intestines are out of balance, chemicals are sent throughout the body alerting other immune cells that there is a state of alarm. These alarm chemicals can lead to collateral damage of many cells, and increase our risk for disease. Additionally, our immune cells need to be fed just like any other cell in the body. Many of us take vitamin C to boost our immunity and decrease the intensity and duration of a cold. Eating whole foods ensures a diet rich in vitamins A, C, and E, and the minerals zinc and selenium which are all needed for optimum immune cell function.

7. To Maintain a Healthy Weight

Food is so much more than the calories it contains. It is a complex, life giving substance rich in nutrients and phytochemicals that acts in our bodies to change the way our genes are expressed. Quality is the most important factor in any healthy diet and weight loss plan, *not quantity*. By eating a whole foods diet you ensure that you are getting the highest quality foods possible and all of the nutrients you need to maintain proper functioning of vital organs and glands. Your thyroid gland for example, can become under active when you have a gluten sensitivity and a diet low in nutrients necessary for healthy thyroid function. Weight gain can be a sign of a dysfunctioning thyroid gland. In addition, cutting calories can send your body into a state of alarm, which increases your cortisol levels, telling your body to store fat. Instead of depriving yourself to reach an ideal weight and state of health, why not nourish yourself? Depriving yourself of nutritious food and calories activates something called Neuropeptide Y in your brain which tells you to search for food. It is highest in the morning, which makes sense after a night's fast. After a nutrient dense meal your stomach secretes a chemical called cholecystokinin, or CCK. CCK stimulates digestion, shuts down appetite, and stimulates the sensation of pleasure in part of your brain called the cerebral cortex. If you don't feel satisfied after a meal then your body secretes Neuropeptide Y to eat more food! Listen to your body's cues for hunger and honor them. Eating foods in their whole form helps to bring on that sense of satisfaction after a meal. When you eat a diet of processed and refined foods or foods that are not in their whole forms, your body, in its natural wisdom, craves the missing parts in your foods. Eating a whole foods diet full of high-quality, nutrient-dense foods will begin to reset your body's natural state of balance to gradually bring on your ideal weight and optimal state of health.

What do Whole Foods Have to Offer?

Greens: *Powerful Phytochemicals and Essential Minerals*

Greens are in a category of their own because they are so vital to the daily diet. Greens provide our bodies with numerous phytochemicals, including *lutein* and *beta carotene*, and the vitamins C, K, E, and folate. Dark leafy greens are also a rich source of the minerals, calcium, and iron. The roots of green leafy plants secrete acids that dissolve rocks in the soil freeing minerals such as calcium, magnesium, and iron. The roots then absorb these minerals into their leaf structures, which is why they are such a good source of minerals, such as calcium.

Phytochemicals in greens support the liver in its ability to increase the production of antioxidants, and excrete toxins from our bodies. This plays an important role in the prevention and treatment of heart disease, arthritis, cancers, cognitive decline, and many other ailments. Try to incorporate both raw and cooked greens into every meal.

Some common types of greens to include in your diet are kale, collard, cabbage, bok choy, Swiss chard, arugula, spinach, and many varieties of lettuce. Try adding greens to your smoothies and soups; use them as an alternative to tortillas to create exciting wraps; or use them with freshly made salad dressings to create refreshing salads.

Vegetables: *Potent Antioxidants and Vitamins*

Vegetables come in so many different shapes, sizes, and colors while providing our bodies with a source for many of the essential vitamins, minerals, trace minerals, essential fatty acids, and antioxidants we need on a daily basis. Dark orange and yellow vegetables such as squash, pumpkin, yams, bell peppers, and carrots are rich in *beta carotene*. Beta carotene is fat soluble and is converted to vitamin A in the liver. Beta carotene is an important antioxidant that boosts the immune system, helps prevent heart disease, protects our eyes from age related damage, and helps to prevent the formation of carcinogens at the molecular level. *Lycopene* is another carotenoid antioxidant that gives food its reddish color; it is found in high concentrations in cooked tomato products. Lycopene plays a role in preventing prostate cancer and heart disease. In fact much of the research available today shows that a diet high in vegetables greatly reduces the risk for many chronic diseases.

Eat a variety of raw and cooked vegetables. Balance your intake of sweet vegetables such as squash, yams, carrots, and potatoes with cleansing vegetables such as celery, cucumber, and bitter greens, to pungent vegetables such as onions and garlic. Try consuming at least six vegetables a day, such as three with lunch and three with dinner. Variety is key to getting your daily dose of protective phytochemicals, antioxidants, vitamins, and minerals; but for most, it will make your diet more enjoyable and sustainable over time.

Fruit: *Potent Antioxidants and Vitamins*

Who can resist the refreshing sweetness of peak-of-the-season organic fruit! Fresh raw fruit provides an easy and deliciously sweet way to consume a wide variety of important phytochemicals, antioxidants, and essential vitamins and minerals. Most fruits contain 80 to 95 percent water and adequate amounts of potassium, iron, calcium, magnesium, and high amounts of vitamin C. Many fruits are also high in soluble fiber, which helps to lower cholesterol levels, regulate blood sugar, and improve bowel function.

Fruits are a rich source of *phenols*, which are a group of natural compounds that can block enzymes which cause inflammation, inhibit tumor formation, and help to prevent cell mutations among many other things. Roughly 8,000 phenolic compounds have been identified, many of them being flavonoids. Phenols are found in high concentrations in red grapes, apples, lemons, strawberries, blueberries, and raspberries. Fruit such as kiwi, mangos, oranges, and papayas contain the carotenoid *zeaxanthin*, which improves the immune response and protects the eyes against macular degeneration. All types of berries are very high in antioxidants and bioflavonoids, which work to prevent and treat many different diseases and conditions.

When shopping, choose a wide variety of organic in season fruit. By eating fruit from all colors of the rainbow, you can be sure you're getting a wide variety of protective phytochemicals and other nutrients. Ripe, fresh fruit can be a cleansing breakfast, eaten raw as a snack, added to smoothies, or made into many fabulous desserts.

Whole Grains: *Protein, Fiber, Vitamins, and Antioxidants*

Whole grains have been a staple food in many cultures for thousands of years. They are rich in protein, fiber, and a host of essential vitamins and minerals. Whole grains provide a rich source of complex carbohydrates, which are readily converted to usable energy, making them an ideal staple for the daily diet.

Whole grains have not undergone any processing which would remove any part of them. The bran, germ, and endosperm are all intact. Refined grains retain only the endosperm or starch—the bran and germ have been removed. The bran and germ provide fiber, which slows both the digestion of starch and release of sugar into the bloodstream. Whole grains also provide trace minerals and vitamins assisting in the digestion of the carbohydrates. Fiber from whole grains has the ability to bind to cholesterol, hormones, and toxins, allowing them to be excreted from our body.

Recent research from Cornell University found that whole grains contain potent disease-fighting chemicals that have equal antioxidant values to those found in fruits and vegetables. Dr Liu, the researcher looking at these compounds in whole grains, summed it up best by saying: "Different plant foods have different phytochemicals. These substances go to different organs, tissues and cells, where they perform different functions. What your body needs to ward off disease is this synergistic effect—this teamwork—that is produced by eating a wide variety of plant foods, including whole grains."

When whole grains are refined, say into white flour or white rice, most of the fibers, phytochemicals, vitamins, and minerals are removed in the refining process. These vital substances protect us from disease. A whole grain that has been processed is easily broken down into simple sugars and then rapidly absorbed into our blood stream. When there is an extra-ordinary amount of sugar circulating in the blood, it has a tendency to stick to proteins. These altered proteins lose their normal function and may even stimulate inflammation by binding to immune cells. As stated earlier, an increase in inflammatory chemicals has been associated with many chronic diseases, including arthritis, heart disease, diabetes, high blood pressure and osteoporosis.

Each whole grain provides a unique taste and nutrient profile, so vary the grains you cook throughout the week. Remember that some whole grains contain gluten, which is a protein that many people are sensitive to. Grains and flours containing gluten include whole wheat berries, spelt berries, rye berries, kamut, barley, and triticale. Oats may contain gluten if processed in the same facility as gluten-containing grains. Gluten-free grains include brown rice, wild rice, quinoa, millet, amaranth, buckwheat, corn, and teff. For information on how to cook whole grains please see *page 212*.

Beans, Lentils, and Soy Foods: *Protein, Fiber, and Vitamins*

Beans, in addition to whole grains, have been a staple food in many cultures for thousands of years. Bean and grain dishes create some of the most exciting dishes found in ethnic cuisine.

Beans are packed with an amazing amount of beneficial amino acids, have very little fat, and no cholesterol. They are a good source of B vitamins, potassium, magnesium, and fiber. In fact, beans are often high in beneficial substances called *phytosterols*, which inhibit the absorption and formation of cholesterol in the body. They are also one of nature's best sources of fibers, which not only promote digestive health and relieve constipation, but help to bind to cholesterol and sweep it out of the intestines. These fibers also slow the absorption of glucose into the blood stream, allowing for a slow rise in blood sugar after eating, which is why eating a diet rich in beans is so helpful in preventing and treating diabetes.

Beans are also a powerful medicine for preventing and treating cardiovascular disease. Beans work to lower blood pressure because they are high in both magnesium and the amino acid L-arginine, which are potent regulators of smooth muscle relaxation in blood vessels. When the vessels can remain relaxed, blood pressure stays low.

A study in the *European Journal of Epidemiology* in 1999 examined food intake patterns and risk of death from coronary heart disease. Researchers followed more than 16,000 middle-aged men in the U.S., Finland, The Netherlands, Italy, former Yugoslavia, Greece and Japan for 25 years. Typical food patterns were: higher consumption of dairy products in Northern Europe; higher consumption of meat in the U.S.; higher consumption of vegetables, legumes, fish, and wine in Southern Europe; and higher consumption of cereals, soy products, and fish in Japan. When researchers analyzed this data, they found that beans were associated with a whopping 82% reduction in risk of death from coronary heart disease.

Choose a variety of beans, lentils, and soy foods and include them in your daily diet. Beans can be made into dips, sandwich spreads, grain and bean salads, soups, stews, and more. See *pages 140 to 143* for how to cook beans.

Nuts and Seeds: *Essential Fats, Minerals, and Protein*

Nuts and seeds are the embryos from which future plants are propagated. Nuts are the edible kernels in hard shells from trees and bushes. Seeds are edible ripened plant ovules containing an embryo. Nuts and seeds are high in protein, calcium, zinc, copper, iron, selenium, folic acid, magnesium, potassium, phosphorus, vitamin E and B2, essential fatty acids, and fiber. Brazil nuts are one of the richest sources of the mineral, selenium. Selenium boosts your ability to neutralize free radicals and is needed for proper thyroid function.

The essential fats in nuts and seeds are needed for proper cell function and brain development. Scientific research has shown that a daily portion of just one ounce of nuts rich in monounsaturated fat can reduce the risk of heart disease by up to ten percent. The nuts highest in monounsaturated fat are almonds, Brazil nuts, hazelnuts, macadamia nuts, pecans, pistachios and walnuts. Other fats in nuts known as phytosterols actually mimic cholesterol and block food-based cholesterol from being absorbed into the blood stream, lowering LDL cholesterol and further decreasing the risk of cardiovascular disease.

Raw nuts and seeds can be eaten as a quick snack or used to add flavor, texture, and beneficial fats to a wide variety of sweet and savory dishes. Raw nuts and seeds can be soaked, toasted, or lightly roasted with flavorings such as tamari and spices.

Choose a variety of fresh raw nuts and seeds, and try to use organic whenever possible.

Sea Vegetables: *Essential Minerals and Trace Minerals*

The ocean contains a host of incredible plants, called sea vegetables, or seaweed. Seaweeds have been a staple in many parts of Asia for thousands of years. Sea vegetables offer us the broadest range of minerals of any food, containing all of the minerals from the ocean which are exactly the 56 essential minerals and trace minerals that are necessary for the human body. Sea vegetables are a rich source of iodine, folic acid, and magnesium, and a good source of iron, calcium, and the B vitamins riboflavin and pantothenic acid. In addition, seaweeds contain good amounts of *lignans*, plant compounds with cancer-protective properties.

Use sea vegetables to add flavor, depth, and minerals to your recipes. Common sea vegetables include wakame, kombu, hijiki, arame, nori, and dulse.

Unrefined Oils: *Essential Fats*

In a whole foods diet, the use of certain fats and oils helps us to feel satisfied and full, thus eliminating the need to overeat and fill up on less healthful foods. Fat is needed by our cell membranes to maintain integrity and to assist in cell communication. The use of healthy fats also provides our brains with the necessary nutrients for proper cognitive function. Avoid using safflower, sunflower, soy, canola, and corn oils because they are more refined and higher in polyunsaturated fats which can feed into inflammatory pathways in the body.

The oils that we recommend using on a daily basis are organic virgin coconut oil and organic extra virgin olive oil. Virgin coconut oil contains the medium-chain triglyceride, lauric acid. Interestingly, lauric acid is the main fat found in human milk. This fat helps to destroy unwanted pathogens in the digestive tract, while promoting the growth of friendly flora. Lauric acid is readily sent to the liver to be burned for energy rather than being stored as fat in the body. Virgin coconut oil is also a rich source of disease-preventing polyphenols. This fat remains relatively stable at higher temperatures and can be used for most of your cooking needs. Extra virgin olive oil is high in monounsaturated fats and natural anti-oxidants; it can be used to make salad dressings, used for sautéing at lower temperatures, and is delicious drizzled over steamed or raw vegetables.

Natural Sweeteners: *Flavor and Minerals*

Natural sweeteners have undergone minimal processing. Unlike refined sweeteners, they retain much of the minerals and vitamins needed to properly metabolize the sugars they contain. Try using natural sweeteners in small amounts in your cooking to enhance the flavor of your dishes. Natural sweeteners also play an important role in creating nutritious desserts and snacks. Natural sweeteners include agave nectar, pure maple syrup, honey, dates, whole cane sugar, stevia, and more.

Dairy Foods: *Flavor and Protein*

Many Americans have been brought up on cow's milk. We were taught that calcium from milk will help us build strong bones. However, authors of a 2005 review article in *Pediatrics* state "we found no evidence to support the notion that milk is a preferred source of calcium." If decreasing or eliminating dairy foods from your diet leaves you concerned about not getting enough calcium, consider eating dark green leafy vegetables. After all, this is where the cows get their calcium. In addition, when you decrease your animal protein consumption, you decrease your need for calcium.

Although dairy foods are not a necessary part of the human diet, they have been a part of our cultural and culinary history for many years. If you desire, dairy foods can be used in small amounts in your dishes to enhance the overall flavor. This is how dairy has traditionally been used in cultures throughout the world. Milk was used raw and cultured and consumed in much smaller quantities than westernized countries consume today. Modern processing of milk makes it difficult to digest and utilize. Commercial dairy products also contain high levels of residual pesticides and herbicides from the food that the animals consume. These chemicals, which are stored in their fatty tissues, are mobilized through the blood stream and into the mammary glands when milk is produced. Non organic, commercial milk also contains detectable levels of antibiotics used on the animal as well as many other environmental contaminants. In addition, fat from conventionally produced milk harbors as much as 400 times as many pesticides found in non-organic fruits and vegetables. Butter, being entirely milk fat, is one of the most concentrated sources of the toxins DDT and PCBs.

Many people consume a high amount of commercial dairy foods, which may be contributing to the current chronic disease problem we face in our western culture. Furthermore, many people are sensitive or allergic to dairy foods and have symptoms ranging from joint pain to migraine headaches. If you do choose to eat dairy, choose cultured and/or raw products made from the milk of cows, goats, or sheep raised on organic pastures and treated in an ethical fashion. Many health food stores and co-ops now sell organic raw and cultured dairy products. Check your local store for availability.

Meat, Poultry, Fish, and Eggs: *Protein and Essential Fats*

Some organically raised animal products can be a very healthy part of a whole foods diet when consumed in small quantities alongside a large serving of fresh vegetables.

Problems arise when these foods become staples in the diet. Red meat is especially problematic because it increases your risk for heart disease and cancer. Most meat, poultry, and fish can contain a significant amount of residual agricultural chemicals which are stored in the fatty tissues of the animal. Additionally, cured meats such as hot dogs, ham, bacon, sausages, and jerky, contain sodium nitrates and/or nitrites that when eaten, react in the stomach with amino acids to form highly carcinogenic compounds called *nitrosamines*. These compounds pose a significant cancer risk to humans, especially children, and should be avoided at all times.

If you choose to eat meat, eat it less often and keep your portion sizes small. Wild game and organic grass-fed meat and poultry are excellent choices when it comes to consuming meat. Wild game contains much less saturated fat than domesticated beef, and both wild game and organic grass fed meats contain higher amounts of omega-3 fatty acids and conjugated linoleic acid (CLA). Omega-3 fatty acids and CLA assist your body in regulating weight and cholesterol. Meat and poultry are excellent sources of protein, vitamin B12, zinc, and selenium. There are many organic farms raising animals in an ethical and healthful fashion. Find a local farm that raises grass-fed beef and organic free-range chickens and buy from them. Your local co-op or health food store may also be a good place to look.

Heavy metals, such as mercury, and PCB's are among some of the chemicals that can be found in significant levels in many fish. PCB's, or polychlorinated biphenyls, are neurotoxic, hormone-disrupting chemicals that have been banned in the U.S. since 1977. Avoid farmed salmon as it is likely the most PCB-contaminated protein source in the U.S. food supply. According to a study published in *Science* in January 2004 these chemicals were found at levels seven times higher in farmed salmon than in wild ones. Also, avoid consuming tuna, swordfish, shark, king mackerel, and tilefish as these fish also contain high levels of pollutants. For more information visit **www.gotmercury.org**.

When buying fish, choose fish from a sustainable fishery in Alaska. Wild fish from Alaska are less polluted than fish from other parts of the world. Wild salmon is an ideal choice when it comes to consuming fish. It is an excellent source of DHA and EPA, two fatty acids that lead into anti-inflammatory pathways in the body. These healthy fats are cardio-protective as well as promote proper brain development in infants and children. A 2005 article from *Archives of Neurology* found that consuming DHA-rich fish at least once a week was associated with a ten percent per year slower rate of cognitive decline in elderly people. Your local co-op or health food store is a good place to shop for fish. You can also call your local fish market and ask them where their fish comes from.

When buying eggs, choose eggs produced from a local certified organic company. Look for Grade AA as these are the freshest grade of eggs. Chickens raised in their natural habitat and left to peck at wild grasses, mosses, and bugs will produce rich, nutritious eggs—very different from commercial factory farmed eggs. Your local egg company may also add flax seeds to the chickens' diet. This makes the eggs a rich source for DHA, an important fat needed for many things in the body including proper cognitive development in developing fetuses, babies, and children.

In short, eat less animal foods and rely more on plant foods. When you do eat animal foods, first and foremost choose organic. Wild Alaskan fish, grass-fed meats and poultry, and local fresh eggs, are excellent choices. Portion sizes need not be larger than three to four ounces a day, or about the size of a deck of cards.

Water: *Detoxification, Lubrication, and Assimilation*

Drinking plenty of pure water throughout the day instead of soft drinks, juice drinks, and coffee will improve your health substantially. Every cell in our body needs water to survive. Water is used in the body to flush out waste and toxins, lubricate tissues and joints, and to help assimilate the food we eat.

Pure water is increasingly difficult to find. Most of our water supply is full of potentially toxic and dangerous chemicals. Not only are chlorine and fluoride routinely added, but a wide range of toxic and organic chemicals can be found in our drinking water. These are largely agricultural and industrial wastes including PCB's, pesticide residues, nitrates, and the heavy metals lead, mercury, arsenic, and cadmium.

Our bodies need about 64 ounces of *pure* water each day. That's about eight glasses. But what constitutes pure? Tap water contains chlorine which increases free radical damage in the body, contributes to certain forms of cancer, and increases the risk for hypertension. Chlorine also contributes to magnesium deficiency while increasing urinary excretion of calcium and phosphorus, thus increasing the risk of osteoporosis. Mineral-rich, rural well-water would be an ideal option if the risk for agricultural chemical contamination wasn't so high. Well-water is so rich in minerals, especially magnesium and calcium, that drinking it is like taking a mineral supplement every day.

Is there a middle ground? Yes, installing an under-the-sink water filtration system would be ideal. Most systems use a solid carbon block filter, which effectively removes chlorine, bacteria, pesticides, and other organic chemicals, yet maintains dissolved minerals such as calcium and magnesium. Filling up reusable water jugs at your local co-op or health food store is a great option if you cannot invest in a home filtration system. These filters are typically the reverse osmosis type, which remove almost all contaminants and dissolved minerals.

It is important to make purified water consumption a regular daily habit. Make sure to use purified water for all of your cooking needs, including the soaking of beans and nuts, the cooking of grains, and the steaming of vegetables.

Sunshine, Fresh Air, Exercise: *Bone Mineralization and Happiness*

The sun is the source for all life on this planet; it connects us to our food, the earth, and life itself. Take time to enjoy its warmth, to watch it bring forth new life, and to let its energy radiate from within you.

The sun gives us vitamin D, a chemical that is actually produced in our bodies when we expose our skin to the sun. Upon exposure to sunlight, a substance within our skin is changed into pre-vitamin D. Our liver and kidneys convert this pre-vitamin D to its active hormone form. The hormone vitamin D binds to portions of our cells, called receptors, which allows for normal gene expression and cellular function. Research shows that vitamin D plays a role in thyroid function, prostate and breast cancer, cardiovascular disease, autoimmune diseases, arthritis, irritable bowel disease, as well as osteoporosis. In addition to maintaining normal blood calcium and phosphorus levels, active vitamin D also calms inflammation which allows for these minerals to stay in the bones. At latitudes above the 35th parallel from about October through April, the sun's rays are at angles that are insufficient to produce significant vitamin D synthesis in our bodies. Also, in the summertime, sunscreens with a sun protection factor of 8 or greater will block UV rays that produce vitamin D. Natural food sources of vitamin D include cod liver oil, wild salmon, and egg yolk; though supplementation is usually needed in the winter months.

Breathing fresh air during deep breathing or exercising relaxes our bodies, clears our minds, and connects our spirits to our life force. Breathing in deep, we take in life— oxygen—which energizes our cells and increases our metabolism. Oxygen is needed at the cellular level to properly metabolize the energy from our food. Exercise increases your heart rate and breathing, thereby increasing your blood flow to bring needed nutrients to every cell in your body. Exercise builds muscle mass which is needed to maintain an optimum metabolism and healthy weight. In addition, daily exercise, in combination with sun exposure or vitamin D supplementation, increases bone mineralization, thus significantly decreasing the risk for osteoporosis later in life. Daily exercise and fresh air provide a deep sense of relaxation. In this state you will be able to reconnect with your body more easily.

Organics, Your Health, and the Planet

"The criteria for a sustainable agriculture can be summed up in one word—permanence—which means adopting techniques that maintain soil fertility indefinitely, that utilize, as far as possible, only renewable resources; that do not grossly pollute the environment; and that foster biological activity within the soil and throughout the cycles of all the involved food chains."

~ Lady Eve Balfour

Organically grown food is an earth-friendly and health-supportive method of farming and processing foods. Weeds and pests are controlled using environmentally sound practices that sustain our personal and planetary health. Organic farming methods were the only ways of farming ever used until the early 1920's, when synthetic pesticides, herbicides, fungicides, and large scale growing techniques were developed. After the Second World War, these techniques were largely in place and the American landscape of small, earth-friendly family farms began to change.

Conventional farming methods adversely affect soil quality, water purity, biodiversity, health of farm workers, survival of small family farms, and the taste and nutritional quality of food. Toxic chemical residues from conventional farming remain in the soil for many years and leech into the groundwater. DDT, a pesticide that is a known carcinogen, which has long been banned in the United States, is still found in our soils. Chemicals from industrial farming include not only pesticides but also heavy metals such as lead and mercury, and solvents such as benzene and toluene. Heavy metals can directly damage nerves, affecting brain function, and possibly contribute to disorders like autism and ADD, and diseases like Parkinson's, Multiple Sclerosis, and Alzheimer's. Solvents damage the immune system, which decreases our ability to resist infections.

For every action there is an equal or greater reaction. We are allowing millions of tons of chemicals to be sprayed on or around our food every single year. As time passes, we realize that many of the chemicals we imagined to be harmless are not harmless at all. What is worse is that we are getting bombarded by over 70,000 different chemicals throughout our lifetime. Eating organic foods dramatically lowers a child's exposure to dangerous chemicals. A study funded by the United States Environmental Protection Agency found that eating organic foods provides children with immediate protection from dangerous organophosphate pesticides, which can cause harmful neurological damage. In 2005, a study was published showing the presence of over 200 chemicals in the umbilical cord blood of newborn infants. From flame retardants and Teflon to pesticides, all the children tested had been exposed to potentially harmful chemicals even before they were born. An article in *Lancet* in November 2006, warned of the potential effects these chemicals might be having on the developing brains of our children. The authors suggested that this overwhelming exposure to chemicals might be causing a "silent pandemic" of brain disorders. If our children really are our future, we might want to invest in organics.

Definition of Organic in the United States:

As of October 21, 2002, all agricultural farms and products claiming to be organic must be guaranteed by a USDA approved independent agency and must meet the following guidelines:

- Abstain from the application of prohibited materials (including synthetic fertilizers, pesticides, and sewage sludge) for 3 years prior to certification and then continually throughout their organic license.

- Prohibit the use of genetically modified organisms and irradiation.

- Employ positive soil building, conservation, manure management and crop rotation practices.

- Provide outdoor access and pasture for livestock.

- Refrain from antibiotic and hormone use in animals.

- Sustain animals on 100% organic feed.

- Avoid contamination during the processing of organic products.

- Keep records of all operations.

Organic farming produces nutrient-rich, fertile soil, which nourishes the plants and keeps chemicals such as pesticides, fungicides, and fertilizers off the land to protect water quality and wild life. Organic farming gives us food that is safer to eat and much more likely to keep us healthy. Research shows that organic food contains substantially higher levels of vitamins, minerals, and phytochemicals than non-organic food. For example, you would need to eat four conventionally grown carrots today to get the same amount of magnesium that you could get from one carrot in 1940.

Organic food often costs slightly more, on average, than conventionally grown food. This is because the cost of production is often higher, the farming methods tend to be more labor intensive, and yields may be less than their conventional counterparts. However, if we were to consider all of the unseen, indirect costs of conventional farming, we would find that industrial farming costs us more than organic farming. Factors such as high health care expenses for conventional farm workers, clean-up efforts for polluted waterways, rivers, and lakes, and the loss of quality top soils would all need to be taken into account when comparing the cost of conventional to organically grown foods. If researchers are correct in finding that autism, Parkinson's disease, Alzheimer's disease, and many cancers are increasing due to our exposure to environmental chemicals, then no price savings at the grocery store could justify the purchasing of chemically grown foods.

The Top 12 Fruits and Vegetables to Buy Organic:

Environmental Working Group, a non-profit organization, created "The Shoppers Guide to Pesticides in Produce." The guide is based on the results of nearly 43,000 tests for pesticides on produce collected by the U.S. Department of Agriculture and the U.S. Food and Drug Administration between 2000 and 2004. The following list contains the top 12 most pesticide contaminated fruits and vegetables in America, or "The Dirty Dozen." For more information please visit **www.ewg.org.**

1. **Peaches**
2. **Apples**
3. **Sweet Bell Peppers**
4. **Celery**
5. **Nectarines**
6. **Strawberries**
7. **Cherries**
8. **Pears**
9. **Grapes (imported)**
10. **Spinach**
11. **Lettuce**
12. **Potatoes**

Organic food products are grouped into these categories:	
"100% Organic"	For a food product to be 100% organic it must be made with 100% organic ingredients to be able to bear the USDA organic seal. The food product also must have an ingredient list and list who the certifying agency is.
"Organic"	In order for a food product to be labeled as "organic" and bear the USDA organic seal, the product must be made from at least 95% ingredients and have an ingredient statement on the label where organic ingredients are listed as organic. Information on the certifying agency also needs to be listed.
"Made with Organic Ingredients"	To claim this statement, a food product must be made with at least 70% organic ingredients and have an ingredient statement on the label where organic ingredients are listed as organic. Information on the certifying agency also needs to be listed.
"Some Organic Ingredients"	Food products with less than 70% organic ingredients cannot bear the USDA seal nor have information about a certifying agency, or any reference to organic content.

Diet and Global Warming

"Nothing will benefit human health and increase chances for survival of life on Earth as much as the evolution to a vegetarian diet."

~Albert Einstein

Global warming is a significant problem that is currently affecting our entire planet. Over the past 100 years, the earth has heated up by about one degree Fahrenheit, and scientists say that by the year 2100 the earth's average temperature could rise between 2.5 and 10 degrees Fahrenheit. This is because the natural layer of greenhouse gases in our atmosphere has thickened due to the Industrial Revolution. The fossil fuels we burn to run our cars, trucks, factories, planes, and power plants have created additional quantities of natural greenhouse gases plus chlorofluorocarbons and other gases. The natural greenhouse gases trap heat from the sun and make the earth warm enough for us to live on; though now we have exceeded the amount of emissions the Earth's capacity has to remove them and are creating an extra-thick heat blanket around the Earth. Scientists say this will lead to an increase in catastrophic natural disasters, such as more frequent and intense hurricanes, flooding, storms, and drought.

We now stand at a tipping point. We can continue with our actions that are causing global warming or we can change them. Many of us don't know that eating meat is a significant contributor to the global warming crisis. Cattle farms, as well as chickens, turkeys and pigs raised in factory farms, produce millions of tons of carbon dioxide and methane gas per year. Both the burning of fossil fuels during food production and the methane emissions from animal waste contribute to global warming. In fact, scientists report that every molecule of methane is more than 20 times as effective as carbon dioxide in trapping heat in our atmosphere. The July 2005 issue of *Physics World* states: "The animals we eat emit 21 percent of all the carbon dioxide that can be attributed to human activity." And statistics from the Environmental Protection Agency show that animal agriculture is the single largest cause of methane emissions in the U.S. Additionally, rainforests are being clear-cut at an extremely rapid rate for cattle farming. Rainforests are called the "lungs of the earth" because they remove massive amounts of carbon dioxide while emitting large amounts of life-supporting oxygen.

Changing to a plant-based diet can be more beneficial in solving the global warming crisis than switching to an energy efficient car. In fact, a calorie of animal protein requires more than 10 times as much fossil fuel input—releasing more than 10 times as much carbon dioxide—than does a calorie of plant protein. This doesn't mean you need to be a strict vegetarian or vegan to make a difference, just start eating less meat and you've already made a difference!

5 Ways to Reduce the Climate Impact of your Diet:

1. **Eat Less Meat**

   A UN report revealed in November of 2006 that livestock farming produces 18 percent of greenhouse gas emissions, and University of Chicago researchers reported that the average meat-heavy American diet produces a ton and a half more greenhouse gases per year than a vegetarian diet. Switching to a more plant-based diet reduces grazing-related deforestation, methane emissions from livestock, and many other climate-change factors associated with raising meat.

2. **Grow Your Own Food**

   According to WorldWatch, an independent research institute for environmental sustainability, US food typically travels more than 1,500 miles from farm to plate, racking up huge climate costs through the burning of fossil fuels for transportation. Growing your own is as local as you can get, with next to zero climate impact. For more information please visit **www.worldwatch.org**.

3. **Buy Local, Organic Food**

   Visit farmers' markets or join a community supported agriculture (CSA) project. Find local sources of food by searching for your city or zip code at **www.localharvest.org**.

4. **Talk to Your Supermarket**

Ask your grocer to carry more local, organic products. Fill out a comment card when you shop, or speak to the manager, and ask your family and friends to do the same.

5. **Bring Local, Organic Food to Schools**

Nineteen states already have established "farm to school" programs to reduce the transportation impact of school lunches and to support local economies. Get active with your state's program or help establish a new program by checking out the resources at **www.farmtoschool.org**.

Source: February 2007 Co-op America Newsletter, **www.coopamerica.org**

Making the Change

"Peace begins with each of us taking care of our bodies and minds everyday"

~Thich Nhat Hanh

Respect yourself for where you are right now in your dietary habits. And if you are reading this book, then your path toward better health is already changing. Living and eating a whole foods diet is not a strict diet. The needs of our bodies, our tastes, and our health are ever-changing. We encourage you to listen to your body's own wisdom when choosing foods for your daily meals. Select foods that give you the most energy, the clearest thinking, the best digestion, the preferred flavors of the moment, and the most overall satisfaction.

Honoring your body and eating with awareness will help to reawaken your mind-body connection. Love yourself by beginning to cultivate thoughts that the food you are consuming is deeply nourishing you. Your gut, or digestive tract, is lined with many nerves, almost as if your digestive system has its own brain. The foods you eat relay messages to your brain through your nervous system. Pay attention to the messages it sends you. Listen to the subtleties of desire for certain foods and flavors. Once you become accustomed to doing this you will regain your inherent gut wisdom and eat foods throughout the days, months, and years which will truly nourish you.

Moving to a whole foods diet can take time. Remember to start small; small changes actually create more lifelong change. Start by cooking one or two recipes in this book each week, then move up to a whole meal, then maybe a few meals a week. As you become more familiar with whole foods and how to prepare them you will naturally want to do more.

Keeping your cooking and eating environment clean and harmonious will help you find your rhythm in preparing and eating whole meals. Your outer environment, or your living space and the people you dine with, is as much a part of your health as the food you eat. Keep your kitchen clean and work to reduce your stress. If preparing an entire meal seems stressful to you then don't do it. Begin with something very simple, maybe just a pot of cooked whole grains or a pot of soup. The more you sit down, relax, and enjoy your meals, especially if you are dining with family and friends, the more fulfilled you will feel by your meals. Food is pleasure, enjoy it to the fullest!

Clear your kitchen and pantry of old and unhealthy foods so it will be easy to follow the messages of your gut wisdom. Enjoy the entire process of meal preparation including shopping for, preparing, eating, and cleaning up afterwards. Every meal is a celebration of life, the seasons, and rhythms of nature. Enjoy being alive and having the opportunity to eat!

Tips for Making the Change:

- **Create a menu plan**—start with 3 days on your menu, then try 5 days the following week. Include recipes and ideas for breakfast, lunch, dinner, and snacks.

- **Make a grocery list** every time you go to the store. It can be overwhelming to walk into a store and decide what foods to buy. After you have made a meal plan, write down all the ingredients you will need for those meals. Include in your shopping list any staple foods you might need.

- **Plan ahead for the following days**—if you have leftovers from dinner, then pack them in a to-go-container for the next day's lunch.

- **Sunday morning breakfast leftovers** can be used for quick breakfasts on Monday and Tuesday mornings.

- **Utilize portions of the previous night's dinner** for the next night's meal.

- **Cook a few different pots of beans** on the weekend to use throughout the week; portions of cooked beans can also easily be frozen for later use.

- **Freeze portions of soups, stews, and casseroles** into small reusable containers. Many of the recipes in this book make large batches—it is much easier to cook a larger batch of a recipe than to cook multiple recipes every day. Once you begin cooking and freezing your freezer will soon be stocked with healthy homemade ready-to-go meals.

- **Utilize the deli at your local co-op or health food store** to buy wholesome prepared bean and grain dishes, vegetable dishes, fresh soups and salads.

- **Get together with others** making dietary transitions or with friends who have already done so. It will be fun to share recipes and meal ideas.

- **Take a guided tour of your local co-op or health food store** to familiarize yourself with many of the ingredients used in this book.

- **Take a cooking class** at your local co-op or health food store. You can learn to prepare, cook and ultimately *taste* unfamiliar foods you are curious about.

- **Let your creativity flow** and try developing your own tantalizing combinations of beans, whole grains and vegetables.

Sample 7 Day Whole Foods Menu

*"One cannot think well, love well, and sleep well,
if one has not dined well."*

~ Virginia Woolf

Creating a whole meal is a work of art—a beautiful balance of colors, flavors, textures, and nutrients. Use the freshest *whole*, *local*, and *organic* ingredients for your meals. Choose foods for your meals that follow the *seasons*. Eating with the seasons helps you to become more in tuned with the natural cycles of the earth and life itself. As you become more familiar with whole foods begin experimenting to find your perfect balance of meal components. Create meals around whole grains, vegetables, and beans. Use meat dishes to accent the rest of your meal if you choose.

If you need to snack between meals, utilize fresh seasonal organic fruit, fresh raw vegetables, and raw nuts and seeds to keep you fueled and energized during the day. Drink purified water throughout the day or try a cup of green or herbal tea. Remember this is just a sample menu. In reality we would utilize either the previous day's leftovers to create meals for the next day or use previously frozen homemade meals to decrease time spent in the kitchen.

The following menu is **free of gluten, dairy, and eggs** to give you an example of the abundance of recipes one can choose from while cooking without these three food groups.

Sunday:

Breakfast
Tofu Scramble, *page 112*
Home Style Potatoes, *page 117*
Breakfast Greens, *page 119*
Peachy Millet Flour Muffins, *page 137*

Lunch
Fresh Vegetable Platter (try cauliflower, carrots, celery, red bell peppers, broccoli)
Hummus, *page 297*
Mediterranean Quinoa Salad, *page 233*

Dinner
Spiced Citrus Salmon, *page 275*
Mango Salsa, *page 307*
Steamed Vegetables with Lemon Garlic Dressing, *page 204*
Lemon Millet Patties, *page 237*
Blueberry Fruit Pie with Raw Nut Crust, *page 334*

Monday:

Breakfast
Minty Green Smoothie, *page 97*
Slice of rice bread spread with raw almond butter

Lunch
Vegetarian Chipotle Chili, *page 159*
Sticky Brown Rice, *page 214*
Arugula Salad with Lime Vinaigrette, *page 177*

Dinner
Sunny Sunflower Seed Burgers, *page 263*
Oven Fries, *page 205*
Cherry Apple Pudding with Almond Cream, *page 320*

Tuesday:

Breakfast
Spiced Apple and Rice Cereal, *page 105*

Lunch
Chicken Noodle and Vegetable Soup, *page 166*
Brown Rice Bread, *page 122*
Autumn Harvest Salad, *page 178*

Dinner
Shiitake Tofu, *page 245*
Lettuce and Cabbage Salad with Creamy Ginger Dressing, *page 183*
Apricot Fruit Gel, *page 324*

Wednesday:

Breakfast
Buckwheat Pancakes, *page 108*
Lemony Cabbage and Cranberry Smoothie, *page 98*

Lunch
Steamed Salmon, Spinach, and Fennel Salad, *page 186*
Pumpkin Spice Bread, *page 127*

Dinner
Fragrant Lentil Soup, *page 148*
Winter Quinoa Salad, *page 236*
Beet and Fennel Salad with Orange Vinaigrette, *page 179*
Dried Fruit Compote with Cashew Cream, *page 323*

Thursday:

Breakfast
Glorious Morning Fruit Bowl, *page 100*
Cherry Almond Smoothie, *page 96*

Lunch
Creamy Butternut Squash Soup, *page 161*
Quinoa and Black Bean Salad, *page 234*

Dinner
Curried Vegetables, *page 203*
Red Lentil Dal, *page 154*
Indian Fried Rice, *page 222*
Chocolate Banana Iced Nut Cream, *page 345*

Friday

Breakfast
Morning Millet Cereal, *page 103*
Fresh Sliced Peaches and Raw Almond Butter to top cereal

Lunch
Tempeh Fajitas, *page 252*

Dinner
Wild Salmon with Lemon, Garlic, and Thyme, *page 277*
Cooked Quinoa, *page 217*
Beet, Kale, and Walnut Salad, *page 189*
Zesty Lemon Tart, *page 333*

Saturday

Breakfast
Tofu and Arame Scramble, *page 113*
Root Vegetable Pancakes, *page 111*
Minty Green Smoothie, *page 97*

Lunch
Roasted Red Pepper Soup, *page 164*
Fresh Vegetable Platter (try cut up carrots, celery, cucumber, red bell peppers)
White Bean and Roasted Red Pepper Dip, *page 298*

Dinner
Sensuous Vegan Vegetable and Bean Enchiladas, *page 266*
Spanish Rice, *page 225*
Arugula Salad with Lime Vinaigrette, *page 177*
Raw Chocolate Hazelnut Brownies, *page 330*

YOUR WHOLE FOODS KITCHEN

Stocking your Whole Foods Pantry

"Whenever you are sincerely pleased, you are nourished. The joy of the spirit indicates its strength. All healthy things are sweet-tempered."

~ Ralph Waldo Emerson

It will be helpful for you to have some of the following items on hand to make most of the recipes in this book. Using fresh ingredients will enhance your recipes and benefit your health. Go through your cabinets, pantry, refrigerator, and freezer and discard any old spices, vinegars, oils, grains, beans, nuts and seeds, old and rancid oils, vinegars and condiments which contain chemical preservatives and any old or unhealthy items you may have hiding in your kitchen. Use the following list to restock your kitchen with fresh, healthful ingredients for your meals. Begin by adding a few items that you think you will use most often and then gradually add more as your cooking repertoire builds. Once your pantry is well-stocked with whole foods you will find that it is easy to prepare nutritious meals and snacks for yourself and your family.

Unrefined Oils:

It is important to discard any old oils and replace them with a few healthful fats and oils. Fats and oils easily become rancid if stored for long periods of time. Only a few oils are needed on hand to use for all of your cooking needs. Store the following oils in a dark place, away from heat or light.

□ **Organic Extra Virgin Olive Oil**

Extra virgin olive oil, which is high in heart-healthy monounsaturated fats and natural anti-oxidants, is made from the first cold-pressing of ripe olives. When purchasing olive oil, look for unfiltered olive oil as it retains more nutrients then its filtered counterpart. Extra virgin olive oil is good for light sautéing and works very well in salad dressings, dips, and spreads. Sometimes I prefer the flavor of olive oil to that of coconut oil for some roasting and therefore I use it occasionally at a higher temperature.

□ **Organic Unrefined Virgin Coconut Oil**

Lauric acid is the main fat found in coconut oil, which helps to keep our digestive system healthy. Virgin coconut oil can be used for most of your cooking needs, from baking to sautéing, since it remains relatively stable at higher temperatures.

□ **Organic Palm Shortening**

Palm shortening is derived from palm oil. Palm oil comes from the tropical palm tree, elaeis guineensis, which is native to tropical areas of Africa. Palm oil is a mixture of saturated and unsaturated fatty acids, with most of the unsaturated fat being monounsaturated fat. Palm shortening is palm oil that has some of its unsaturated fats removed, giving it a very firm texture and high melting point. Organic palm shortening is trans-fat free and a great replacement for butter in biscuits, shortbreads, scones, pie crusts, and other desserts. Two brand names of this product are Tropical Traditions and Spectrum.

□ **Organic Toasted Sesame Oil**

Sesame oil is very high in linoleic acid, one of the two essential fatty acids our bodies cannot produce. Research has shown that diets high in sesame oil can lower cholesterol. Unrefined sesame oil contains an antioxidant called sesamol which protects it from becoming rancid. Sesamol has been found to inhibit the damage caused by free radicals on our DNA. We like to use sesame oil in salad dressings, marinades, sauces, and as a garnish for stir-fries.

□ **Hot Pepper Sesame Oil**

Hot pepper oil is delicious added to miso soup, sauces, salad dressings, or used to garnish dark leafy green dishes.

Vinegars:

Vinegars and cooking wines are secret ingredients that will help your meals shine. Used as a garnish at the end of cooking time, they enhance the natural flavor and sweetness in foods, especially bitter greens. Store your vinegars in a dark place, away from heat or light.

□ **Organic Raw Apple Cider Vinegar**
Raw apple cider vinegar is highly regarded for its healing, cleansing, and energizing properties. It is made from the juice of fresh, crushed, organically grown apples and allowed to age in natural wooden barrels. Apple cider vinegar is very tangy and can be used in salad dressing or sprinkled on steamed vegetables. One tablespoon can be taken before meals to increase digestion and absorption of food.

□ **Organic Seasoned Brown Rice Vinegar**
Brown rice vinegar is made by an alcohol fermentation of mashed brown rice. It then undergoes another fermentation to produce vinegar. To create seasoned brown rice vinegar, organic grape juice concentrate and sea salt are added. Brown rice vinegar is more acidic than other vinegars. It is delicious added to stir-fries, salad dressings, and marinades. It compliments tamari very well and is widely used in Asian cooking.

□ **Organic Red Wine Vinegar**
The word "vinegar" is derived from the Old French *vin aigre*, meaning "sour wine." Red wine vinegar is produced by fermenting red wine in wooden barrels. This produces acetic acid, which gives it that distinctive vinegar taste. Red wine vinegar has a characteristic dark red color and red wine flavor. It is delicious used in salad dressings, sauces, soups, and marinades.

□ **Organic White Wine Vinegar**
White wine vinegar is a pale and moderately tangy vinegar made from a various blend of white wines. The wine is fermented, aged, and filtered to produce a vinegar with a slightly lower acidity level, making it milder that other vinegars. It is great added to dips to create a little more tang; it can also be used in salad dressings, sauces, and marinades. A dash or two of wine vinegar added at the end of cooking time to soups and stews deepens the flavors.

□ **Organic Balsamic Vinegar**
Balsamic Vinegar is a thick, aromatic vinegar made from concentrated grape must. Grape must is the freshly pressed juice of the grape which also contains pulp, skins, stems, and seeds. The must is then boiled down to a sap and aged in wooden barrels for six months to twelve years. Some very expensive balsamic vinegars are aged up to 25 years.

□ **Ume Plum Vinegar**
Ume Plum Vinegar is made from ume plums, water, sea salt, and the shiso leaf. Traditionally used in macrobiotic cooking, ume vinegar can be used in salad dressings, miso soup, dips, or sprinkled over sautéed dark leafy greens. Ume plum vinegar is very salty, and therefore can be used as a salt substitute.

☐ **Sherry Vinegar**
   Sherry vinegar has a deep, complex flavor and a dark reddish color. It is made from three different white grape varieties grown the Jerez region in Spain. Most of the Sherry vinegar produced comes from this region making it a popular ingredient in Spanish cooking. Sherry vinegar can be used in salads, sauces, and whole grain dishes. Balsamic or red wine vinegar can replace sherry.

Salts and Salt Seasonings:

Salt brings depth to the food it is cooked with. Conventional salt production uses chemicals, additives, and heat processing to reach the final end product we call table salt. Unrefined sea salt, on the other hand, contains an abundance of naturally occurring trace minerals. Tamari is another great salt seasoning that works well as a replacement for traditional soy sauce.

☐ **Unrefined Sea Salt**
   We like to use Redmond RealSalt®, **www.realsalt.com**, for our sea salt needs, which can be found at your local co-op or health food store. This sea salt comes from a dried ancient sea bed that has never been exposed to modern day pollution, making it one of the purest sea salts available. RealSalt contains over fifty minerals and trace minerals, including calcium, potassium, magnesium, manganese, zinc, and iodine.

☐ **Herbamare®**
   Herbamare, which is a flavorful sea salt and herb blend, works great to make flavorful soups and stews. Herbamare is made by steeping fresh organic herbs and vegetables in sea salt for several months before being vacuum dehydrated.

☐ **Wheat-Free Tamari**
   Tamari is a natural, aged soy sauce made from soybeans, water, sea salt and sometimes added wheat. If avoiding gluten, look for wheat-free tamari. Shoyu is very similar to tamari, except that it contains wheat. Nama Shoyu, which also contains wheat, is a cultured soy sauce rich in enzymes and beneficial bacteria.

☐ **Miso**
   Miso is a sweet, fermented soybean paste usually made with some sort of grain. It comes unpasteurized and in several varieties from robust red to sweet white. It can be made into a soup or a sauce or used as a salt substitute. If you are gluten-sensitive, then be sure to look for miso that says "gluten-free" on the label. This is because miso made with brown rice can have gluten in the *koji*, which can contain either barley or wheat. Look for a miso that uses *rice koji* instead. The South River Miso Company produces a gluten-free miso. Check your local health food store or co-op for availability or visit **www.southrivermiso.com**.

Condiments:

Having a few different healthful, organic condiments available is useful to completing a recipe or rounding out a meal.

☐ **Organic Ketchup**
   We usually keep a bottle of organic ketchup on hand for topping our Sunny Sunflower Seed Burgers, *page 263*, or for dipping homemade oven fries in. Conventional ketchup usually contains highly refined high fructose corn syrup. Look for ketchup that is sweetened only with agave nectar, making it an ideal condiment for people with blood sugar imbalances.

☐ **Organic Dijon Mustard**
   I like to keep a jar of organic Dijon mustard on hand to help create delicious sauces and to use in our salad dressings because it works to emulsify, or to mix together, the oils and vinegars.

☐ **Organic Raw Cultured Vegetables and Raw Sauerkraut**
   Raw cultured vegetables and raw sauerkraut, which provide an abundance of health-promoting friendly bacteria and enzymes to assist with digestion and absorption, are found in the refrigerated section of your local co-op or health food store. Simply place a spoonful or two on your plate along with the rest of your meal. Please see *page 175* for instructions on making your own cultured vegetables.

☐ **Wasabi**
   Wasabi is a Japanese horseradish. Wasabi is dried into a pale green powder that, when mixed with water, makes a potent, fiery paste that is typically served with sushi and sashimi. Buy your wasabi as a dry powder and use as needed. Be sure to store it in a tightly covered glass jar away from heat or light.

Natural Sweeteners:

Natural sweeteners are closer to their whole form than refined sugar and sweeteners. Refined sugar, such as white sugar and brown sugar, has most or all of its natural vitamins and minerals removed during the refining process. These vitamins and minerals are the very nutrients that help to metabolize the sugar you consume, therefore preventing the "sugar blues." Remove all refined sugar and sweeteners from your pantry and stock your pantry with wholesome, natural sweeteners. Also be sure to keep all artificial sweeteners out of your diet as they contribute to a host of health problems. Natural sweeteners contain flavors that are deeper and richer than their refined counterparts so your recipes will turn out much better also. We use natural sweeteners not only for creating delicious wholesome desserts but also to make salad dressing, sauces, and more.

☐ **Agave Nectar**
Agave Nectar is a liquid sweetener naturally extracted from the Americana Agave, a cactus-like plant native to Mexico. It has an amber color and a very natural, light taste which is milder than honey or maple syrup. It dissolves easily and can replace honey, maple syrup or other liquid sweeteners cup for cup. Agave Nectar has a very high fructose content, and therefore a low glycemic index, so it absorbs slowly into the bloodstream. Agave nectar does not significantly raise blood sugar levels and is acceptable for people with diabetes and hyperglycemia.

☐ **Blackstrap Molasses**
Molasses is a dark, thick syrup made as a by-product of making refined sugar. It contains all of the minerals from the cane juice in a concentrated syrup. Rich in iron and other minerals, molasses has a strong, deep flavor and can be added to breads and muffins or drizzled on top of hot cereal. Look for "unsulphured molasses" which indicates that no sulphur was used in the extraction process.

☐ **Brown Rice Syrup**
Brown Rice Syrup is made from brown rice that has been soaked, sprouted, and cooked with an enzyme that breaks the starches into maltose. Brown rice syrup has a light, mild flavor and a similar appearance to honey, though less sweet. Rice syrup can be substituted one for one for honey or maple syrup. Lundberg Brown Rice Syrup is gluten-free.

> ### *Sweetener Substitutions*
>
> *The following list gives amounts for replacing dry, granulated sugar in any recipe.*
>
> • **Agave Nectar:** replace 1 cup sugar with ½ cup agave nectar and reduce liquids by ¼ cup
>
> • **Brown Rice Syrup:** replace 1 cup sugar with 1 to 1 ¼ cups brown rice syrup and reduce liquids by ¼ cup
>
> • **Honey:** replace 1 cup sugar with ½ cup honey and reduce liquids by ¼ cup
>
> • **Maple Syrup:** replace 1 cup sugar with ½ cup maple syrup and reduce liquids by ¼ cup
>
> • **Molasses:** replace 1 cup sugar with ½ cup molasses, no need to reduce liquids
>
> • **Stevia:** replace 1 cup sugar with 1 teaspoon dry Stevia, no need to reduce liquids

☐ **Frozen Fruit Juice Concentrate**
Frozen Fruit Juice Concentrate can be used to sweeten fruit pies, crisps, or other desserts—simply thaw and use.

☐ **Honey**
Honey is a sweet substance made from plant nectar and acid secretions by the honey bee. About 40% of the sugar in honey is fructose. The source of the

nectar determines the color, flavor, and texture of honey. Alfalfa and clover honey are the most common types, though other types can be found also. Honey is sold in liquid or crystallized form, and is available raw or pasteurized. Commercial honey is heated to 150 to 160 degrees F to prevent crystallization and yeast formation. Organic or raw honey has not been heat-treated. Honey is sweeter than other liquid sweeteners but can be substituted cup for cup for any of them.

☐ **Maple Syrup**

Maple Syrup is made from the boiled sap of sugar maple trees. Forty gallons of sap is needed to make one gallon of syrup. Maple syrup comes in two grades, A and B. Grade A is lighter and more refined. Grade B is darker, richer and the least refined, containing more minerals, such as manganese and zinc. Since Grade B is less refined, we use it exclusively when maple syrup is needed.

☐ **Sorghum**

Sorghum is a thick, dark syrup similar in flavor to molasses. It comes from the sweet sorghum plant, a grain related to millet that is similar in appearance to corn. The juice is extracted from the plant and then boiled down to a syrup.

☐ **Whole Cane Sugar**

Whole cane sugar, also called dried cane juice, is made from the dried juice of the sugar cane plant. Many of the minerals from the plant are still present which helps to digest the sugars. Dried cane juice resembles brown sugar in appearance and taste, though is less sweet. It can be substituted for white sugar cup for cup in baked goods. Trade names for this type of sugar are Rapadura and Sucanat, Rapadura being the least refined.

☐ **Date Sugar***

Date Sugar is made from ground dehydrated dates. It has a similar taste and appearance to brown sugar, but the taste is slightly less sweet. It can be substituted cup for cup in baked goods. *Although dates themselves are gluten-free, oat flour is often added when processing date sugar, making this type of sweetener unsuitable for the gluten-sensitive individual.*

☐ **Medjool Dates**

Dates can be used in combination with other dried fruits and nuts to make nutritious raw desserts or snacks. We like to use the medjool date, which has a nice moisture content and a very sweet, delicate flavor.

☐ **Stevia**

Stevia is derived from the leaves of a South American shrub, *Stevia rebaudiana.* Stevia is about 300 times sweeter than cane sugar, or sucrose. Stevia is not absorbed through the digestive tract, and therefore has no calories. Stevia does not affect blood sugar levels and is therefore acceptable for people with diabetes or hyperglycemia. Stevia can be found in either the natural sweetener or dietary supplement section of your local co-op or health food store. It comes in several forms: dried leaf, liquid extract, or a powdered extract.

Basic Herbs and Spices:

Herbs and spices are the musical notes that form the orchestra of your meal. They are the essential component to a flavorful and delicious meal. Spices enhance the natural sweetness of foods. Herbs provide color and a diverse array of flavors to foods. If your recipes have not been turning out well, then your old spices could be to blame. Throw away any old spices and herbs that you may have to make way for new, fresh ones.

An herb is the leaf, root, stem, or flower of a plant that usually grows in a temperate climate. Fresh herbs have more flavor and more nutritional value than dried herbs. Use 1 teaspoon of dried herb for 1 tablespoon fresh herb in a recipe. A spice is the whole or ground bud, fruit, flower, seed, or bark of a plant that usually grows in a tropical climate. Always use your dried herbs and ground spices within *six months*, otherwise, they will lose their color and flavor and become bitter. Whole spices such as cloves, nutmeg and cinnamon sticks maintain quality for two to three years if stored properly. Spices and dried herbs should be stored in a glass jar with an air-tight lid. Keep the jars in a closed cupboard well out of reach from direct sunlight and heat.

Your local food co-op or health food store is usually a great place to buy *organic* dried herbs and spices. You can utilize their bulk bins and buy spices in smaller quantities, more often. It may also help to buy spices in their whole form, and then grind them as you need them. Use a mortar and pestle or a coffee grinder to grind whole spices.

☐ **Dried Thyme**
Thyme is one of my all time favorite herbs. It is a member of the mint family and its use dates back to at least 3500 BC. Thyme has a strong, aromatic flavor and a bright, sharp taste. It is used in vegetable dishes, soups and stews, and meat dishes. Thyme acts as a digestive aid, stimulating the production of gastric fluids.

☐ **Dried Rosemary**
Rosemary is an evergreen shrub of the mint family native to the Mediterranean region. It contains the oil of camphor, which gives it that pungent flavor and wonderful aroma. Though I always prefer to use fresh rosemary in recipes, having a jar of dried rosemary stocked in your spice cabinet definitely comes in handy. When using dried rosemary, it is best to crush it with a mortar and pestle

before using. Rosemary is delicious added to soups and stews, meat dishes, sprinkled on top of vegetable dishes, and the fresh flowering tops can even be added to salads.

☐ **Dried Oregano**

Oregano is native to Europe and a member of the mint family. Oregano varies in flavor from mild common oregano and the more strongly flavored Greek and Spanish oregano, to the intensely flavored Mexican oregano, which is used in chili powders blends and other dishes. Oregano enhances the flavor of almost anything it is cooked with, from potato dishes and marinara sauces to savory stews and enchiladas.

☐ **Bay Leaves**

The fragrant bay tree is native to the Mediterranean basin. Bay leaves are strongly flavored if freshly dried and should be used sparingly. They offer a strong spicy flavor reminiscent of pine, nutmeg, and pepper. The whole leaves are usually added to simmering beans, meat dishes, stews, and soup stocks. The leaves are then removed from the dish before it is served.

☐ **Italian Seasoning**

Italian seasoning usually consists of a blend of dried oregano, marjoram, thyme, basil, rosemary, and sage. It is great to have on hand for making Mediterranean style soups, stews, and sauces.

☐ **Black Peppercorns**

Pepper is the small berry of a tropical vining shrub from the Malabar Coast of India. It was first cultivated around 1000 BC. It was soon carried to other parts of the world; and in medieval Europe, it was so precious that it was classed with gold, silver, and gems. Black peppercorns are berries that are picked when unripe but full-sized and allowed to dry in the sun to develop their color and flavor. It is best to use whole black peppercorns and then grind them as needed in a hand held pepper mill. Ground black pepper loses its flavor and volatile oils quickly and turns bitter if ground too far in advance. In addition most preground black pepper is toasted, and once toasted, it acts as an irritant to the gut. Use freshly ground pepper to spice up just about any savory dish. Whole peppercorns can be added to soup stocks, pickles, and marinades.

☐ **Cumin Seed and Ground Cumin**

Cumin is indigenous to the eastern Mediterranean region, especially near the upper Nile. Cumin, with its strongly aromatic, spicy, yet somewhat earthy flavor, can be toasted in a hot skillet in its whole seed form to deepen its flavor or can be used in its ground form. Ground cumin loses its flavor and freshness very quickly, so buy smaller amounts and replace it frequently. The whole seed can be ground with a mortar and pestle when needed. Cumin is used in curry dishes, soups, stews, and Mexican dishes such as beans, rice, and chili. Cumin acts as a natural digestive aid and carminative. It aids in the secretion of digestive juices and helps to relieve pain and cramping in the abdomen.

☐ **Ground Coriander**
Coriander seeds are the seeds of the cilantro plant. Coriander is indigenous to the Mediterranean regions of Africa and Asia and is one of the most ancient herbs still in use today. Coriander was cultivated in Egyptian gardens thousands of years before the birth of Christ. Freshly ground coriander seeds have a distinctive spicy-sweet aromatic flavor. They are one of the main spices in curries, but can also be used to flavor cakes, desserts, and other savory dishes.

☐ **Cinnamon**
Strongly aromatic and sweet-tasting, cinnamon is the dried inner bark of a tropical evergreen laurel tree native to India and Sri Lanka. The flavor of cinnamon becomes stronger once it has been ground, though it quickly becomes stale in its ground state. It is best purchased in small quantities and constantly replaced. Cinnamon adds a warm flavor to many desserts, whole grain breakfast cereals, curries, sauces, and pilafs.

☐ **Cardamom**
The cardamom plant is a tropical shrub of the ginger family native to Ceylon and India. Cardamom is a warming spice that acts as a carminative and sweetens the breath. Cardamom is the world's third most expensive spice, behind saffron and vanilla, because each seedpod must be hand-picked. It is such an intensely flavored spice that only a small amount is needed in cooking. It is available both in its ground form and in its whole pod form. Because it rapidly loses flavor when ground, it is best purchased in its whole form and then ground as needed. If purchasing the ground spice, be sure to only buy small amounts and then replace as needed.

☐ **Ginger powder**
The warm spiciness of ginger powder is a fantastic addition to many desserts. I like to use fresh ginger in most savory soups and stews, but occasionally if I am out of fresh ginger I will replace it with dried.

☐ **Garlic Powder**
Garlic powder offers a mild garlic flavor to bean dips and other dishes. It can be used to replace fresh garlic when the taste may be too strong for some, like children, breastfeeding moms, or for people who simply cannot tolerate a lot of garlic.

☐ **Turmeric**
Turmeric is an East Indian tropical plant of the ginger family. The bright orange-yellow rhizome is peeled, dried, and ground into a fine powder. Occasionally you may be able to find fresh turmeric at your local market or

health food store. The fresh rhizome can be peeled and finely diced and then added to curry dishes. Turmeric powder is one of the main ingredients in curry powder and is what lends curry dishes their bright yellow color. Turmeric is one of the best anti-inflammatory and anti-carcinogenic spices.

☐ **Cayenne Pepper**
Cayenne pepper is made by grinding dried red peppers. A high quality, fresh cayenne pepper should be used sparingly as its flavor will be very intense. It can be used to enliven flavors of almost any dish but it is most commonly used in soups and stews. Cayenne pepper is a natural stimulant, producing warmth and improving circulation. It aids in digestion and provides a cleansing effect on the bowels.

☐ **Chili Powder**
Chili powder is a blend of cayenne pepper, cumin, oregano, paprika, garlic powder, and sometimes salt. Chili powder is used in chili and other spicy soups and stews.

☐ **Chipotle Chili Powder**
Chipotle chili powder is made by first roasting jalapeño peppers, then drying them and grinding them to a powder. Chipotle chili powder imparts a smoky flavor to any dish it is added to.

☐ **Curry Powder**
Curry powder is a combination of many different spices, from as few as five to as many as fifty different ingredients. The base of most curry powders include ground red chili peppers, turmeric powder, and coriander. Other ingredients may be added such as cumin, allspice, caraway, cardamom, cinnamon, cloves, fenugreek, ginger, white or black pepper, saffron, and many others. Curry powder has been shown to increase metabolism, help with breathing difficulties, and reduce cholesterol.

☐ **Garam Masala**
Garam Masala is a sweetly pungent blend of spices common in Indian cuisine. It is usually a mix of cinnamon, cumin, cloves, nutmeg, black pepper, and cardamom, and sometimes coriander and fennel.

☐ **Mexican Seasoning**
Mexican Seasoning is usually a blend of ground chili peppers, dehydrated garlic, dehydrated onion, paprika, cumin, celery seed, oregano, cayenne pepper, and bay leaf. It is a great blend to have on hand for making casseroles, bean dishes, or to simply sprinkle over sautéed vegetables.

Raw Nuts and Seeds:

Raw nuts can create nutritious desserts and also be used to accent other dishes. Raw seeds work well to accent salads or other vegetable dishes or can be eaten as a simple snack. Flax seeds can also be used as an egg replacement in baked goods. Store raw, shelled nuts and seeds in either the refrigerator or freezer to prevent them from becoming rancid.

☐ **Cashews**

Cashews are an excellent source of copper, which is needed for antioxidants and tissue-forming enzymes in the body. Cashews are also high in the heart-healthy monounsaturated fat, oleic acid. Cashews can be blended into a sweet cream and used to top desserts or blended with water to be used as a replacement for dairy in cream soups and ice cream. They can also be lightly roasted in the oven with a little sea salt and used to top curries or stir-fries.

☐ **Almonds**

Almonds are the seed of a stone fruit, similar to an apricot. Almonds are high in manganese and vitamin E, two nutrients utilized for antioxidant functions in the body. Numerous research studies have shown that eating almonds lowers cholesterol, increases antioxidant levels in the body, assists with weight loss, and regulates blood sugar. Almonds are delicious as a snack. They can also be soaked overnight and added to smoothies, or can be ground into a flour to increase nutrients in baked goods.

☐ **Walnuts**

Walnuts are an excellent source of antioxidants and omega-3 fatty acids, in fact, a ¼ cup serving provides over 90% of your daily need for these essential fats. Lightly roasted walnuts are a delicious addition to salads or as a topping to whole grain breakfast cereals. They can also be eaten raw as a snack in combination with organic dried fruit.

☐ **Hazelnuts**

Widely grown in the Pacific Northwest, hazelnuts add a delicious nutty flavor to salads, main courses, and desserts; we even like to add them to our whole grain cereals in the morning. Hazelnuts are high in heart-healthy monounsaturated fats, vitamin E, B vitamins, and a host of phytochemicals that benefit the immune system. Hazelnuts are also high in arginine, an amino acid that relaxes blood vessels, and folic acid. In fact, hazelnuts have the highest concentration of folic acid among all the tree nuts.

☐ **Pecans**

Pecans are an excellent source of both the gamma and alpha tocopherol forms of vitamin E. Pecans are also an excellent source of plant-based zinc. Zinc is usually found in higher concentrations in animal foods. Pecans are also rich in antioxidants, calcium, magnesium, phosphorus, potassium, and B vitamins, including folic acid. Pecans can be used in whole grain dishes, salads, and used to make many decadent raw desserts.

☐ Brazil Nuts

Brazil nuts originated in Brazil and grow wild in the Amazon Rainforest of South America. Brazil nuts are an excellent source of selenium, in fact 6 to 8 nuts provides a whopping 840 micrograms! Brazil nuts are also a good source of magnesium and thiamin. Brazil nuts make a great snack, can be used to top whole grain breakfast cereals, or can be used to replace other nuts in raw dessert recipes.

☐ Pine Nuts

Pine nuts are the edible seeds of the pine tree. They are found on the pine cone where they are covered by a hard shell. Most of the pine nuts available today come from Southern Europe, particularly from the Stone Pine, which has been cultivated for over 6,000 years. Pine nuts in the United States, from the Colorado Piñon tree, have been harvested by Native Americans for over 10,000 years. Pine nuts contain about 31 grams of protein per 100 grams of nut, the highest of any nuts and seeds. They are also rich in monounsaturated fats. Pine nuts are probably best known for their appearance in pesto, though they can also be used in desserts, whole grain dishes, or as a garnish for many savory dishes. Pine nuts can become rancid very quickly. They can be stored in an airtight glass jar in the refrigerator for up to one month or frozen.

☐ Pumpkin Seeds

Pumpkin seeds, also known as pepitas, are flat, dark green seeds. Pumpkin seeds are very rich in minerals, particularly, manganese, magnesium, phosphorus, iron, copper, and zinc. They are also high in vitamin K and the amino acid, tryptophan. Pumpkin seeds are delicious lightly toasted and added to salads, they can also be ground to a powder in a coffee grinder and mixed into whole grain baby cereals for babies 10 months and older.

☐ Sunflower Seeds

Sunflower seeds come from the beautiful sunflower. Sunflower seeds are high in polyunsaturated fat, manganese, magnesium, selenium, and vitamin B_1. Sunflower seeds are also a fantastic source of vitamin E, the body's primary fat soluble anti-oxidant. Sunflower seeds can be added to salads, combined with whole grains and spices to make vegetarian burgers, used as a garnish for vegetable dishes, or used in combination with other nuts to make delicious raw desserts.

☐ Sesame Seeds

The use of sesame seeds as a condiment dates back to as early as 1600 BC. Sesame seeds add a delicious nutty flavor to a variety of Asian dishes, such as stir-fries and noodle dishes. They are also the main ingredient in tahini (sesame seed paste). Sesame seeds are very rich in copper, calcium, and manganese. They are also a great source of magnesium, iron, phosphorus, zinc, and vitamin B₁.

☐ **Flax Seeds**

Flax seeds are available in two varieties, golden and brown. They are a fantastic source of omega-3 fatty acids, though they need to be ground in order for the body to utilize these fats. Omega-3 fatty acids help to calm inflammation in the body and have been shown to benefit many disease states. Unfortunately, foods that are high in omega-3 fatty acids, like flax, spoil very quickly. Flax seeds and flax oil should be stored in the refrigerator or freezer. Flax seeds can be added to smoothies, or ground and sprinkled on top of just about any food, from whole grain cereals to vegetable dishes. Flax seeds also work as an egg replacement in baked goods. Use 1 heaping tablespoon ground flax mixed with 2 to 3 tablespoons hot water. This will replace 1 egg in any baked good.

Nut & Seed Butters:

Nut and seed butters, which are rich in protein, work well to make a quick sandwich or to spread onto whole grain toast. They are also very useful in making rich-tasting, healthful sauces. Store opened jars in the refrigerator. It is also nice to have some fruit spreads on hand, try organic apricot fruit spread which does not have any added sugar. Some other more unusual nut and seed butters include pecan, hemp, and pumpkin seed. Check your local co-op or health food store for availability.

☐ **Raw Almond Butter**

Raw almond butter, with its sweet taste and smooth texture, is delicious for making sandwiches, can be used to make savory sauces, and can be used as a dip for fruits and vegetables.

☐ **Cashew Butter**

Cashew butter can be used to make savory sauces and gravies, or simply spread onto toast in the morning. It can be found raw or roasted in the nut butter section of your local co-op or health food store.

☐ **Unsalted Peanut Butter**

Peanuts, contrary to their name, are not actually true nuts. They are a member of a family of legumes related to peas, lentils, chickpeas and other beans. Peanut butter is rich in manganese, vitamin E, niacin, folic acid, and protein. Peanut skins also contain the phenolic antioxidant, *resveratrol*, which is also found in red grapes and red wine. Unsalted peanut butter can be used to make a quick sandwich or a delicious sauce to top steamed greens, noodle dishes, and more.

☐ **Sesame Tahini**

Sesame tahini is simply made from ground sesame seeds. It comes salted and unsalted and also roasted or raw.

☐ **Fruit Juice Sweetened Apricot Jam**

Apricots are very beneficial for intestinal health as they help to feed the friendly bacteria in the gut. Apricot jam is great used in combination with raw almond butter and brown rice bread to make a delicious sandwich. The brand of apricot jam we recommend is Bionaturae.

Whole Grains:

Keep a variety of whole grains on hand to create filling yet energizing meals. Only buy what you think you would use within a few months. Whole grains should be stored in airtight containers in a cool dark place. Grains stored this way can be kept for up to *six to nine months*. It is also helpful to have a variety of whole grain pastas on hand to make as part of a quick meal. **All of the following grains are gluten-free.** Check our resource guide in the back of the book for a source of certified gluten-free oats.

☐ **Short Grain Brown Rice**

Brown rice is an excellent source of manganese and a good source of selenium, magnesium, and fiber. When cooked, short grain brown rice tends to stick together, making it an ideal component to vegetarian burgers, croquettes, puddings, risotto, or rice balls.

☐ **Sweet Brown Rice**

Sweet brown rice, sometimes called glutinous brown rice, has a sweet taste and sticky texture when cooked. It can be ground and cooked into a delicious, creamy breakfast cereal, or used in combination with short grain brown rice as a filling for nori rolls (sushi).

☐ **Brown Jasmine Rice**

Brown jasmine rice is an aromatic long grain rice originally grown in Thailand. When it is being cooked, the delicate, nutty aroma will fill your kitchen. Brown jasmine rice can be used to make pilafs, fried rice, or simply used as a base to flavorful curries and stews.

☐ **Brown Basmati Rice**

Brown basmati rice is another long grain aromatic rice. It can be used interchangeably with brown jasmine rice. Brown basmati rice is ideal for making pilafs, fried rice, stuffing, or used as a base for fragrant curries and stews.

☐ **Millet**

Millet is a small, round, yellow grain with a sweet, earthy taste. Millet is a good source of manganese, phosphorus, magnesium, and fiber. Millet is native to the East Indies and North Africa, though now it is used throughout the world as a staple grain. Millet can be used for making savory grain-based casseroles, breakfast cereals, croquettes, and more.

☐ **Quinoa**

Quinoa, an ancient Incan grain, comes from the Andes Mountains in South America. Although considered a grain, quinoa is actually a seed from a plant similar to spinach and chard. Quinoa is an excellent source of plant-based protein, containing all nine essential amino acids. It is also a great source of manganese, magnesium, and iron. Quinoa's light fluffy nature makes it ideal for creating grain-based salads. It is also great in pilafs, breakfast cereals, or used as a base for savory stews.

☐ **Amaranth**

Amaranth, an ancient Aztec grain, is high in protein, calcium, and iron. Amaranth sustained the Aztec culture until 1521, when Cortez arrived and banished the crop. It survived in remote wild areas and was then rediscovered in 1972 by a United States botanical research team. Amaranth, like quinoa, is a seed of a broad-leafed plant. The leaves and stems of amaranth are also edible and extremely nutritious, being particularly high in calcium. Amaranth greens can substitute spinach in any recipe. The grain can be used to make savory casseroles, puddings, and breakfast cereals.

☐ **Buckwheat**

Buckwheat, a hardy plant that grows in poor, rocky soil and extreme climates, is native to Manchuria and Siberia. The grain is actually the seed of a plant related to rhubarb. After harvesting, the black, hard, inedible outer shell needs to be removed in order to access the inner kernel. The kernel is then split into pieces, called groats, which are sold either roasted or raw. The roasted groats, also called *kasha*, have a strong robust flavor. The raw groats are much milder in flavor. Buckwheat can be made into a cereal, pilaf, or ground into flour and made into a noodle, which is very popular in Japan. Buckwheat is especially famous for its blood sugar regulating properties, and is therefore very useful for diabetics.

☐ **Teff**

Teff is a very tiny grain that is available in three colors—white, red, or brown—each with its own distinct flavor. Teff originated in Africa where it was once a foraged wild grass before it was cultivated as a staple grain for the Ethiopians. Teff is very high in protein and iron. Teff can be cooked into a delicious nutty breakfast porridge, used to make casseroles, or used as an alternative to corn in polenta.

☐ **Thick Rolled Oats**

Oats, originally from Western Europe, help to regulate blood sugar, regulate the thyroid, and sooth the digestive system. Oats also support the nervous system and improve resistance to stress. Rolled oats are made from hulled oats that have been steamed and rolled flat. Instant or quick-cooking oats have been precooked in water, dried, and then rolled superthin. Although they cook faster than thick rolled oats they have much less nutritional value due to the high heat processing. Rolled oats are subject to rancidity within one to three months after milling; it is therefore advisable to store large quantities in the refrigerator to prevent rancidity. Rolled oats can be cooked into a delicious, warming breakfast cereal, ground into flour to make pancakes, or used to make many decadent desserts.

☐ **Polenta**

Polenta is made by coarsely grinding dried corn kernels. It is then cooked with water and salt and baked in the oven to make a warming casserole. It is often served with chicken or fish stews and is also delicious topped with a fresh marinara sauce. It is easy and quick to cook making it a great component to any evening meal. Corn is high in thiamin, folic acid, and fiber. It is also a great source of the antioxidant carotenoid, *beta-cyrptoxanthin*.

☐ **Popcorn Kernels**

Popcorn kernels are great to have stocked in your pantry. Popcorn cooks up easily and quickly on the stove, making it a great, healthful snack. Look for organic popcorn kernels in the bulk section of your local co-op or health food store.

☐ **Brown Rice Noodles**

Brown rice noodles are great to have stocked in your pantry. They can help be part of a very quick meal, used in broth-based soups, or used to make more complex noodle dishes. Look for a brand that says "gluten-free" on the label. A brand that we like to use is Tinkyáda, **www.tinkyada.com**.

☐ **Quinoa Noodles**

Quinoa noodles are a nutritious blend of quinoa flour and corn. They are gluten-free and come in different shapes and sizes. Quinoa noodles can be added to broth soups at the end of cooking time, or simply cooked up plain for a fun snack.

Whole Grain Flours:

Go through your pantry and cabinets and discard any old whole grain flours as they can spoil easily. The oils found in the germ and bran of whole grains can go rancid quite easily when ground into flours. Store your whole grain flours in the refrigerator or freezer if you will not be using them right away. Brown rice flour, buckwheat flour, teff flour, millet flour, quinoa flour, amaranth flour, sorghum flour, and tapioca flour are naturally gluten-free. Be sure to **look for a gluten-free symbol on the label** as some flours may be processed in the same facility as gluten-containing flours and therefore cross-contaminated.

☐ **Brown Rice Flour**
Brown rice flour is a staple gluten-free baking flour in our house. Its subtle flavor makes an ideal base for cakes, breads, muffins, and desserts. For a more nutrient-dense baked good, substitute half or more of the brown rice flour with teff, sorghum, buckwheat, quinoa, or amaranth flour. Authentic Foods makes a Superfine Brown Rice Flour that is ideal for making pie crusts and tart shells; it can be found online at **www.glutenfreemall.com**.

☐ **Buckwheat Flour**
The packaged buckwheat flour you buy in the store is ground from roasted buckwheat groats, so it has a very strong, robust flavor. I prefer to grind my own from raw buckwheat groats. They grind up very quickly to a fine powder in a coffee grinder and even faster if you own a grain grinder. Buckwheat flour makes a delicious pancake, and can also be used to make muffins, quick breads, and some desserts.

☐ **Teff Flour**
Teff's tiny size makes it impractical to hull or degerm, so the entire grain is milled leaving all of the nutrients intact. Teff flour is highly nutritious, being particularly high in iron, protein, fiber, and complex carbohydrates. It comes in two varieties, ivory or brown. The rich, buttery flavor of teff flour makes an ideal addition to most baked goods. Use it to make pancakes, brownies, cookies, yeast breads, quick breads, and more. You can replace half of the brown rice flour in our recipes with teff flour with good results.

☐ **Millet Flour**
Millet flour's light, yellow color and sweet flavor works well in cakes, quick breads, and muffins. It can be substituted for brown rice flour in most recipes.

☐ **Quinoa Flour**
Quinoa flour has a strong flavor and should be used in combination with other mild flours such as brown rice flour. Quinoa flour is very high in protein making it a great addition to quick breads and muffins.

☐ **Amaranth Flour**
Amaranth flour has a distinct, sweet, nutty flavor, though can sometimes leave a bitter aftertaste. It is high in protein and iron and can be used in combination with other flours in baking.

☐ **Sorghum Flour**
Sorghum flour adds delicious flavor and texture to gluten-free baked goods. It is a good substitute for whole wheat flour, as it has a familiar taste and texture.

☐ **Tapioca Flour**
Tapioca flour comes from the ground starch of the cassava root. A small part of tapioca flour is used in combination with other gluten-free flours in baked goods to help them stick together. Gluten and egg-free baked goods made without tapioca flour may crumble and fall apart once baked.

Beans:

Beans need to be fresh in order to cook properly. Discard all of your old beans and restock your pantry with small amounts of your favorite beans. Buy organic dried beans in bulk from your local health food store or food co-op. Store your dried beans in the coolest and driest place in your kitchen. This will preserve their freshness and make them last longer. Beans stored in this way can be kept for up to *six months*. Mark the date of purchase on your bean containers so you will know to discard them if they are older than six months. Organic canned beans are an acceptable substitute for dry beans, especially if you are not accustomed to planning ahead for your meals. Keep a few cans of each of your favorite beans stocked in your pantry.

☐ **Dried Kidney Beans**
Kidney beans are great for making chili, spicy Cajun dishes, or can be used in bean salads. As with most beans, kidney beans are very high in molybdenum, folic acid, tryptophan, fiber, manganese, and protein.

☐ **Dried Black Beans**
Black beans are so versatile; they can be used to make spicy soups and stews, used in enchiladas, grain and bean salads, or used for breakfast with eggs and salsa. Black beans are rich in antioxidant compounds called, *anthocyanins*, which work to protect against cancer.

☐ **Dried Garbanzo Beans**
Garbanzo beans, also called chickpeas, are used in a wide variety of ethnic cuisine from Mediterranean to Indian cooking. They can be used to make soups, stews, curries, grain and bean salads, bean dips, such as hummus, and more.

☐ **Dried White Beans**
Small white beans, such as navy or great northern, are delicious in savory soups and stews or vegetable and bean salads.

☐ **Dried Pink Beans**
Pink beans can be used to make Mexican dishes and are delicious in savory vegetable-bean soups. They can be used interchangeably with pinto beans.

☐ **Dried Pinto Beans**
Pinto beans can be used in combination with kidney beans and black beans to make fabulous chili, or used in a variety of soups and stews.

☐ **Dried Red, Green, and French Lentils**
Lentils are so versatile and quick to cook that they are a staple in our house. Very high in protein, iron, and other minerals they are essential to the well-stocked pantry. Lentils can be made into delicious Indian stews, called *dal*, or can be made into savory soups, grain and bean salads, and more.

☐ **Yellow and Green Split Peas**
Yellow and green split peas, like lentils, cook up rather quickly. They can be used to make savory split pea soups, and are often used in Ethiopian cooking to make spicy stews.

☐ **Tempeh**
Tempeh, pronounced TEM-pay, is a traditional Indonesian food. It is made from fully cooked soybeans that have been fermented with a mold called *rhizopus* and formed into cakes. Tempeh needs to be refrigerated or frozen. Tempeh takes on the flavor of whatever it is marinated with. Lime, lemon, vinegar, tamari, herbs, and spices can be combined in varying combinations to make fabulous marinades. After the tempeh has marinated, we sauté it in olive oil or coconut oil.

☐ **Tofu**
Tofu, or bean curd, is made from soy beans that have been cooked, made into milk and then coagulated. Different types of coagulants may be used for making tofu, including calcium sulfate, nigari and magnesium chloride. The soymilk curdles when heated and the curds are then skimmed off and pressed into blocks. Tofu can be found extra-firm, firm, or soft in the refrigerated section of your local co-op or health food store. Tofu can be marinated and sautéed like tempeh, crumbled into enchiladas and lasagna, or made into tofu scramble.

Organic Canned Tomato Products:

Tomatoes can add depth and flavor to your meals, especially in bean soups and stews. It will be helpful to have the following tomato products on hand to use for some of the recipes in this book. Choose organic whenever possible as they will be lower in sodium and residual chemicals. Of course it is even better if you grow your own tomatoes and can them yourself. I prefer to use fresh tomatoes in recipes where chopped tomatoes are called for, but I don't always have them on hand, so canned organic tomatoes work as an acceptable substitute.

☐ **Crushed Tomatoes**
Crushed tomatoes are a great addition to most soups or stews because their acidic nature deepens the flavors.

☐ **Diced Tomatoes**
Canned diced tomatoes can replace diced fresh tomatoes in most recipes, especially soups and stews.

☐ **Crushed Fire Roasted Tomatoes**
Crushed fire roasted tomatoes add a smoky flavor to spicy soups and stews. Use crushed tomatoes when you want the broth of the soup to have a tomato base.

☐ **Diced Fire Roasted Tomatoes**
Diced fire roasted tomatoes add a smoky flavor to spicy soups and stews. Use the diced variety when you want chunks of tomatoes in your soup or stew.

☐ **Tomato Sauce**
Tomato sauce can be used to make flavorful sauces or added to stews and soups to give them a distinct tomato flavor.

☐ **Tomato Paste**
Small amounts of tomato paste can be added to dull tasting bean or vegetable stews and soups to enliven the flavors. Tomato paste can also be used to make savory sauces. We like to use the brand Bionaturae because it comes in glass jars.

Frozen Foods:

Frozen foods offer some variety when fresh is not in season. Of course choosing fresh whenever possible will yield a more flavorful dish with a slightly higher nutrient value. We like to buy from our local Farmer's Market, or harvest our own fruits and vegetables when they are in season and freeze them. Please see *page 87* for freezing tips.

☐ **Organic Corn**
Frozen corn can be used when fresh corn is out of season. Corn is great added to casseroles, soups, stews, and grain salads. It adds a beautiful color and a detectable crunch to everything it is added to.

☐ **Organic Peas**
Frozen peas are nice to have on hand to cook up for a quick side dish, especially for hungry children. They are also delicious added to split pea and other soups, curries, grain salads, and more.

☐ **Organic Spinach**
Frozen spinach can be added to many different soups and stews for color, texture, and a host of valuable nutrients, such as, vitamin K, vitamin A, manganese, folic acid, magnesium, iron, and calcium.

☐ **Organic Cherries**
Frozen cherries provide a delicious, quick frozen snack. They can also be added to smoothies, used to make iced nut cream, or pureed to be used as a baby food. We like to harvest our own cherries in July or buy them from the market, pit them, and stock our freezer full.

☐ **Organic Blueberries**
Frozen blueberries are another healthful, frozen snack. In fact, our children have been eating them that way since they were about nine moths old. Frozen blueberries can be added to whole grain cereals in the morning, used to make smoothies, or blended up with other fruits and frozen into popsicle molds for a delicious snack.

☐ **Organic Peaches**
Frozen peaches are a fantastic addition to smoothies and homemade iced nut cream. They can also be thawed and pureed to be used in our Peachy Millet Flour Muffins, *page 137.*

Sea Vegetables:

The use of sea vegetables helps to round out the flavors in your recipes. Sea vegetables lend a natural saltiness to foods. Seaweed can be used as a snack or added to soups, salads, stews, and grain and bean dishes. The naturally occurring glutamic acid in seaweeds also acts as a flavor enhancer in your recipes. Sea vegetables can be found in the dried form either in the bulk section or in packages in the macrobiotic section of your local co-op or health food store. Store your sea vegetables in glass jars or sealed containers in your pantry away from heat and light.

☐ **Kombu**

The use of the seaweed kombu, or kelp, is essential in cooking beans as it contains glutamic acid, which helps to break down the indigestible, gas-producing sugars, *raffinose* and *stacchiose*, in beans. Kombu is also one of the main ingredients used in Japanese soup stocks and broths. Kombu reduces blood cholesterol and lowers hypertension.

☐ **Wakame**

Wakame is a brown Japanese seaweed that grows in long, ribbon like strands. It can be soaked in water, cut up, and then added to salads, vegetable dishes, nut pates, and more. The Japanese use it to flavor fish stock (dashi). It is also delicious in miso soup.

☐ **Hijiki**

Hijiki has been used for hundreds of years in Japan where it is known as "the bearer of wealth and beauty." The harvested plants are cut and sun-dried, boiled until soft, and then dried again. Hijiki is very rich in minerals, especially calcium and iron. It should be soaked before use because it will quadruple in volume. Hijiki makes an excellent addition to Asian noodle salads, grain dishes, and tofu dishes.

☐ **Arame**

Arame, which is one of the richest sources of iodine, is a member of the kelp family closely related to kombu and wakame. Arame is harvested not only in Japan, but also Peru and the Pacific North American coast. Arame grows in wide leaves up to a foot in length. After harvesting, the leaves are cut into long strands, cooked for seven hours, sun-dried, and packaged. Arame has a mild, sweet flavor which many people enjoy. Arame is best soaked before use. It can be added to stir-fries, soups, stews, even tofu scramble.

☐ **Nori**

Nori comes in thin sheets and is used to make sushi. It can also be wrapped around rice balls, cut into strips and used for a garnish, or broken into pieces and added to salads or soups. We also love to eat plain nori as a snack. Nori has the highest protein content of all the seaweeds and is the most easily digested. Nori contains an enzyme that helps to breakdown cholesterol deposits in the body.

☐ **Dulse Flakes**

Dulse flakes, which are rich in iron, can be used much like sea salt to enhance the flavor and saltiness of your dishes. Dulse grows in temperate to frigid zones of the Atlantic and Pacific. The use of dulse as a food dates back to the eighteenth century in the British Isles where it was commonly eaten with fish, potatoes, and butter.

Non-Dairy Milks:

Keeping a few different containers of non-dairy milk in your pantry will be helpful to make a variety of the recipes in this book. Smoothies, desserts, and some main dish recipes are a few examples. Non-dairy milks come in many flavors such as plain, vanilla, chocolate, and carob and can be found in aseptic packages on the shelf of your local health food store, co-op, and now in many grocery stores. If you are gluten sensitive, then be sure to purchase a gluten-free rice or soy milk. Some brands contain a very small percentage of barley malt or wheat. Check the label to find out.

☐ **Rice Milk**

Rice milk is made from brown rice, water, sea salt, and usually a small amount of oil. It is a very light, sweet tasting beverage that can replace cow's milk in most recipes.

☐ **Almond Milk**

Almond milk is made from almonds, water, sea salt, and usually some type of sweetener. It works well as a substitute for cow's milk in baked good recipes. For a warming drink in the winter it can be simmered on the stove with spices, such as cinnamon, cloves, and ginger.

☐ **Hemp Milk**

Hemp milk is a thick, rich, non-dairy milk made from hemp seeds, water, and brown rice syrup. It is rich in healthy Omega-3 fatty acids, protein, and essential vitamins and minerals. Because of its high nutrient content, we use it almost exclusively where non-dairy milk is called for.

☐ **Soy Milk**

Soymilk is made by grinding soybeans, mixing with water, and cooking. Finally, the liquid is pressed from the solids and then filtered. Soymilk can be found unsweetened, sweetened, or in flavors like vanilla and chocolate.

☐ **Canned Coconut Milk**

We always have a few cans of organic coconut milk in our pantry for making quick curries, soups, and even homemade popsicles. Use the regular coconut milk for cooking instead of the "light" variety.

Dried Fruit:

Dried organic fruit is essential to a well-stocked pantry. It is wonderful eaten as a quick, nutritious snack when away from home. Dried fruit can also be added to desserts, whole grain dishes, stews, and salads. Look for dried fruit that is darker in color than the fresh fruit of the same kind. Dried fruit that is the same color as the fresh fruit means that it has been preserved with sulfur dioxide. Fresh, in-season fruit can be harvested yourself or bought from your local Farmer's Market and then dried in a food dehydrator. It typically takes about five pounds of fresh fruit to equal one pound of dried fruit. Living in the Pacific Northwest, we have access to an abundance of fresh local fruit that is excellent for drying. Our favorite fruit to dry is the Italian Plum—it grows everywhere here and in abundance. We slice the ripe plums into strips and dry them in our food dehydrator. Unfortunately, they don't even last until winter because they are such a delicious treat! When purchasing dried fruit, always choose organic! Store dried fruit in tightly covered glass jars in your pantry.

☐ **Raisins**
Raisins are made by dehydrating grapes. Look for sun-dried raisins as some companies use a higher heat mechanical process that destroys nutrients. Raisins are one of the top sources of the trace mineral boron, which is important for bone health and converting vitamin D to its active form. Raisins are rich in anti-oxidants which prevent free radical damage in the body. The phytochemicals in raisins, particularly oleanolic acid, are effective in killing bacteria that cause cavities and gum disease. Raisins can be eaten as a delicious, sweet snack, used to top salads, or used in spicy stews.

☐ **Zante currants**
Zante currants, which are actually dried Corinth grapes, are very similar to raisins in their anti-oxidant values and nutrient content. Zante currants are delicious added to salads, stews, grain pilafs, quick breads, and trail mixes.

☐ **Dried Cranberries (fruit juice sweetened)**
The cranberry plant is a small evergreen shrub related to the blueberry. It is native to open bogs and swampy marshes from Alaska to Tennessee. Dried cranberries are so versatile they can be used in whole grain pilafs, sprinkled atop whole grain breakfast cereals, used in many desserts and quick breads, or eaten as a sweet snack. When buying dried cranberries, look for the organic, fruit juice sweetened variety.

☐ **Dried Cherries**
Dried cherries can be used to top breakfast cereals in the morning, used to make dried fruit compotes, used in trail mixes, whole grain pilafs, and stuffing. Look for organic, unsweetened dried cherries when purchasing from the store. Cherries are on the list for the top 12 fruits and vegetables to have the highest levels of chemical pesticides used on them. Always buy organic cherries.

☐ **Dried Apricots**
Dried apricots are a super-concentrated source of nutrients. They are high in iron, potassium, beta-carotene, phosphorus, and fiber. Dried apricots are also an amazing source of fructo-oligosaccharides, which are long chain fruit sugars that feed beneficial bacteria in out gut. Dried apricots can be cooked with meats or fish, added to quick breads, muffins, and desserts, or eaten as a delicious snack.

☐ **Dried Apples**

Dried apples are fun to make in autumn when there is an overabundance of them. Simply cut them into slices, with their peels intact, and spread them out onto a food dehydrator. Dehydrate at a low temperature until dry. Dried apples make a great snack in the wintertime; they can also be added to trail mixes, and desserts, such as our Dried Fruit Compote, *page 323*.

☐ **Dried Pears**

We dehydrate pears in autumn with the same method used on apples as described above. Dried pears make an excellent, sweet snack; and can be added to desserts, trail mixes, and stews.

☐ **Dried Figs**

Dried figs make a superb snack. They are also great chopped up and sprinkled on top of stews, fish dishes, or vegetables. We like to use fresh figs when they are in season, though dried figs can replace fresh in any recipe.

☐ **Dried Plums (prunes)**

Both the fresh and dried version of plums are nutritional powerhouses. High in beta-carotene, potassium, fiber, copper, and antioxidants, they make a great addition to the whole foods pantry. Plums, both dried and fresh, are high in special phytochemicals called *neochlorogenic* and *chlorogenic acid.* These compounds act as antioxidants in the body scavenging free radicals and helping to prevent oxygen-based damage to fats. Dried plums make an exquisite, sweet-tasting snack; and can also be made into delicious desserts, or chopped and added to quick breads and muffins.

☐ **Goji Berries**

Goji berries, native to Tibet and Mongolia, contain more protein than whole wheat, more beta carotene than carrots and 500 times more vitamin C by weight than oranges. Goji berries are packed with numerous antioxidants, trace minerals, and essential vitamins, including vitamins B_1 and B_6. Goji berries are wonderful eaten as a snack, can be soaked in water and added smoothies, and are great as part of a trail mix. Goji berries can be found at your local health food store or co-op and can also be ordered online.

Specialty Items:

☐ **Olives**

Olives are a fruit that must be cured before they are edible. A brine made from salt and water is typically used, though kalamata olives are cured in a salted vinegar brine. Look for olives that are made with sea salt and avoid brands that have been treated with preservatives. Olives are an essential part of a well-stocked pantry. They can be used to make dips, spreads, salads, main dishes, or simply eaten as a nutritious snack. Olives come in green and black varieties and can be found flavored with many things such as garlic, lemon, and chili peppers. Green olives are younger and tend to be lighter and fruitier in flavor. Black olives are ripe and more mature. Olives can be stored in their brine in the refrigerator for several months.

☐ **Capers**

Capers are the unopened green flower buds of the *Capparis spinosa* bush. Manual labor is required to gather capers because the buds must be picked each morning just as they reach the proper size. After the buds are picked, they are usually sun-dried, then pickled in a salted vinegar brine. Capers are a delicious addition to sauces, dips, vegetables dishes, or as a garnish for meat or fish.

☐ **Sun-Dried Tomatoes**

Sun-dried tomatoes are a flavorful and nutritious way to add an extra bit of zest to your recipes. Look for organic sun-dried tomatoes. Most commercial varieties process their sun-dried tomatoes at high temperatures which destroys precious nutrients. Some companies also add sulfur dioxide as a preservative. Store dry pieces in a glass jar in your pantry. Sun-dried tomatoes also come packed in extra virgin olive oil. These are found in glass jars at your local co-op or health food store. A good company to buy from is Mediterranean Organic. Olive oil packed sun-dried tomatoes do not need to be soaked in water before using, ultimately making them more convenient.

Other Items:

The following list of miscellaneous foods will be helpful to have stocked in your pantry to make many of the recipes in this book.

☐ **Organic Vanilla Extract**

Vanilla extract can be either made with alcohol or glycerine (non-alcoholic). We typically like to use the non-alcoholic variety for dishes that are not cooked, such as raw desserts. The alcohol in traditional vanilla extract will evaporate with heat in cooked desserts. Vanilla extract enhances the sweetness to whatever it is added to.

☐ **Almond Extract**

Almond extract comes from the bitter almond, an unpalatable relative of the sweet almond. The highly valued oil is extracted by heating the almond and then pressing the oil. The bitterness is destroyed with the heat. Almond extract can be made with alcohol or glycerin (non-alcoholic). We usually use Almond Flavoring which is non-alcoholic.

☐ **Lemon Flavoring**

Lemon flavoring is the essential oil extract of the lemon peel combined with a carrier oil. It can replace lemon zest in baked goods or be used in sauces and soups to create a hint of lemon flavor. The brand Simply Organic makes a great lemon flavoring, which can be found at your local food co-op or health food store.

☐ **Organic Chocolate Chips**

Chocolate chips are only as good as the chocolate they are made from. Look for a high-quality, organic dark chocolate chip, such as Dagoba Chocodrops, which are gluten-free. Enjoy Life makes mini-chocolate chips, though not organic, they are gluten, dairy, egg, soy, and nut-free. Antioxidant-rich dark chocolate chips can be added to cookies, chocolate cakes, or melted to create a decadent frosting.

☐ **Organic Cocoa powder**

The cacao tree is native to tropical America and can grow up to thirty feet tall. The ripe pods that grow on the tree are seven to twelve inches long and dark reddish brown or purple in color. The pods are split open and the pulp and seeds are removed and then piled in heaps and laid out on grates for several days. During this time, the seeds and pulp undergo "sweating", where the thick pulp liquefies as it ferments. The fermented pulp drains away, leaving cocoa seeds behind. The cocoa seeds are then roasted or left raw and cracked. Now called cocoa nibs, they are ground into a thick, oily paste called chocolate liquor. The cocoa fat is rendered into a yellowish cocoa butter and the remaining powder is cocoa powder. Cocoa powder can be found raw or roasted. Raw cocoa powder has about seven times as many antioxidants as roasted cocoa powder! They can both be used interchangeably in recipes where cocoa powder is called for. Dagoba Cocoa Powder is gluten-free.

☐ **Raw Carob Powder**

The carob tree is native to southwestern Europe and western Asia and is widely cultivated in the Mediterranean region. In the United States, carob is grown mostly in California. The carob tree bears pods which are harvested in September. After the pods are sun-dried, the seeds are removed and the pulp is ground into carob powder. Carob powder can be found roasted or raw, we prefer to use raw. It can be used in place of cocoa powder in most recipes.

☐ **Kudzu**

Kudzu is a coarse, high-climbing, twining, trailing, perennial vine which grows in Asia and the southeastern United States. Kudzu powder is a starch from the kudzu root. The powder comes in crumbly white chunks and is used to thicken sauces or create a gel when cooked with a liquid and then cooled.

☐ **Agar flakes**

Agar flakes are the product of the mucilage of several species of seaweeds. The flavorless mucilage is formed into bars and then flakes or powder. Agar will gel a liquid much like gelatin does though it will have a firmer texture. 3 tablespoons flakes equal ¼ teaspoon powder. 1 tablespoon flakes will gel 1 cup of liquid. Agar flakes can be used to make healthful gelled desserts.

☐ **Arrowroot Powder**

Arrowroot Powder is made from the dried and ground rootstalks of the arrowroot plant. It has a very similar appearance to cornstarch. It is used as a thickener in sauces, stews, and gravies, or in flour blends to replace wheat flour. If you are gluten sensitive then make sure your arrowroot is truly gluten-free as some companies mill wheat on the same equipment that the arrowroot is ground, therefore cross-contaminating it. We buy ours from Authentic Foods.

☐ **Tapioca Pearls**

Tapioca Pearls are made from the starch obtained from the tuberous root of the cassava plant. They make a delicious pudding when combined with other ingredients such as nuts and fruit. Tapioca pearls usually need to be soaked for a few hours before using.

☐ **Xanthan Gum**

Xanthan gum is produced from the fermentation of corn sugar by a bacterium. Xanthan gum is used in gluten-free baking as a substitute for gluten, providing the structure and mouth-feel that gluten-free flours lack. Guar Gum can replace xanthan gum in any recipe.

Essential Cooking Equipment

"And in the end it's not the years in your life that count.
It's the life in your years."

~Abraham Lincoln

N ow that your pantry is stocked and you are ready to prepare a meal, we thought you might like to know what types of cooking equipment you will need. Having the proper cooking equipment is essential to creating great meals. Though not all of it is absolutely necessary, some of it will cut down on preparation time considerably. If you are new to cooking and do not own many kitchen items, then simply begin by adding one item at a time.

Pots and Pans

Stocking your kitchen with a high quality set of stainless steel pots and pans will be essential to your cooking and to your health. Recent research on non-stick cookware reveals that it is made using the chemical perfluorooctanic acid (PFOA). The Environmental Protection Agency advisory panel calls PFOA "a likely human carcinogen." According to research from Johns Hopkins Hospital in 2004, PFOA was found in the umbilical cord blood of 99 percent of 300 babies born there. When these non-stick pots and pans are heated they release at least six different toxic gasses, some of which have been found to be carcinogenic. We recommend that you take all of your non-stick cookware out of your house and replace them with some high quality alternatives.

Look for 18/10 stainless steel pots and pans with a thick aluminum core. The 18/10 refers to the proportion of chromium to nickel in the stainless steel alloy. The aluminum core maintains and distributes heat evenly which helps to prevent burning and sticking and is essential for cooking whole grains. If you can not afford to buy a set of new cookware then we recommend buying one 11-inch stainless steel skillet, one 3-quart stainless steel saucepan, and one 8-quart stainless steel stock pot. These three pots and pans will get you through most of the recipes in this book. I like to use stainless steel pots and pans that have a glass lid so you can easily see how the food is cooking without disturbing it. You may also choose to use a totally non-reactive, enamel-lined, cast iron cookware such as Le Creuset® for all of your cooking needs. This cookware is typically more expensive than stainless steel, so you can decide what works best for you.

- ☐ **8-inch stainless steel skillet**
- ☐ **10-inch stainless steel skillet**
- ☐ **11 or 12-inch deep stainless steel skillet with lid**
- ☐ **1 stainless steel wok**
- ☐ **1.5-quart stainless steel saucepan with lid**
- ☐ **2-quart stainless steel pot with lid**
- ☐ **3 or 3 ½-quart stainless steel pot with lid**
- ☐ **6-quart stainless steel pot with lid**
- ☐ **8-quart stainless steel stockpot with lid**
- ☐ **10 to 12-inch cast iron deep skillet**
- ☐ **10-inch enamel-lined, cast iron Dutch oven, at least 4 inches deep**

Baking Dishes

Stocking your kitchen with a few pieces of high quality baking equipment will be essential for creating many of the baked goods and other recipes in this book. Having a variety of glass bakeware, stoneware, and other items instead of aluminum and non-stick bakeware, will not only create better tasting dishes but will also benefit your health. We realize it is not always possible to have the highest quality bakeware. Favor glass or stone baking dishes and avoid aluminum and non-stick to the best of your ability.

- ☐ **10 x 14-inch glass or stone baking dish**
- ☐ **1 or 2 glass or stone 9 x 5-inch bread pans**
- ☐ **1 or 2 glass or stone 9 x 13-inch baking dishes**
- ☐ **1 square glass 8 x 8-inch baking dish**
- ☐ **1 stone or stainless steel muffin tin**
- ☐ **1 stone or stainless steel bundt pan**

- [ ] 2 stone or stainless steel cookie sheets
- [ ] 9-inch glass pie plate
- [ ] 9.5 or 10-inch stone or glass deep dish pie plate
- [ ] A variety of sizes of glass or stone casserole dishes with lids

Electric Equipment

The use of electric equipment is a relatively new invention. Throughout the history of cooking, people have relied upon their own power and strength to create meals, where today we often use some sort of electrical device. People formerly used large stone mortar and pestles for grinding grain and grinding seeds, nuts, cooked beans, and herbs to create flour, sauces, and more. Now we have food processors, blenders, grain grinders, and more that do the work for us. This has enabled us to cut down on food preparation time considerably, though in the process we have lost the intimate connection that people used to have with their food. For those of you who would like to keep food preparation time to a minimum, myself included, the following items will be helpful to have in your kitchen.

- [ ] 10 to 14 cup Food Processor (Cuisinart is our favorite)
- [ ] Blender with a very sharp blade or a Vita-Mix blender
- [ ] Immersion Blender
- [ ] Coffee grinder

Kitchen Gadgets and More

The following items will be useful to have in your kitchen to make many of the recipes in this book. Having a few high-quality, sharp knifes that feel good to work with will keep cutting and chopping fun and easy.

- [ ] 1 paring knife
- [ ] 1 serrated knife
- [ ] 1 chef's knife
- [ ] 1 mandoline
- [ ] 1 high-quality garlic press
- [ ] 1 ginger grater
- [ ] 1 Microplane for grating citrus peel
- [ ] 1 citrus juicer
- [ ] 1 fine mesh strainer with handle
- [ ] 1 long stainless steel spoon and 1 slotted spoon
- [ ] A variety or wooden and stainless steel spatulas and spoons
- [ ] A variety of sizes of silicone spatulas
- [ ] 4, 2, and 1 cup liquid glass measuring cups
- [ ] 1 large wooden cutting board for cutting vegetables and fruits
- [ ] 1 small plastic cutting board for cutting meat and fish

Food Storage Containers:

When you cook your own food, instead of eating packaged meals from the supermarket or eating out, you will need containers to store leftover food in. Most of the recipes in this book make large batches. This makes it easier to stick to a healthy diet because you will have ready-made meals in your fridge at most times.

We prefer to use glass storage containers such as Pyrex® to store our leftovers in. Be sure to have a few different sizes on hand to store everything from large batches of soup to small amounts of ground grains or seeds.

Reusable plastic containers work well for freezing meals in. Be sure to wait until hot food has cooled before placing into the plastic container because these types of containers leach toxic plastic compounds into the foods they contain. This is why it is always preferable to store your food in glass whenever possible.

We like to store our homemade salad dressing in used glass nut butter jars. After you are done with your nut butter, simply rinse out the jar and run it through the dishwasher. When you are ready to make a dressing, just add all the ingredients to the jar, shake well, and store unused portions in the refrigerator.

- ☐ **Glass storage containers, in a variety of shapes and sizes**
- ☐ **Plastic storage containers, in a variety of shapes and sizes**
- ☐ **Clean, used nut butter glass jars or other clean glass jars**

Definition of Cooking Techniques

"Joy is a return to the deep harmony of body, mind, and spirit that was yours at birth and that can be yours again; that openness to love, that capacity for wholeness with the world around you, is still within you."

~Deepak Chopra

Cooking and preparing meals is an art of intuition and a science of basic cooking knowledge. Blending the two together will help to create fabulous meals. Below is a list of basic cooking techniques that are used throughout this cookbook. It will be helpful to familiarize yourself with them before moving on to the recipes. When making a recipe, use your intuition as to whether or not you should add more or less of certain ingredients and how long to cook some dishes. No recipe can ever be perfect because of the incredible variations in ingredients, cooking equipment, and the person who is preparing the recipe.

Cutting Techniques

Chiffonade: This cutting technique can be used for leafy greens, such as chard, kale and collards, and fresh herbs, such as basil and mint. Stack the leaves one on top of another. Then tightly roll lengthwise. Slice with a sharp knife horizontally to make long, thin strips.

Chopping: A chef's knife is typically used for chopping. This general technique involves cutting the food into pieces where no specific size or shape is called for.

Dicing: Dicing food produces small even squares or cubes. Diced vegetables are typically in an eighth to quarter-inch cubes. Slice the food item into long strips, and then cut across the slices to make cubes. This technique can be used for onions, tomatoes, bell peppers, cucumbers, yams, as well as many other vegetables and fruits.

Julienne Cut (Matchsticks): The julienne cut creates small matchstick pieces. This technique is used for cutting vegetables that go into sushi rolls, as well as for many other recipes. Simply take your vegetable, a carrot for example, and cut it diagonally into eighth-inch slices. Then take each slice and cut into thin strips lengthwise.

Mincing: Mincing is a technique used for cutting food into very small pieces. Strong-flavored foods such as garlic, shallots, onions, ginger, and hot peppers are typically minced to incorporate flavors evenly. Use a chef's knife and start by slicing the food, then chop back and forth in a rocking motion until the food is in small, fine pieces.

Shredding: Shredded vegetables add a juicy, delicate flavor to salads and can also be used to add extra nutrients to baked goods. Food can be shredded by hand with a hand-held stainless steel grater or in a food processor with the grating disc in place. For vegetables, the finer the shred, the sweeter the flavor.

Slicing: Slicing is a broad term used for cutting food into various shapes, such as discs, wedges, or strips. Recipes typically will explain the nature of the slice. Green onions can be sliced into rounds, carrots into rounds too. A bell pepper can be sliced lengthwise into long strips or sliced horizontally into rings. Apples can be sliced into thin wedges and potatoes can be sliced into rounds or wedges.

Zesting: Zesting is used to remove the outer portion of citrus skin where all of the delicate oils hide. You can zest a citrus fruit with a specialized zesting tool or with a fine grater. The key is to just remove the outer skin and not the bitter white pith beneath.

Preparation Techniques

Marinating: Pouring a liquid that contains an acidic and/or salty substance, such as vinegar, citrus, or tamari, over the food and allowing it sit for a period of time so that the flavors will penetrate the food.

Soaking: Place food in a bowl and cover with a liquid, usually purified water, so the food can rehydrate by absorbing the liquid. Keep the bowl on your kitchen counter at room temperature. This technique is used for soaking nuts, seeds, beans, whole grains, and dried fruit.

Puréeing: Puréeing food turns it into a thick smooth liquid. A blender works best to purée foods, though a food processor or hand held immersion blender may also be used. Place food such as steamed squash, frozen or fresh fruit, or cooked soups into a blender. To blend hot foods, fill bender no more than half full, place a towel over the lid and firmly hold it in place. Start on the lowest speed and gradually increase as food is blending.

Roasting Bell Peppers: Place peppers in a baking dish under the broiler until the skin is charred, turning frequently, about 8 to 10 minutes. Remove peppers from pan and place them into a paper bag or a covered glass bowl, let stand at room temperature for about 10 minutes. Remove peppers and peel off charred skin. Cut peppers and remove the seeds.

Storing Tofu: When you open a package of tofu and only use part of it, the unused portion needs to be stored properly to keep it from spoiling. Rinse tofu under cool water then place it into a container, fill the container with purified water to cover the tofu. Change the water every day until you use the remaining tofu.

Freezing: Freezing your own fruits and vegetables that you have either harvested yourself or bought from the Farmer's Market is a great way to preserve food. Also, freezing your leftovers will make it easy to have healthy homemade meals on nights you may not want to, or have time to cook. Be sure to label and date your food and use it in about 3 to 6 months.

> **Bananas:** Remove the peel, cut into 2-inch slices and place into a reusable plastic container in your freezer.
>
> **Berries:** Freeze on baking sheets then transfer into reusable plastic storage containers and place back into freezer.
>
> **Beans:** Cook beans according to directions on *page 140* , then place into 2 to 3-cup plastic storage containers, add bean cooking liquid to cover beans, and place into freezer.
>
> **Muffins:** Cool your freshly cooked muffins to room temperature then place into a plastic bag in a single layer. Place in your freezer.
>
> **Leftovers:** In general, foods that have a higher liquid content, such as soups, casseroles, bean dips, and pureed vegetables and fruits freeze well. Place cooled food into reusable plastic storage containers and freeze. To use, run the container under hot water to release food. Place frozen food in a pot to reheat.

Warming Tortillas: Corn tortillas and brown rice tortillas are best warmed before you use them to prevent cracking and breaking. An easy way to warm any type of tortilla is to place it on top of steaming hot food, either in the oven, in a pot, or on your plate. We usually use this approach when making burritos or some kind of wrap with brown rice tortillas. When making enchiladas, you can lightly sauté each corn tortilla in a small amount of olive oil or coconut oil or you can dip each tortilla in the hot enchilada sauce—which is what we usually do.

Cooking Techniques

Baking: Place food in a baking dish into a preheated oven. Moisture is released from the food while it is baking and circulates in the oven. When you are baking more than one dish at a time be sure to stagger the dishes so that the air may circulate. All oven temperatures will vary slightly, so you may need to adjust your temperature and/or cooking time to your oven.

Blanching: Quickly boiling vegetables, usually for only a few minutes, and then placing them in a cold water bath to stop cooking. This technique works to preserve colors and nutrients in food.

Boiling: Placing a food into water or a cooking liquid, such as stock, in an uncovered pot that has reached a temperature of about 212 degrees F or where bubbles are visible on the surface. The food is cooked by the rapidly moving liquid. The boiling point can be defined as the temperature at which the vapor pressure of a substance is equal to the external, or atmospheric, pressure. When cooking at higher elevations, the boiling point of a liquid will be lower due to the drop in atmospheric pressure. For each 1000 feet above sea level the boiling point drops by about 2 degrees Fahrenheit. Water-soluble substances, such as salt and sugar, raise the boiling point of water.

Braising: Food is lightly sautéed, then a small amount of a flavored liquid is added and the pan is covered while the food cooks and absorbs part of the liquid.

Broiling: Turn your oven dial to "broil" and place food in an oven-safe dish on the rack level indicated in your recipe.

Par-Boil: To partially cook a food in boiling water; the cooking is then completed by some other method.

Poaching: Food is cooked by submerging it into a liquid that is just barely simmering. Be sure the food is covered in the cooking liquid by about ½ to 1 inch. The cooking liquid is usually stock or water with an acid added to it, such as lemon juice or vinegar. Fresh or dried herbs and a salt or salt seasoning are also added (except for eggs—do not add salt while poaching eggs). This technique works to retain the original shape of the food.

Pressure Cooking: Cooking with a pressure cooker decreases cooking times tremendously. Temperatures inside a pressure cooker can reach 250 degrees F, much higher than boiling temperature. Never fill a pressure cooker more than half full and be sure to use the recommended amount of liquid.

Roasting: Cooking food by dry heat in an oven, usually with some kind of fat added.

Sautéing: Add a small amount of oil or fat to a heated skillet, then add your cut food. Keep the food moving in the pan to prevent burning and sticking. Sautéing is a quick-moving process that necessitates having all of the ingredients within arm's reach and ready for use. If your food begins to stick to the pan during cooking then add extra fat, water, wine, or stock to the pan.

> **Water-Oil Sauté**: If you would like to lessen the amount of oil in a dish, you can replace half of it with water. Continue to sauté as directed above.

> **No-Oil Sauté:** It is not necessary to always sauté in oil. Instead, you may add a small amount of water, broth, or white wine to the pan and sauté as directed above.

Simmering: Cooking a liquid on the stove where bubbles are barely breaking the surface is simmering. This is usually done by bringing the liquid and food to a boil first then turning heat to low to medium-low and cooking with a lid on the pot.

Steaming: Steaming is a great way to barely cook vegetables until they are crisp-tender. This method of cooking retains more nutrients than other methods. Place about 2 inches of water in a pot, then place a steamer basket in the pot and add your food. Place a lid on the pot and cook for a certain amount of time. You can test doneness with a fork—food should pierce easily but the fork should not easily go all the way through the piece of food.

Steeping: Steeping extracts color, flavor, and nutrients from the substance being steeped. Place food or herbs into a ceramic or glass dish and pour boiling water over them. Place a cover on the dish and steep for directed amount of time. Herbs or food are then strained out of the liquid.

Stir-frying: Place your cut food in piles on your cutting board or in separate dishes and line up from longest cooking to shortest cooking. You may use a wok or a large skillet, but be sure to use stainless steel, no non-stick. Heat your pan over medium-high heat and add some fat—usually coconut oil. Begin by placing the longest cooking food in first then move up to the shortest cooking food. Keep the food moving in pan constantly to prevent burning—this process usually only takes a few minutes. Then add a small amount of liquid to the pan and cover with a lid to quickly finish the cooking by steaming.

Toasting: Raw seeds can be toasted to improve flavor and digestibility. To toast seeds, heat a thick-bottomed stainless steel skillet over medium heat. Add enough seeds to pan to create one layer. Keep the pan moving over the heat source to prevent burning. When the seeds are lightly golden or you have heard "popping" sounds, then the seeds are done. Immediately transfer them to a plate to cool. Seeds that can be toasted include pumpkin, sunflower, and sesame.

THE RECIPES

Breakfast

"Wisdom begins in wonder."

~Socrates

T he word "breakfast" literally means to break the fast. This is a time of the day when your body is ready to receive nourishment after a night of fasting. The mind and body function much better throughout the day if they are fed upon awakening.

Skipping breakfast may lead to overeating at later meals. This is because you will be hungrier and will tend to eat faster and larger portions to relieve the hunger and desire for food. When you are very hungry it is easier to eat too much as well as to eat foods which have a high fat and sugar content.

One of the fastest ways to boost your metabolism is to simply eat a nutritious breakfast every morning. Choose foods such as whole grain cereals, any combination of nuts and fruits, organic eggs, tofu, or even miso soup with fish added to it. All of these foods eaten first thing in the morning readily give your metabolism a boost for the entire day and provide your body with the nutrients you need to start your day. If you are unaccustomed to consuming food in the morning then it may take a little more planning until you get in the habit of morning meals. Plan your breakfast before you go to bed the night before. Set out any items to be used to prepare your breakfast and be sure your kitchen is clean.

Quick Nutritious Breakfast Ideas:

- **Rice bread, raw almond butter, and apricot jam sandwich** with a piece of seasonal organic fruit

- **Plain cooked millet or quinoa** with chopped raw nuts and fresh or dried fruit on top. See *page 212* for how to cook whole grains

- **Toasted rice bread spread with cashew butter** and a glass of your favorite green smoothie

- **2 organic hard boiled eggs**, steamed kale, cooked quinoa, and a spoonful of raw cultured vegetables on the side

- **A bowl of your favorite seasonal organic fruit** topped with plenty of soaked raw almonds

- **Leftover beans and grains** wrapped up in a brown rice tortilla, lettuce leaf, or cabbage leaf with your favorite fixings

- **Leftover cooked salmon** over Breakfast Greens, *page 119*

- **Leftover tempeh and some cooked grains** combined with any raw or cooked vegetable

- **Simple bowl of fresh chopped seasonal fruit** with raw nuts and seeds sprinkled on top

- **Gluten-free muffin** and a fresh green smoothie

- **Basic Buckwheat**, *page 215*, cooked with dates and topped with chopped Brazil nuts

Energizing Berry Nut Smoothie

This smoothie makes for a quick breakfast on the go or a nourishing afternoon snack. You can even add a few handfuls of fresh spinach or lettuce while blending for a more nutrient packed drink. To freeze your ripe bananas, simply remove the peels, break the banana into pieces, and then place them into plastic storage containers in the freezer.

SERVES 1 TO 2

1 cup raw cashews
1 cup water or rice milk
1 cup frozen banana pieces
½ cup frozen blueberries
½ cup frozen cherries

> *Going Dairy-Free Tip*
>
> Raw cashews blended with water can easily replace yogurt or milk in any smoothie recipe.

1. Place raw cashews and water or rice milk in a blender fitted with a sharp blade. Blend on high until smooth and creamy.

2. Add frozen banana chunks, blueberries, and cherries. Blend on medium-high until smooth.

Cherry Almond Smoothie

This nutrient packed smoothie will protect your arteries and can help lower your blood pressure. Almonds are a rich source of magnesium; in fact, ½ cup provides almost 200 mg which is about 50% of the daily value for this mineral. Magnesium helps your blood vessels to relax, which improves the flow of blood and oxygen throughout the body.

SERVES 1 TO 2

> ½ cup raw almonds, soaked
> ½ cup water
> 1 ripe pear, cored and cut into wedges
> 1 cup organic fresh or frozen cherries

1. The night before you plan to make this smoothie, soak the almonds by placing them in a small dish or jar. Cover them with purified water and set them on the counter to soak overnight or up to 8 hours.

2. In the morning drain off the soaking water and rinse the almonds. Place them in the blender with the cup of water. Blend on high until thick and creamy.

3. Add pear and cherries and blend for another minute until very creamy.

Minty Green Smoothie

Drinking your greens in a smoothie is an easy and digestible way to get many of the green vegetables you need daily to support and recharge your body. Kale is a powerful, medicinal food providing ample protective phytochemicals that work to prevent and treat many different forms of cancer. We like to make variations of this smoothie every morning and drink it throughout the day. Try substituting the banana for another pear and add the juice of one lime.

SERVES 1 TO 3

> 1 ripe banana, peeled and broken into pieces
> 1 medium apple, cored and cut into chunks
> 1 ripe pear, cored and cut into chunks
> 1 lemon, juiced
> 2 to 3 cups water
> 3 to 4 lettuce or spinach leaves, rinsed
> 3 to 4 kale leaves, rinsed and torn
> ¼ cup fresh parsley leaves
> 2 to 4 tablespoons fresh mint leaves

1. Remove the tough stems from the kale and break the kale into pieces. Place the banana pieces, apple chunks, pear chunks, lemon juice, and water into the blender. Blend on high, stopping as needed to push the fruit down.

2. Then add the lettuce leaves, kale pieces, parsley, and mint leaves; blend again until very smooth Add more water if needed and blend until completely smooth and brilliant green.

Lemony Cabbage and Cranberry Smoothie

This smoothie has a beautiful pink hue from the cranberries and is as medicinal as it is delicious. Cabbage is a rich source of cancer-fighting phytochemicals called glucosinolates. Cranberries are also a rich source of phytochemicals including proanthocyanidins which work in the body to prevent and treat urinary tract infections, quinic acid which helps to prevent kidney stones, and anthocyanidins which have been shown to inhibit the development of atherosclerosis, cancer, and other degenerative diseases. Fresh cranberries have the highest antioxidant levels compared to dried or processed juices.

SERVES 1 TO 3

2 medium apples, cored and cut into chunks
2 ripe pears, cored and cut into chunks
1 cup water
1 to 2 lemons, juiced
½ cup fresh or frozen cranberries
5 Napa or Savoy cabbage leaves, rinsed and torn
1 to 2 inch piece fresh ginger, peeled and sliced

1. Place the apple chunks, pear chunks, water, and lemon juice into a blender fitted with a sharp blade or a Vita-mix and blend until smooth and creamy.

2. Add the cranberries, cabbage leaves, and sliced ginger and blend again on high until very smooth.

Tom's Fruity Medicine Chest Smoothie

Tom makes a large batch of this smoothie nearly every morning. The fruit in it changes according to the seasons. In the summer we use peaches and nectarines instead of pears and apples. This smoothie has been paramount in the lives of many people we have helped. It can literally change your health in a matter of days and hours. The fruit is a rich source of soluble fiber and a host of vitamins and antioxidants. The greens offer powerful phytochemicals. Cabbage is a potent food that affects many pathways in the body. Ginger is a powerful anti-inflammatory. The lemon offers vitamin C and bioflavonoids. And yes, it tastes great, as many of the people in our cooking classes will tell you. This smoothie makes enough to fill a Vita-Mix so divide the recipe in half if you are using a regular blender.

SERVES 2 TO 4

2 apples, cored and cut into chunks
2 ripe pears, cored and cut into chunks
1 to 2 cups water
2 lemons, juiced
1 to 2-inch piece fresh ginger, peeled and sliced
5 kale leaves, rinsed and torn
5 romaine lettuce leaves, spinach leaves, or collard greens, rinsed
1 cup coarsely chopped green cabbage, optional

Optional Additions:
1 to 2 kiwi fruit
1 handful of fresh parsley or mint leaves
2 to 3 tablespoons flax seeds
½ cup soaked goji berries

1. Place the apple chunks, pear chunks, water, and lemon juice into a blender fitted with a sharp blade or a Vita-Mix and blend until smooth and creamy.

2. Add the ginger, black kale, romaine lettuce, and green cabbage, and blend again until very smooth. Add more water for a thinner smoothie.

3. You can taste it now and if it is too "lettucy" for you then add another pear and blend again. Add more water for a thinner consistency.

Glorious Morning Fruit Bowl

The flavors of this fruit bowl are quite exotic and glorious. This makes for a very light breakfast for those days when you feel a little sluggish in the morning and could use a light meal.

SERVES 2 TO 4

½ **cup raw organic almonds, soaked overnight, then chopped**
1 **ripe mango, peeled and cut into chunks**
1 **ripe banana, sliced**
2 **kiwis, peeled and diced**
1 **ripe pear, cut into chunks**
2 **tablespoons lime juice**
2 **to 4 tablespoons organic shredded coconut**

1. Soak the almonds in a bowl with 1 ½ cups purified water at room temperature for 8 to 10 hours or overnight.

2. In the morning drain off the soaking water and rinse well. Place almonds onto a cutting board and chop.

3. Place almonds and all other ingredients into a bowl and gently mix together.

Cinnamon Spiced Granola

This easy-to-make granola is perfect to have on hand for busy mornings. It can top fresh fruit, be served with a dollop of organic yogurt, or served as a breakfast cereal with hemp milk or another non-dairy milk. You can add any dried fruit after it has been cooked. If you have a nut allergy, then substitute sunflower seeds and pumpkin seeds for the nuts.

MAKES ABOUT 5 CUPS

3 cups rolled oats
1 cup coarsely chopped walnuts
1 cup coarsely chopped almonds
1 tablespoon cinnamon
½ teaspoon nutmeg
¼ teaspoon cloves
¼ teaspoon ginger
¼ teaspoon sea salt
½ cup maple syrup
½ cup melted coconut oil or ¼ cup apple juice + ¼ cup coconut oil
1 teaspoon vanilla

Optional Additions:
chopped dried apple
raisins
dried cranberries
dried cherries
shredded coconut
sunflower seeds
pumpkin seeds

> ### Going Gluten-Free Tip
>
> Oats can sometimes contain traces of gluten if processed in a facility that also processes gluten-containing grains. Be sure to use Certified Gluten-Free Oats.

1. Preheat oven to 300 degrees F. Place the rolled oats, chopped nuts, and spices into a medium-sized bowl. Mix well.

2. Add the maple syrup, melted coconut oil and vanilla to the oat mixture. Toss together using two spoons. Add shredded coconut and any seeds if desired, toss again.

3. Spread mixture onto a large cookie sheet and place in the oven. Bake for 35 to 40 minutes, turning occasionally with a spatula.

4. Remove from oven and stir in any dried fruit if desired. Let cool completely before transferring to a large glass jar.

Blueberry Almond Oatmeal

Oatmeal makes for a quick and nutritious breakfast. The almonds and blueberries add more nutrients and flavor to brighten up plain oats. Make sure you buy the thick cut rolled oats as they are processed less than the quick cooking variety.

SERVES 3 TO 4

2 cups thick rolled oats
4 cups water
pinch sea salt
maple syrup or agave nectar
blueberries, fresh or frozen
raw almonds, ground
cinnamon

> **Going Gluten-Free Tip**
>
> If you are gluten sensitive then use Certified Gluten-Free Oats.

1. Place oats, water, and sea salt into a medium saucepan. Turn heat to medium, cook oatmeal until it begins to bubble then turn heat to low.

2. Continue stirring until oatmeal is thick and cooked, about 10 minutes.

3. Grind raw almonds in a coffee grinder to a fine meal.

1. Place desired amount of oatmeal into a serving bowl, top with a little maple syrup or agave nectar, a handful of blueberries, and a tablespoon or two of ground almonds. Sprinkle with cinnamon if desired.

Morning Millet Cereal

This delicious breakfast cereal is wonderful by itself or can be topped with chopped dates and nuts. You can save time by rinsing, toasting, and grinding the millet a few days ahead of time. Store ground millet in a jar with a tight fitting lid in your refrigerator for up to two weeks. Use one heaping cup of ground millet per four cups of water and a pinch of sea salt. Millet is a good source of manganese, phosphorus, and magnesium.

SERVES 3 TO 4

1 cup millet
4 cups water
pinch sea salt

1. First rinse the millet in a fine mesh strainer under warm running water for a minute or two. Drain off any excess water.

2. Then place millet into a large skillet and heat over medium heat. Stir and keep millet moving in the pan so the moisture will evaporate, about 5 to 10 minutes.

3. Once this process is complete place millet into an electric grinder and grind to a fine powder.

4. Place ground millet into a medium saucepan with the four cups of water and pinch of sea salt. Whisk together then turn heat to medium high and continue whisking until bubbling. Turn heat to low and continue to stir occasionally until cereal has thickened and millet is cooked, about 15 minutes.

5. Top with maple syrup or chopped dates, berries, and nuts if desired.

Sweet Rice Cereal

*This delightful cereal is best topped with a little maple syrup and a spoonful of virgin coconut oil. The rice can be ground ahead of time and stored in a glass jar in the refrigerator for up to two weeks. This cereal is great for babies **8 months** and older. Brown rice is an excellent source of manganese and a good source of selenium and magnesium.*

SERVES 3 TO 4

> **1 cup sweet brown rice, ground**
> **3 cups water**
> **pinch sea salt**

1. Grind the rice in an electric grinder or coffee grinder to a fine powder.

1. Place the ground rice, water, and sea salt in a medium saucepan and whisk together. Turn heat to medium-high and bring cereal to a boil. Then turn heat to low and continue to whisk until completely cooked and thickened, about 15 minutes.

Spiced Apple and Rice Cereal

Serve this warming cereal on a cool fall morning before work or school. In the summertime we use fresh peaches instead of apples for the topping and freshly ground raw almonds instead of walnuts for the garnish. Since peaches have more liquid than apples simply reduce the water to just a few tablespoons when making the topping. You may use brown jasmine rice instead of the brown basmati if you desire.

SERVES 3 TO 4

1 cup brown basmati rice, ground
1 cup hemp milk, rice milk, soy milk, or almond milk
2 to 3 cups water
½ teaspoon cinnamon
¼ teaspoon ground cardamom
pinch sea salt

Apple Topping:
2 teaspoons virgin coconut oil
2 to 3 tart apples, cored and thinly sliced
¼ cup Zante currants, optional
2 to 3 tablespoons maple syrup or whole cane sugar
1 teaspoon cinnamon
¼ teaspoon ground nutmeg
½ cup water

chopped raw walnuts, for garnish

1. Grind rice in a coffee grinder until finely ground. Place into a 2-quart pot with the milk, water, cinnamon, cardamom, and sea salt.

2. Bring to a boil, then turn heat to a low simmer and stir frequently until cooked, about 15 minutes. Add more water as needed for a thinner consistency. Remove from heat when cooked.

3. In a medium skillet, heat coconut oil; add the apples, Zante currants, maple syrup or sugar, cinnamon, and nutmeg. Sauté for about 2 minutes then add water and simmer for about 5 minutes, uncovered, stirring frequently.

4. Place rice cereal into individual serving bowls and spoon apple mixture over each. Garnish each bowl with chopped walnuts if desired.

Teff Breakfast Porridge

Teff, an ancient Ethiopian grain, is very high in protein and iron. It cooks up quickly and easily making it an ideal quick breakfast. Try topping the porridge with dried cranberries or cherries and finely chopped nuts. In the summertime we top this with sliced peaches or nectarines, ground raw almonds, and a drizzle of agave nectar.

SERVES 2 TO 3

3 cups water
pinch sea salt
1 cup teff grain

1. In a medium pot, bring water and sea salt to a boil. Add teff and stir a little. Cook for 15 to 20 minutes, covered. Towards the end of cooking time, stir occasionally.

2. Top with dried or fresh fruit and chopped nuts if desired.

Warming Three Grain Morning Cereal

The combination of the quinoa, millet, and amaranth make this morning porridge especially nutritious and very high in protein. The nutty flavor of the three grains lends some heartiness to your morning meal. Try adding some ground toasted pumpkin seeds on top with sliced apples and a dash of honey or maple syrup.

SERVES 3 TO 4

¾ cup quinoa, rinsed
¾ cup millet, rinsed
¾ cup amaranth, rinsed
5 cups water
pinch sea salt

1. Rinse the grains in a very fine mesh strainer. Let warm water run through them while you move them around with your hand. Rinsing is very important step to remove the bitter saponin coating on the outside of the grains.

2. Place the washed grains into a 2 or 3-quart pot with the water and sea salt. Cover and bring to a boil, then reduce heat to low and simmer for about 25 minutes. Remove from heat and serve with your favorite toppings.

Buckwheat Pancakes

These rich yet light pancakes are always a crowd pleaser. Try serving with pure maple syrup, fresh plum or apricot slices, and a sprinkling of cinnamon. These pancakes are also delicious served with the Warm Berry Sauce on page 315. I prefer to grind my own buckwheat flour from raw buckwheat groats in a coffee grinder just prior to making these. I find the flavor superior to packaged buckwheat flour. Many people who dislike the strong flavor of buckwheat will enjoy these when made with the freshly ground flour.

MAKES 5 TO 7 PANCAKES

Going Egg-Free Tip

Try using 1 heaping tablespoon ground flax seeds whisked with 3 tablespoons boiling water to replace 1 egg in any baked good recipe.

1 heaping cup buckwheat flour
¼ cup tapioca flour
1 teaspoon baking powder
½ teaspoon baking soda
¼ teaspoon sea salt
1 to 1 ½ cups hemp, almond, soy, or rice milk
1 organic egg
2 tablespoons melted virgin coconut oil or organic butter
1 tablespoon maple syrup or agave nectar

virgin coconut oil or organic butter for cooking

1. In a medium bowl mix together the dry ingredients. In a separate bowl whisk together the wet ingredients. Add the wet to the dry and gently mix until ingredients are combined. Let the batter sit a few minutes to thicken up.

2. Heat a thick-bottomed stainless steel skillet over medium heat. Add a few teaspoons of coconut oil or butter. When skillet has heated, add about ½ cup of batter. Cook for about 1 to 2 minutes or until top begins to bubble, flip and cook for a minute or so more on the other side. Repeat this process until all of the batter has been used. Add a little coconut oil or butter in between cooking each pancake to prevent sticking.

3. Place pancakes onto a warm plate and serve.

Rice Flour Pancakes

These easy-to-make pancakes are well loved by children. Serve them with Grade B pure maple syrup and a glass of freshly squeezed orange juice for a classic breakfast.

MAKES 5 TO 7 PANCAKES

1 cup brown rice flour
¼ cup tapioca flour
1 teaspoon baking powder
½ teaspoon baking soda
¼ teaspoon xanthan gum
¼ teaspoon sea salt
1 ½ cups hemp, soy, almond, or rice milk
1 organic egg
2 tablespoons melted virgin coconut oil or organic butter
1 tablespoon pure maple syrup or agave nectar

virgin coconut oil or organic butter for cooking

> ### Going Egg-Free Tip
>
> Try using 1 heaping tablespoon ground flax seeds whisked with 3 tablespoons boiling water to replace 1 egg in any baked good recipe.

1. In a medium bowl, mix the dry ingredients together. You can place the dry mixture into a glass jar and store in your pantry to have on hand for those mornings when you are pinched for time. Just be sure to place a label on the jar with the name, date, and directions for adding wet ingredients to the mixture.

2. Whisk the wet ingredients in a separate bowl. Add the wet ingredients to the dry and gently mix together.

1. Heat a 10-inch stainless steel skillet over medium heat. Add a little virgin coconut oil or organic butter for cooking. When the pan is hot, add about ½ cup batter. Cook for about 1 to 2 minutes or until top begins to bubble, flip and cook for a minute or so more on the other side. Repeat this process, adding more coconut oil or butter in between pancakes, until all of the batter has been used.

Variations:
- Add 1 mashed banana to the batter for banana pancakes
- Add 1 tablespoon lemon juice to the milk and fresh or frozen blueberries to the batter for blueberry "buttermilk" pancakes
- Add 1 grated apple + 1 teaspoon cinnamon to the batter for apple cinnamon pancakes
- Replace half of the rice flour with amaranth flour for a more nutrient-dense pancake
- Replace rice flour with teff flour for a hearty, nutrient-dense pancake. Try adding ¼ cup mashed banana for a teff banana pancake

Oatmeal Blueberry Banana Pancakes

*This pancake makes a great breakfast for wheat or gluten intolerant people. It is also well loved among small children and babies older than **9 months**. Serve with raw almond butter and pure maple syrup.*

MAKES 5 TO 7 PANCAKES

1 ½ cups thick rolled oats
1 teaspoon baking powder
½ teaspoon baking soda
1 ¼ cups rice, almond, or hemp milk
2 tablespoons melted virgin coconut oil
1 tablespoon maple syrup
1 small banana, lightly mashed
½ cup blueberries, fresh or frozen

virgin coconut oil for cooking

> ## Going Gluten-Free Tip
>
> Some brands of non-dairy milk contain a small amount of barley malt. Barley is a gluten-containing grain and not safe for someone intolerant of gluten. Also, be sure to use Certified Gluten-Free Oats.

1. Grind oats to a fine powder in an electric grinder, or coffee grinder. Place ground oats, baking powder, and baking soda in a medium sized mixing bowl and stir together.

2. In a separate bowl, combine rice milk, coconut oil, maple syrup, and mashed banana and stir together. Pour the wet ingredients into the dry and mix together. Be sure to not over mix batter! Gently fold in the blueberries. Add more rice milk if batter seems too thick.

3. Heat a skillet over medium-low heat. Add a little coconut oil and drop the batter by the ½ cup full into the pan. Cook for about 2 minutes on each side. Watch temperature very carefully to avoid burning. Add more coconut oil to the pan before you cook the next pancake. Repeat this process until all the batter has been used.

Root Vegetable Pancakes

Serve these hearty pancakes with one of the tofu scramble recipes on the following two pages and a green smoothie for a nutrient and energy-packed breakfast. I like to use my food processor for these; first I mince the onion with the "s" blade, then I put in the grating disc and grate the vegetables. It only takes a minute or two to do all this. To get the pancakes on the table faster, try cooking them in two or three skillets at once.

MAKES 5 TO 7 PANCAKES

    1 small onion, minced
    1 small yam, peeled and grated
    2 medium yellow or red potatoes, grated
    1 carrot, grated
    ¼ to ½ cup brown rice flour or sorghum flour
    1 teaspoon dried thyme
    ½ teaspoon Herbamare or sea salt
    1 tablespoon dulse flakes
    extra virgin olive oil for cooking

1. Place the minced onion and grated vegetables into a large bowl. Add the brown rice flour, dried thyme, Herbamare, and dulse flakes; mix well.

2. Heat a medium sized stainless steel skillet over medium heat. Form the mixture into thin patties with your hands. They will fall apart when raw but when cooked the starches will be released and they will hold together.

3. Add some olive oil and one or two patties to the heated skillet. Cover the skillet with a lid and cook for approximately 5 minutes, then flip, cover, and cook for another 5 minutes. Place onto a serving platter. Add a little more olive oil to the pan for each batch you cook. You may need to adjust the temperature to prevent any burning.

Tofu Scramble

Tofu is a good source of protein. In fact, recent research shows that regular intake of soy protein can help to lower total cholesterol levels, lower triglyceride levels, and reduce the tendency of platelets to form blood clots. Serve this dish with the Minty Green Smoothie on page 97, or the Breakfast greens on page 119 for a balanced meal.

SERVES 3 TO 4

> 1 tablespoon extra virgin olive oil
> 5 green onions, sliced into rounds
> 1 ½ cups chopped mushrooms
> 1 small red bell pepper, diced
> 1 teaspoon dried thyme
> 1 teaspoon garlic powder, or 2 cloves crushed
> ½ to 1 teaspoon turmeric
> 1 teaspoon sea salt or Herbamare
> 1 pound firm tofu, crumbled

1. Heat olive oil in a skillet over medium heat. Add the green onions, mushrooms, and red bell pepper. Sauté until tender, about 5 to 7 minutes.

2. Add spices, herbs, and sea salt, sauté a minute more and stir to coat.

3. Add crumbled tofu, mixing it into the vegetables. Sauté 2 minutes more. Add a few tablespoons water if mixture seems dry.

Tofu and Arame Scramble

Arame is a sea vegetable that is harvested off the coast of Ise, Japan. With its sweet mild flavor, Arame is a good sea vegetable to start with if you are unfamiliar with the flavors of seaweeds. It is rich in iodine, magnesium, calcium, and vitamin A. It is also a source of potassium, iron, vitamin B2, zinc and many essential trace minerals. Serve this delicious tofu scramble with Root Vegetable Pancakes on page 111, and Breakfast Greens on page 119 for a meal that will keep you going all morning long.

SERVES 3 TO 4

¼ cup arame, soaked in water for 10 minutes
1 tablespoon extra virgin olive oil
1 bunch green onions, sliced into rounds
1 small red bell pepper, diced
3 cloves garlic, crushed
1 ½ teaspoons ground coriander
1 teaspoon turmeric
1 pound firm tofu, crumbled
2 tablespoons wheat-free tamari
chopped cilantro, for garnish

1. Drain arame and place into a small pot with a cup of water and simmer for 10 minutes; drain and set aside.

2. Heat a large skillet over medium heat. Add olive oil, green onions, diced red pepper and crushed garlic. Sauté for about five minutes or until red pepper is tender.

3. Add coriander, turmeric, crumbled tofu, and arame; cook for five to seven minutes stirring occasionally. Remove from heat, add tamari, mix well, and garnish with chopped cilantro if desired.

Buckwheat and Tempeh Hash

A diet high in buckwheat has been associated with lowered total cholesterol, lowered LDL cholesterol, and a high ratio of HDL cholesterol to total cholesterol. Buckwheat is high in flavonoids, particularly rutin, which help to maintain blood flow, keep platelets from clotting excessively, and protect LDL from free radical oxidation. Serve this hearty breakfast dish with the Breakfast Greens on page 119, and a fresh apple for a balanced breakfast.

SERVES 3 TO 4

1 ½ cups water
¼ teaspoon sea salt
1 cup roasted buckwheat (kasha)

one 8-ounce package tempeh, cut into small cubes
3 tablespoons wheat-free tamari
1 tablespoon brown rice vinegar
2 cloves garlic, crushed

1 tablespoon extra virgin olive oil
1 small red onion, diced
½ teaspoon oregano
½ teaspoon freshly ground black pepper
2 cups finely chopped Swiss chard leaves

1. In a small 1 ½ quart pot, bring water and sea salt to a boil. Add roasted buckwheat, cover, and simmer for 15 to 20 minutes or until all of the water has been absorbed. Remove pot from heat and let stand for 10 minutes.

2. While buckwheat is cooking, place the tempeh cubes into a dish with the tamari, brown rice vinegar, and garlic to marinate. Let marinate for about 15 to 20 minutes.

3. In a large skillet, heat olive oil over medium heat. Add diced onion and sauté until soft, about 5 minutes. Then add the marinated tempeh cubes, oregano, and black pepper. Sauté for a few more minutes to cook the tempeh.

4. Add the chopped Swiss chard and cooked buckwheat and sauté, stirring frequently, until the chard has wilted but is still bright green. Remove from heat, taste, and adjust seasonings if necessary.

Fun Scrambled Eggs

This is a tasty way to add more flavor and nutrients to plain scrambled eggs. Serve with toasted Honey Whole Grain Bread, page 124, and home-style potatoes if desired. Grade AA eggs are the freshest source of eggs that you can buy at the store. Buying from a local organic company will usually ensure their freshness.

SERVES 2

4 large grade AA organic eggs
2 tablespoons water
organic butter for cooking
½ cup chopped cherry tomatoes
¼ cup chopped cilantro
4 green onions, thinly sliced
a few dashes of your favorite natural hot sauce
sea salt or Herbamare

1. Crack eggs into a medium bowl, add water and whisk together.

2. Heat a stainless steel skillet over medium-low heat. Add about 2 to 3 teaspoons of organic butter and heat until melted. Add eggs and scramble them with a silicone spatula, being very careful not to brown.

3. Remove from heat and add tomatoes, cilantro, and green onions; stir gently. Add hot sauce and sea salt or Herbamare to taste.

Vegetable Frittata *with Potato Crust*

Serve this delicious dish for a Sunday morning breakfast with some fresh gluten-free muffins (see next chapter) and a fresh green salad. For a quicker version of this recipe, try eliminating the potato crust. It is just as delicious!

SERVES 4

> 2 cups grated potato, about 1 large baking potato
> ½ teaspoon sea salt
>
> 2 teaspoons organic butter or extra virgin olive oil
> 1 small onion, diced small
> 2 cloves garlic, chopped fine
> 1 small red bell pepper, diced small
> 1 ½ cups finely chopped broccoli
> 1 ½ teaspoons dried thyme
> ½ teaspoon freshly ground black pepper
> ½ teaspoon Herbamare or sea salt
> 6 Grade AA organic eggs, lightly beaten
> ½ cup grated raw organic jack cheese, optional

1. Preheat oven to 375 degrees F.

2. Place the grated potato into a small bowl with the sea salt. Let rest for about 10 minutes. Then squeeze out the excess water. Oil a 9-inch deep dish pie plate with olive oil or butter. Place grated potato into pie plate and press evenly into bottom of dish.

3. In a medium skillet heat the 2 teaspoons olive oil or butter; add diced onion and garlic and sauté over medium heat until soft, about 5 minutes.

4. Place cooked onion and garlic into a bowl with the diced red bell pepper, chopped broccoli, dried thyme, black pepper, and sea salt. Mix well.

5. Add the eggs and cheese. Mix well then pour egg and vegetable mixture over potato crust. Sprinkle the top with extra grated cheese if desired. Place into the preheated oven and bake for 25 to 30 minutes or until eggs are cooked through.

Home Style Potatoes

These potatoes are great for a hearty Sunday morning breakfast. Serve with Tofu Scramble, page 112, or scrambled eggs and a fresh green salad for a balanced meal.

SERVES 4

> **6 medium red potatoes, washed and cut into chunks**
> **1 tablespoon extra virgin olive oil**
> **1 medium red onion, chopped**
> **½ teaspoon sea salt or Herbamare**
> **1 teaspoon garlic powder**
> **1 teaspoon dried oregano**
> **½ teaspoon ground cumin**
> **¼ teaspoon freshly ground black pepper**

1. Place potatoes in a steamer basket in a medium pot filled with about 2 inches of water, cover, and steam until tender but not all the way cooked, about 10 minutes depending on the size of the potato chunks. Remove and let cool.

2. In a large stainless steel skillet (11-inch works well) or pot, sauté onions in olive oil until golden, about 5 to 7 minutes. Add sea salt, garlic powder, oregano, ground cumin and black pepper, sauté one minute more.

3. Add potatoes to onion mixture and sauté for 5 to 10 minutes or until golden brown, being careful not to burn. Add more olive oil if potatoes begin to stick to pan.

Zucchini and Potato Hash

The combination of the zucchini, potatoes, and kale make a tasty and very nutritious combination to get you going in the morning. If you have a mandoline you can use it to quickly slice the potatoes and zucchini very thinly. It is a very useful kitchen tool to have on hand. Otherwise, just use a sharp knife to slice the vegetables into thin rounds. Serve this dish with scrambled tofu or eggs and a piece of fruit for a hearty, balanced breakfast.

SERVES 4

1 to 2 tablespoons extra virgin olive oil
1 small onion, cut into half moons
5 to 6 small yellow or red potatoes, sliced into thin rounds
2 medium zucchini, sliced into thin rounds
½ bunch black kale, chopped small
1 to 2 teaspoons dried thyme
1 teaspoon garlic powder, or 1 clove crushed garlic
sea salt or Herbamare to taste

1. In a large stainless steel (11-inch works well) or cast iron skillet heat olive oil over medium heat.

2. Add onions and sauté for 2 to 3 minutes. Add potatoes and stir into the onions Put a cover on the skillet and let cook for about 5 to 7 minutes, stirring occasionally and adding any necessary water to prevent burning.

3. Then add zucchini slices, kale, thyme, garlic powder, and salt; gently mix. Put the cover back onto the skillet and cook for another few minutes until the zucchini and kale are tender, stirring occasionally. Taste and add more sea salt or Herbamare if necessary.

Breakfast Greens

Greens for breakfast? Yes! Greens are great any time of day. Eating fresh organic leafy greens throughout the day will provide you with abundant vitality and health. Greens help to get your digestive juices flowing in the morning and also are rich in enzymes which help to digest other parts of your meal. Try fresh greens with your favorite salad dressing or simply top with the lemon-olive oil dressing below.

SERVES ABOUT 2

fresh organic salad greens

Dressing:
1 lemon, juiced
3 to 4 tablespoons extra virgin olive oil
2 to 3 teaspoons tamari or ¼ to ½ teaspoon sea salt
1 clove garlic, crushed

1. Place fresh salad greens in a bowl.

1. Place ingredients for dressing into a jar with a tight-fitting lid. Shake well. Taste and adjust salt if necessary.

3. Drizzle dressing over fresh greens. Dressing will keep in the refrigerator for up to a week

Warming Miso Soup

Miso is a thick paste and is made by fermenting cooked soybeans, koji, sea salt, and different grains for six months to two years. It is a live food and contains significant amounts of friendly bacteria that promote intestinal health. It is important to not cook the miso for this reason but rather to add it to already cooked foods. Consuming miso helps to create an alkaline condition in the body, promoting resistance against disease. The salty flavor of miso stimulates digestion which is why it has been a traditional breakfast food in Japan for centuries. Adding some cooked fish to the soup will help to boost your metabolism even more at your morning meal. For information on gluten-free miso see page 54.

SERVES 4

> 2 teaspoons toasted sesame oil
> 2 carrots, peeled and cut into matchsticks
> 3 to 4 shiitake mushrooms, sliced thin
> 1 clove garlic, finely chopped
> 2 to 3 teaspoons finely chopped fresh ginger
> 4 cups water
> 1 small strip wakame seaweed, broken into pieces
> 1 cup thinly sliced baby bok choy leaves
> 2 to 3 green onions, cut into thin rounds
> 2 to 3 tablespoons gluten-free miso
> hot pepper sesame oil
> wheat-free tamari
> brown rice vinegar

1. In a 3-quart pot heat toasted sesame oil over medium heat. Add carrots, mushrooms, garlic, and ginger and lightly sauté for 3 to 4 minutes, being very careful not to brown the vegetables.

2. Add water and wakame seaweed, bring to a simmer, cover pot, and cook for about 7 to 10 minutes or until vegetables are tender.

1. Turn off heat and add bok choy, green onions, and miso that has been mixed with a little water. Stir well, and garnish with a few dashes of hot pepper sesame oil (only if you like some spice), tamari, and brown rice vinegar. Taste and adjust seasonings as necessary.

Fresh Breads &Muffins

"What lies behind us and what lies before us are tiny matters,
compared to what lies within us."

~Ralph Waldo Emerson

Baking is an especially fun activity for children. I have many fond memories of baking bread with my mother when I was a child. All of the recipes in this chapter are **gluten-free** *and* **egg-free**! Using flours such as brown rice, teff, millet, quinoa, and buckwheat can create some of the tastiest and nutritious treats around. Please see *pages 68 through 69* for a detailed description of these highly nutritious gluten-free flours.

Remember, gluten is a protein found in grains such as wheat, spelt, kamut, rye, and barley, and sometimes oats (oats can be contaminated with gluten if processed in the same facility).

Try making one of our yeasted breads to use as sandwich bread or for toast in the morning. Muffins are a great way to sneak in extra nutrients to your diet. Try adding raisins, chopped nuts, frozen berries, or shredded or pureed vegetables to your muffins for added flavor and nutrients. Be sure to store your gluten-free, dairy-free, and egg-free baked goods in the refrigerator to make them last longer. Butter and eggs in baked goods actually preserves them and helps them to last longer at room temperature without spoiling. We like to store our gluten-free muffins in large rectangular glass Pyrex® containers in the refrigerator.

Brown Rice Bread

If you have a gluten sensitivity or are just someone looking for an alternative to whole wheat bread, then this bread is ideal for you. It is a dense, moist loaf that is easy to make and has a wonderful texture and flavor. We like to spread freshly made hummus on it for a snack!

MAKES 1 LOAF

> 1 ½ cups warm water (100 to 110 degrees F)
> 1 teaspoon whole cane sugar
> 1 package active dry yeast (2 ¼ teaspoons)
> 1 teaspoon sea salt
> ¼ cup honey or agave nectar
> 2 tablespoons melted virgin coconut oil or extra virgin olive oil
> 3 cups brown rice flour
> ½ cup tapioca flour
> 2 teaspoons xanthan gum

1. In a large bowl combine the warm water and sugar; add the yeast and whisk together until yeast is dissolved. Let stand 5 to 10 minutes, or until the yeast begins to get foamy and bubbly.

2. Add the sea salt, honey, and oil, stir well.

3. Next add the brown rice flour, tapioca flour, and xanthan gum; mix well with a wooden spoon. Continue to mix the dough with the spoon for another 1 to 2 minutes. Dough will still be a bit moist and sticky.

4. Place dough into an oiled 9 x 5-inch bread pan and cover with waxed paper. Place pan in a very warm spot (85 to 90 degrees F) and let rise for about 60 to 70 minutes. Sometimes, if my kitchen is cool, I will fill a 9 x 13-inch glass baking dish with very hot water and then place the bread pan into it. This helps the bread to rise at the correct temperature.

5. Preheat oven to 375 degrees F. Remove waxed paper and bake for 35 to 45 minutes.

Herbed Foccacia Bread

Here is a quick gluten-free yeast bread recipe that can be made without a lot of preparation time. Try replacing the dried herbs with chopped fresh herbs and chopped garlic for a richer, more flavorful bread. This bread is delicious used for dipping in a high quality olive oil.

SERVES 6 TO 8

1 ¾ cup warm water (100 to 110 degrees)
1 teaspoon whole cane sugar
1 package active dry yeast (2 ¼ teaspoons)
¼ cup extra virgin olive oil
2 tablespoons honey or agave nectar
1 tablespoon apple cider vinegar
1 ½ cups brown rice flour
1 cup arrowroot powder
½ cup tapioca flour
1 teaspoon xanthan gum
¾ teaspoon sea salt
½ teaspoon baking soda
1 teaspoon dried thyme
1 teaspoon dried oregano
½ teaspoon dried basil
¼ teaspoon dried crushed rosemary

1. Oil a 9 x 13-inch pan with about 2 tablespoons olive oil.

2. Place warm water and sugar into a small bowl or liquid measuring cup and stir to dissolve. Add the yeast and whisk it into the warm water; let rest for about 5 to 10 minutes to activate the yeast. It should become foamy or bubbly, if not start over with fresh yeast and water.

3. Then add the olive oil, honey, and apple cider vinegar. Whisk together.

4. In a medium-sized bowl, mix all of the remaining dry ingredients together. Pour the wet mixture into the dry and quickly whisk together. Continue to whisk for about 30 to 60 seconds, until the dough thickens. Spoon dough into the oiled pan and place into a warm spot to rise. Let rise for about 30 to 35 minutes.

5. Preheat oven to 375 degrees. Drizzle the top of the dough with olive oil and sprinkle with coarsely ground sea salt. Bake for about 20 to 25 minutes. Let cool for 5 to 10 minutes before slicing.

Honey Whole Grain Bread

This moist and delicious gluten-free bread will remind you of a traditional whole wheat bread with its squishy texture and crusty exterior. Though the list of ingredients may seem daunting, making this recipe isn't.

MAKES 1 LOAF

1 ½ cups warm water (100 to 110 degrees F)
1 teaspoon whole cane sugar
1 package active dry yeast (2 ¼ teaspoons)
¼ cup honey
2 tablespoons extra virgin olive oil
1 tablespoon apple cider vinegar
½ cup arrowroot powder
½ cup tapioca flour
½ cup brown rice flour
½ cup sorghum flour
½ cup teff flour
¼ cup buckwheat flour (I use freshly ground flour from raw buckwheat)
¼ cup amaranth flour
1 ½ teaspoons xanthan gum
1 teaspoon sea salt
½ teaspoon baking soda

> **Ingredient Tip**
>
> For a slightly sweeter tasting bread, you can replace the amaranth and buckwheat flours for equal amounts of sorghum flour if desired.

1. Preheat oven to 200 degrees F and oil a 9 x 5-inch loaf pan. Place the warm water and teaspoon of sugar into a small bowl (a 2-cup liquid measure works well). Make sure the water is the right temperature. If the water is too cold the yeast will not become active and if the water is too hot it will kill the yeast. Add the yeast and stir. Proof the yeast by allowing it to stand for 5 to 10 minutes. It should become bubbly, if not start over with fresh yeast and water. Then add the honey, oil, and apple cider vinegar. Stir well with a fork or wire whisk.

2. In a large bowl, add the arrowroot powder, tapioca flour, brown rice flour, sorghum flour, teff flour, buckwheat flour, amaranth flour, xanthan gum, sea salt, and baking soda. Combine the flours with a wire whisk. Pour the wet ingredients into the dry and whisk them together as you are pouring to avoid lumps. Continue to whisk for another 30 to 60 seconds or so, or until the batter thickens and becomes smooth.

3. Transfer batter to an oiled 9 x 5-inch loaf pan and gently spread out with the back of a spoon. Place pan, uncovered, into the 200 degree oven. Let rise for 30 to 35 minutes with the oven door cracked <u>open</u>. After it has risen, close the oven door and turn the oven temperature up to 375 degrees F. Bake for 30 minutes. Loosen sides with a knife and place onto a wire rack to cool.

Orange Currant Millet Bread

This gluten-free bread can be made any time but is especially good for special occasions or holiday brunches. If you can't find millet flour try replacing it with brown rice flour or sorghum flour. Try adding about ¼ teaspoon ground cardamom to the dough for a nice twist.

MAKES 1 LOAF

> 1 cup warm water (100 to 110 degrees F)
> 1 teaspoon whole cane sugar
> 1 package active dry yeast (2 ¼ teaspoons)
> ½ cup freshly squeezed orange juice
> 1 to 2 teaspoons orange zest
> 1 teaspoon almond extract
> 1 teaspoon sea salt
> ¼ cup honey or maple syrup
> 2 tablespoons melted virgin coconut oil
> ½ cup Zante currants
> 1 ½ cups millet flour
> 1 ½ cups brown rice flour
> ½ cup tapioca flour
> 2 teaspoons xanthan gum

1. In a large bowl combine the warm water and sugar; add the yeast and whisk together until yeast is dissolved. Let stand 5 to 10 minutes, or until the yeast begins to get foamy and bubbly.

2. Then add the orange juice, orange zest, almond extract, sea salt, maple syrup, and coconut oil; stir well. Add the Zante currants and mix again.

3. Next add the millet flour, brown rice flour, tapioca flour, and xanthan gum; mix well with a wooden spoon. Continue to mix the dough with the spoon for another 1 to 2 minutes. Dough will still be a bit moist and sticky.

4. Place into an oiled 9 x 5-inch bread pan and cover with waxed paper. Place pan in a very warm spot (85 to 90 degrees F) and let rise for about 60 to 70 minutes. Sometimes, if my kitchen is cool, I will fill a 9 x 13-inch glass baking dish with very hot water and then place the bread pan into it. Putting the pan into a 100 degree oven with the door cracked open also works well. This helps the bread to rise at the correct temperature.

5. Preheat oven to 375 degrees F. Remove waxed paper and bake for 35 to 45 minutes.

Quinoa Zucchini Bread

This gluten-free quick bread can be made with all brown rice flour if quinoa flour is unavailable. Make this bread in late summer when fresh garden zucchini is in abundance. This bread can be cut into squares after it has cooled and placed in little containers ready to go for a breakfast on the run.

MAKES ABOUT 15 SMALL SQUARES

1 cup quinoa flour
1 cup brown rice flour
½ cup tapioca flour
1 ½ teaspoons baking soda
1 ½ teaspoons xanthan gum
¾ teaspoon sea salt
1 teaspoon cinnamon
¼ teaspoon nutmeg
¾ cup applesauce
¾ cup maple syrup
⅓ cup extra virgin olive oil or melted virgin coconut oil
2 tablespoons apple cider vinegar
1 teaspoon vanilla
2 cups grated zucchini
½ to 1 cup chopped walnuts or pecans
½ cup organic chocolate chips

1. Preheat the oven to 350 degrees F. Oil a 9 x 13-inch baking pan.

2. In a large bowl, mix together the quinoa flour, brown rice flour, tapioca flour, baking soda, xanthan gum, sea salt, cinnamon, and nutmeg; set aside.

3. In another bowl whisk together the applesauce, maple syrup, olive oil, apple cider vinegar, and vanilla. Add this mixture to the dry ingredients and gently mix together with a large wooden spoon.

4. Fold in the grated zucchini, walnuts, chocolate chips and gently mix.

5. Immediately place mixture into oiled 9 x 13-inch pan. Spread out batter evenly and place into the oven. Bake for 25 to 30 minutes. When cool cut into squares and serve.

Pumpkin Spice Bread

Serve this gluten-free treat at your next Thanksgiving or Christmas or simply serve with a bean soup, such as the Fragrant Lentil Soup on page 148, for an easy weekday meal. You can even replace the pumpkin with butternut squash for equally delicious results. For directions on how to bake squash and pumpkins please see page 210.

MAKES 1 LOAF

2 ¼ cups brown rice flour
½ cup tapioca flour
⅔ cup whole cane sugar, lightly ground
2 teaspoons baking powder
1 ½ teaspoons xanthan gum
1 teaspoon baking soda
2 teaspoons cinnamon
1 teaspoon ground ginger
½ teaspoon ground cloves
¼ teaspoon nutmeg
½ teaspoon sea salt
2 ¼ cups sugar pie pumpkin puree
¼ cup water (add only if needed)
⅓ cup melted virgin coconut oil or organic butter
2 teaspoons vanilla
1 cup chopped pecans, optional
1 cup Zante currants, optional

> ### Chef's Tip
>
> To make pumpkin or squash puree, scoop out the freshly baked flesh from the outer skin and place into a food processor. Process for about 2 minutes, or until very smooth. Measure out desired amount of puree. You may freeze the remainder in 2-cup containers.

1. Preheat oven to 400 degrees F. Oil one 9 x 5-inch bread pan or two 8 x 4-inch bread pans.

2. In a large bowl combine the brown rice flour, tapioca flour, sugar, baking powder, xanthan gum, baking soda, spices, and salt. Mix well.

3. Place pumpkin puree in a small bowl and whisk it together with the water, melted coconut oil, and vanilla. Pour the wet ingredients into the dry and gently mix together being careful not to over mix. Add the ¼ cup of water if your batter seems too dry. Your pumpkin puree may have enough moisture already. Fold in chopped pecans and Zante currants if using.

4. Place batter into an oiled bread pan. (You can also make these into muffins). Bake for about 50 to 60 minutes for 9 x 5-inch loaf or 35 to 45 minutes for two 8 x 4-inch loaves or until a knife inserted in the center comes out clean. Loosen sides with a knife and gently take out of pan and place onto a wire rack to cool.

Rosemary Olive Dinner Rolls

These gluten-free dinner rolls are quick to prepare and quick to bake. If you don't have fresh rosemary on hand, just skip it. Dried rosemary is just too dry and won't work as a replacement. Serve these rolls with a warming winter stew or soup. They are great served with our Chicken Noodle and Vegetable Soup on page 166. You could also try serving them with the Tempeh and Mushroom Stroganoff on page 250 or our White Bean and Vegetable Stew on page 270. Either way they are bound to become a family favorite!

MAKES 1 DOZEN ROLLS

1 ½ cups warm water (100 to 110 degrees F)
1 teaspoon whole cane sugar
1 package active dry yeast (2 ¼ teaspoons)
3 tablespoons honey or agave nectar
3 tablespoons extra virgin olive oil
1 tablespoon apple cider vinegar
1 cup sorghum flour
½ cup brown rice flour
½ cup teff flour
½ cup arrowroot powder
½ cup tapioca flour
1 ½ teaspoons xanthan gum
1 teaspoon sea salt
½ teaspoon baking soda
½ cup chopped kalamata olives
2 to 3 tablespoons chopped fresh rosemary

1. Preheat oven to 200 degrees F and oil a 12-cup muffin pan.

2. Place the warm water and teaspoon of sugar into a small bowl (a 2-cup liquid measure works well). Make sure the water is the right temperature. If the water is too cold the yeast will not become active and if the water is too hot it will kill the yeast. Add the yeast and stir. Proof the yeast by allowing it to stand for 5 to 10 minutes. It should become foamy and/or bubbly, if not start over with fresh yeast and water.

3. Add honey, olive oil, and apple cider vinegar. Stir well with a fork or wire whisk.

4. In a large bowl, add the sorghum flour, brown rice flour, teff flour, arrowroot powder, tapioca flour, xanthan gum, sea salt, and baking soda. Combine the flours with a wire whisk. Pour the wet ingredients into the dry and whisk them together as you are pouring to avoid lumps. Continue to whisk for another 30 to 60 seconds or so, or until the batter thickens and becomes smooth.

5. Quickly add the chopped olives and rosemary and stir into the batter. You don't want to wait too long and disturb the dough as the baking soda and vinegar will start to react right away and form little air bubbles. You want these air pockets so your rolls will be light and airy like wheat bread, otherwise they may end up too dense.

6. Spoon batter about ⅔ of the way full into oiled muffin cups. Place pan, uncovered, into the 200 degree oven. Let rise for 20 to 25 minutes with the oven door cracked <u>open</u>.

7. After they have risen, close the oven door and turn the oven temperature up to 375 degrees F. Bake for 20 minutes. Allow rolls to cool for a few minutes in the pan and then remove each roll with a knife and place onto a wire rack to cool.

Variations:
- Omit olives and rosemary for a plain Whole Grain Roll
- Use 1 tablespoon of Italian seasoning and about ¼ cup coarsely chopped fresh garlic in place of the olives and rosemary for a Herbed Garlic Roll
- Replace olives and rosemary with about ½ to 1 cup chopped pecans and 2 to 3 teaspoons cinnamon, and sprinkle the top of each roll with whole cane sugar and cinnamon for a Cinnamon Pecan Sweet Roll.

Grandma's Cinnamon Rolls

These ooey, gooey and oh-so-delicious cinnamon rolls taste just like Grandma's, but there's one difference: they are gluten and dairy-free! Serve these rolls as a fun treat on special occasions. Christmas morning, Mother's Day, and Easter would be fun!

MAKES APPROXIMATELY 10 ROLLS

½ cup water (100 to 110 degrees F)
1 teaspoon whole cane sugar
1 package active dry yeast (2 ¼ teaspoons)
1 cup hemp milk or soy milk, warmed
¼ cup honey or agave nectar
2 tablespoons virgin coconut oil
1 cup cooked & whipped potatoes (about 2 medium baking potatoes)
2 ½ cups brown rice flour
½ cup tapioca flour
1 ½ teaspoons xanthan gum
1 teaspoon sea salt

Filling:
virgin coconut oil
whole cane sugar
cinnamon

1. Place the warm water, yeast, and sugar in a large bowl. Stir to dissolve the yeast. Let stand about 5 minutes or until foamy and bubbly.

2. In a small pot gently warm the hemp milk, honey, and coconut oil. Be very careful not to get too hot; 100 degrees F is a good temperature. If it gets too hot it will kill the yeast and your rolls won't rise.

3. Add mixture to the yeast and water and whisk well. Then add the whipped potatoes (a regular hand held electric mixer works well to whip potatoes). Beat wet ingredients together using an electric mixer.

4. In a separate bowl, mix together the brown rice flour, tapioca flour, xanthan gum, and sea salt. Add dry ingredients to the wet and continue to beat with the electric mixer until completely combined, about 2 minutes.

5. Form dough into a ball and roll out onto a floured surface (using brown rice flour). Roll dough into a large rectangle.

6. Spread coconut oil over the entire surface with your hands (about a ¼ cup). Then sprinkle whole cane sugar over the top of the oil (about ¼ to ½ cup). And lastly, sprinkle 2 to 4 tablespoons cinnamon over the sugar.

7. Now you are ready to roll! Be sure to have three pie plates or cake pans out and greased with coconut oil. Set aside. Now take the long end of the dough and begin to roll. Keep it tight and when you get to the end pinch the dough together all along the length of the roll.

8. Use a serrated knife to cut dough into rolls. Make a cut every 1 ½ to 2 inches. Place rolls in the pans (about 5 rolls per pan). Cover with waxed paper and let rise in a warm spot for about 45 minutes.

9. Preheat oven to 350 degrees F. After rolls have risen, place pans, uncovered, in the oven for approximately 30 to 35 minutes.

Easy Gluten-Free Biscuits

My grandmother used to make the most delicious biscuits in the world—using white flour of course! So I created this recipe in hopes of continuing her tradition of biscuit making, now gluten-free. They are wonderful to make for a weekend breakfast and also great as part of a weekday dinner. Our children like to add a little cinnamon and sugar to the dough to satisfy their sweet tooth. Try spreading them with jam when they are hot out of the oven, yum!

MAKES APPROXIMATELY 10 BISCUITS

2 cups brown rice flour
½ cup tapioca flour
2 teaspoons baking powder
1 teaspoon xanthan gum
¾ teaspoon sea salt
½ cup cold organic butter, palm shortening, or virgin coconut oil
¾ cup soy milk or hemp milk

1. Preheat oven to 425 degrees F.

2. Combine the brown rice flour, tapioca flour, baking powder, xanthan gum, and sea salt in a large mixing bowl.

3. Add the fat. Mix together with your fingers until well combined and crumbly.

4. Slowly add the milk, stirring with a wooden spoon as you pour. Gently knead the dough with your hands until just combined, being careful not to over mix!

5. Roll out dough on a floured surface until about ½-inch thick. Cut into rounds with a knife, biscuit cutter, or a cup. Place onto an ungreased cookie sheet or baking dish. You may also drop batter onto cookie sheet by the large spoonfuls for an even easier way of making these.

6. Bake for about 10 to 12 minutes, or until done. Cool slightly on a wire rack and enjoy warm! They are great spread with fruit jam and butter or coconut butter.

Banana Walnut Muffins

These muffins are gluten, dairy, soy, and egg-free, making them a great alternative for people sensitive to those foods. Try adding 1 to 2 cups fresh or frozen blueberries to the batter when you add the walnuts for a nice twist. You can also make this recipe into four mini-loaves; we like to make two plain and two with chocolate chips.

MAKES 1 TO 1 ½ DOZEN MUFFINS

2 ½ cups brown rice flour
½ cup tapioca flour
½ cup whole cane sugar
2 teaspoons baking powder
1 ½ teaspoons xanthan gum
1 teaspoon baking soda
½ teaspoon sea salt
2 cups mashed ripe bananas, about 4 large
1 cup vanilla hemp milk, soy milk, almond milk, or rice milk
¼ cup melted virgin coconut oil
2 teaspoons vanilla
1 cup chopped walnuts, optional
organic chocolate chips, optional

1. Preheat oven to 375 degrees F. Lightly oil muffin tins or line with paper muffin cups.

2. In a large bowl combine the brown rice flour, tapioca flour, sugar, xanthan gum, baking soda, baking powder, and sea salt. Mix well.

3. Place the bananas into a 4-cup glass measuring cup and mash with a fork; it should equal approximately 2 cups.

4. Add the milk to the mashed bananas and whisk it together with the melted coconut oil and vanilla. Pour the wet ingredients into the dry and gently mix together being careful not to over mix. Gently fold in the chopped walnuts and chocolate chips if using.

5. Spoon batter into oiled muffin tins. Bake at 375 degrees F for about 20 to 25 minutes. Loosen sides with a knife and gently take out of tins and place onto a wire rack to cool.

Carrot Raisin Buckwheat Muffins

If you are a buckwheat lover then you will to enjoy these gluten-free muffins. Try adding more carrots, raisins, some shredded apple, or any chopped nut for a denser, more nutritious treat. These muffins work great as a quick breakfast, simply serve with a green smoothie for a balanced and energizing meal.

MAKES 1 TO 1 ½ DOZEN MUFFINS

2 ½ cups buckwheat flour
½ cup tapioca flour
½ cup whole cane sugar
2 teaspoons baking powder
1 teaspoon baking soda
½ teaspoon sea salt
2 teaspoons cinnamon
1 teaspoon ginger powder
2 cups applesauce
¼ cup melted virgin coconut oil
2 teaspoons vanilla
1 cup grated carrots
½ to 1 cup raisins, soaked for 10 minutes in ¼ cup water

1. Preheat oven to 375 degrees F. Lightly oil muffin tins or line with paper muffin cups.

2. In a large bowl combine the buckwheat flour, tapioca flour, sugar, baking soda, baking powder, sea salt, and spices. Mix well.

3. Place apple sauce into a separate bowl and add the melted coconut oil, vanilla, carrots, and raisins; whisk together. Pour the wet ingredients into the dry and gently mix together being careful not to over mix.

4. Spoon batter into oiled muffin tins. Bake at 375 degrees F for about 25 to 30 minutes. Loosen sides with a knife and gently take out of tins and place onto a wire rack to cool.

Cranberry Apple Spice Muffins

These muffins are gluten, dairy, soy, and egg-free, perfect for individuals with multiple food sensitivities. For extra spice try adding some freshly grated ginger to the batter. Another great addition is about 2 teaspoons of freshly grated orange zest.

MAKES 1 TO 1 ½ DOZEN MUFFINS

2 ½ cups brown rice flour
½ cup tapioca flour
½ cup whole cane sugar
2 teaspoons baking powder
1 ½ teaspoons xanthan gum
1 teaspoon baking soda
½ teaspoon sea salt
2 teaspoons cinnamon
½ teaspoon ginger powder
¼ teaspoon ground nutmeg
¼ teaspoon ground cloves
2 ¼ cups applesauce
¼ cup melted organic virgin coconut oil
1 teaspoon vanilla
1 small tart apple, grated or finely diced
½ to 1 cup fresh or frozen cranberries
1 cup chopped pecans, optional

1. Preheat oven to 375 degrees F. Lightly oil muffin tins or line with paper muffin cups.

2. In a large bowl combine the brown rice flour, tapioca flour, sugar, xanthan gum, baking soda, baking powder, sea salt, and spices. Mix well.

3. Place applesauce into a separate bowl and add the melted coconut oil and vanilla; whisk together. Pour the wet ingredients into the dry and gently mix together being careful not to over mix.

4. Gently fold in the diced apples, fresh or frozen cranberries, and optional chopped pecans.

5. Spoon batter into oiled muffin tins. Bake at 375 degrees F for about 25 to 30 minutes. Loosen sides with a knife and gently take out of tins and place onto a wire rack to cool.

Quinoa Banana Apple Muffins

You can find quinoa flour in the baking section at your local co-op or natural foods store. If you can not find quinoa flour try substituting brown rice flour. This recipe was developed by my friend, Jenna Boudreau, for her daughter, Elle, who cannot tolerate gluten.

MAKES 1 TO 1 ½ DOZEN MUFFINS

½ cup melted virgin coconut oil
½ cup whole cane sugar
3 bananas, mashed
1 cup applesauce
1 medium apple, cored and grated
1 cup raisins
1 teaspoon vanilla
1 ½ cups quinoa flour
1 cup brown rice flour
1 teaspoon xanthan gum
1 ½ teaspoons baking powder
1 teaspoon baking soda
½ teaspoon sea salt
1 teaspoon cinnamon
½ cup chopped walnuts, optional

1. Preheat oven 375 degrees F. Lightly oil muffin tins or line with paper muffin cups.

2. In a large bowl, cream together coconut oil and sugar with an electric mixer. Stir in bananas, applesauce, grated apple, raisins, and vanilla.

3. In separate bowl mix quinoa flour, brown rice flour, xanthan gum, baking powder, baking soda, sea salt, and cinnamon together. Add wet ingredients to dry ingredients and gently mix together. Fold in chopped walnuts, if using.

4. Spoon batter into oiled muffin tins.

5. Bake for about 30 minutes, or until knife inserted comes out clean. Cool in pan 10 minutes. Then place muffins onto a wire rack to cool.

Peachy Millet Flour Muffins

Millet is a gluten-free grain, though if you can't find millet flour you may replace it with sorghum flour or brown rice flour. You can also try grinding your own millet flour in a Vita-Mix or a grain grinder. If fresh peaches are out of season you may thaw out two 10-ounce bags of organic frozen peaches and it will equal exactly two cups pureed.

MAKES 1 TO 1 ½ DOZEN MUFFINS

2 ½ cups millet flour
½ cup tapioca flour
½ cup whole cane sugar
2 teaspoons baking powder
1 ½ teaspoons xanthan gum
1 teaspoon baking soda
½ teaspoon sea salt
2 cups pureed peaches
¼ cup melted organic virgin coconut oil
2 teaspoons vanilla

1. Preheat oven to 375 degrees F. Lightly oil muffin tins or line with paper muffin cups.

2. In a large bowl combine the millet flour, tapioca flour, sugar, xanthan gum, baking soda, baking powder, and sea salt. Mix well.

3. Puree peaches in a blender until smooth, measure out two cups. Place peach puree in a small bowl and whisk it together with the melted coconut oil and vanilla. Pour the wet ingredients into the dry and gently mix together being careful not to over mix.

4. Spoon batter into oiled muffin tins. Bake for about 20 minutes. Loosen sides with a knife and gently take out of tins and place onto a cooling rack.

Corn-Free Baking Powder

Here is a recipe for an allergen-free baking powder. In addition to being sensitive to gluten, dairy, and eggs, many people also have allergies or sensitivities to corn. Corn starch is one of the main ingredients in baking powder. You can store your homemade baking powder in a tightly covered glass jar almost indefinitely. Just be sure to label it!

MAKES ¾ CUP

   ¼ cup baking soda
   ½ cup cream of tartar
   ½ cup arrowroot powder

1. Place all ingredients into a glass jar and shake well.

2. Store your baking powder in a cool, dry place.

Soups

"Of soup and love, the first is best"

~Old Spanish Proverb

Soup is probably as old as the history of cooking as food historians say. The act of combining different ingredients in a large pot to create a nutritious, filling, and easily digested food was inevitable. Soups, stews, and porridges evolved according to local ingredients and tastes.

Soup is a wonderful way to enjoy a variety of vegetables, herbs, beans, and meats in a savory form. The ingredients in the simmering soup slowly release their vital nutrients into the liquid; which includes many minerals and trace minerals, vitamins, and phytochemicals. Serve soup with a fresh green salad or cultured vegetables to maximize digestion of vital nutrients. Soup, which is very economical, is easy to make and can be made in large batches and then frozen for later use.

The following pages contain important information on how to cook beans, this will be necessary to make many of the soup and vegetarian main dish recipes in this book.

How to Cook Beans:

It is important to buy dried beans from a store that has a rapid turnover. Buy organic beans that are in the bulk bins from your local co-op or health food store. It is best to use dried beans within a few months of purchasing them.

Store dried beans in glass jars or another type of airtight container in the coolest and driest place in your kitchen. This will preserve their freshness and make them last longer. Beans stored in this way can be kept for up to *six months*. Mark the date of purchase on your bean containers so you will know to discard them if they are older than six months. Older beans become very dry and hard and will take much longer to cook until tender.

Sort though your beans and pick out any stones, foreign matter, or discolored, shriveled beans. Then rinse them to remove any dirt or debris. You may do this by placing the dried beans into a bowl and adding cool water, then take your hand and swirl the beans around. Pour off the water through a strainer and give them one final rinse with cool water.

Soaking your beans decreases cooking times dramatically and allows the gas-producing sugars in beans to be released into the soaking water.

> *Smaller beans do not require any soaking*, these include: green or brown lentils, red lentils, green or yellow split peas, black-eyed peas, mung beans, and adzuki beans.

> *Larger beans need be soaked* by either of the two methods below, these include: garbanzo beans, pinto beans, pink beans, black beans, lima beans, navy beans, kidney beans, great northern beans, Christmas limas, and cannelini beans.

> **Traditional Slow Soak:** In a large bowl, place rinsed beans with twice as much water as beans. So for 1 cup of dry beans use 2 cups of water. Soak for 6 to 8 hours or overnight. Drain and rinse the beans.

> **Quick Soak:** In a stockpot, bring the same proportion of water and beans to a boil. Boil for 2 to 3 minutes. Turn off heat, cover, and let soak at room temperature 1 to 2 hours. Drain and rinse the beans then follow cooking instructions on the following pages.

Cooking Beans on the Stove:

For Small Beans: (green or brown lentils, red lentils, green or yellow split peas, black-eyed peas, mung beans, and adzuki beans)

1. **Place the rinsed beans into a heavy stainless steel pot.** Use 2 to 2 ½ cups water per cup of dry beans.

2. **Add herbs or spices if desired**, and one 2-inch piece of **kombu** seaweed. Herbs that aid in digestion of beans include *cumin*, *fennel*, *ginger*, and *winter savory*.

3. **Bring beans, water, and kombu to a boil.** Reduce heat, cover, and simmer. See bean cooking chart on *page 143* for cooking times. Salt beans at the end of cooking time.

For Large Beans: (garbanzo beans, pinto beans, pink beans, black beans, lima beans, navy beans, kidney beans, great northern beans, Christmas limas, and cannelini beans)

1. **Place the soaked, rinsed beans in a heavy stainless steel pot**. Use 3 cups of fresh water per 1 cup dry beans that have been soaked.

2. **Add herbs or spices if desired**, and one 3-inch piece of kombu seaweed.

3. **Bring the beans, water, and kombu to a boil.** Reduce heat, cover, and simmer. Add water as needed during cooking to make sure beans are always covered with liquid. A well-cooked bean can easily be mashed on the roof of your mouth with your tongue. See bean cooking chart on *page 143* for cooking times.

Chef's Tip

Remember to never add salt or acids to your pot of cooking beans. These include tomatoes, vinegars, and citrus. These will toughen the outer layer of the beans and may prevent them from cooking thoroughly. Always add salt and any acid at the **end** of cooking time. Salt and acids help to bring out the flavor of beans and are important in creating a delicious bean dish.

Pressure-Cooking Beans:

*Directions below are for both **small unsoaked beans** and **large soaked beans**.*

1. **Place the rinsed beans into the pressure cooker.** Use about 3 cups water per cup of dry beans. The beans need to be completely covered with water to cook evenly.

2. **Add herbs or spices if desired,** and one 2 or 3-inch piece of **kombu** seaweed.

3. **Lock the lid into place,** turn stove to medium-high, and bring cooker to high pressure.

4. **Cook for time indicated on the following page.** The timing begins when full pressure is reached.

5. **Let the pressure come down naturally.** Then remove the lid and test for doneness.

6. **If the beans are almost done** then simmer on the stove until done. If they need considerable more time then place the lid back on and bring to high pressure. Cook for only a few minutes more.

7. **Now add salt and flavorings if desired.**

Ingredient Tip

Kombu is a sea vegetable that contains glutamic acid which helps to tenderize and breakdown the indigestible, gas-producing sugars, *raffinose* and *stacchiose*, in beans. Kombu is also a rich source of many important trace minerals. These minerals are released into the cooking water of the beans. Kombu can be purchased in the dried form in either the bulk or macrobiotic section from your local co-op or health food store.

The chart below gives approximate cooking times for *large soaked beans* and *small unsoaked beans*. Always check beans for doneness at least 5 to 10 minutes before minimum time indicated (stovetop method) for small beans and 20 to 30 minutes before minimum time indicated for large beans.

*Note: Large lima beans and black soybeans have delicate skins and need salt added to the cooking water to keep them intact during stovetop cooking. When pressure cooking large lima beans and soybeans, add 2 tablespoons oil per cup of beans.

**Pressure cooking times are for minutes under high pressure only. Timing begins when full pressure has been reached.

Beans (1 cup dry)	Approximate Stovetop Cooking Times	Approximate Pressure Cooking Times	Yield Cooked Beans in Cups
Adzuki	1 hour	10 to 15 minutes	2 cups
Black (turtle)	1 ½ to 2 hours	5 to 10 minutes	2 cups
Black-eyed Pea	30 minutes	8 to 11 minutes	2 ¼ cups
Cannelini	1 to 1 ½ hours	8 to 12 minutes	2 cups
Christmas Lima	1 to 1 ½ hours	8 to 10 minutes	1 ¼ cups
Cranberry	1 ½ to 2 hours	8 to 11 minutes	2 ¼ cups
Garbanzo	1 to 1 ½ hours	12 to 16 minutes	2 ½ cups
Great Northern	1 to 1 ½ hours	8 to 11 minutes	2 ¼ cups
Kidney	1 ½ to 2 hours	10 to 14 minutes	2 cups
Lentils (brown or green)	40 to 50 minutes	6 to 8 minutes	2 cups
Lima (large)*	45 minutes to 1 hour	4 to 6 minutes	2 cups
Lima (baby)	45 minutes to 1 hour	5 to 6 minutes	2 ½ cups
Navy	1 to 1 ½ hours	6 to 8 minutes	2 cups
Pink	1 to 1 ½ hours	4 to 6 minutes	2 cups
Pinto	1 to 1 ½ hours	4 to 6 minutes	2 ¼ cups
Red Lentil	20 to 25 minutes	—	2 cups
Scarlet Runner	1 ½ to 2 hours	12 to 14 minutes	1 ¼ cups
Soybeans (beige)	2 to 3 hours	8 to 12 minutes	2 ¼ cups
Soybeans (black)*	1 ½ hours	20 to 22 minutes	2 ½ cups
Split Peas	45 minutes	8 to 10 minutes	2 cups

Bean Conversions:

- One 15-ounce can of beans = 1 ½ cups cooked, drained beans
- One pound dry beans = 6 cups cooked, drained beans
- One pound dry beans = 2 cups dry beans
- One cup dry beans = approximately 2 to 3 cups cooked, drained beans

Homemade Vegetable Soup Stock

Making your own vegetable broth is very easy. I like to save vegetable scraps from a few days worth of cooking and make a large pot of broth on the weekends. You can create many different flavors of stock by varying the herbs and vegetables you use. You can also add bone-in meat to this recipe for a richer stock. The minerals and acids in the vegetables help to extract the healing properties found in the marrow of the animal bones. Use the cooked meat to add to your favorite vegetable and bean stews or it can be used as part of a filling for enchiladas or used to top fresh green salads. Freeze your stock in 4-cup containers for later use.

MAKES ABOUT 10 CUPS

> 12 cups water
> 1 large onion, skins left on and coarsely chopped
> 1 leek, chopped
> 2 carrots, chopped
> 4 stalks celery, chopped
> 4 cloves garlic, skins left on and chopped
> one 4-inch piece kombu
> ½ bunch parley
> 3 bay leaves
> 1 teaspoon black peppercorns
> fresh herbs (thyme, rosemary, savory, marjoram)
> vegetable scraps (carrot peels, celery tops, onion skins)
> 1 teaspoon Herbamare or sea salt

1. Place all ingredients into an 8-quart stockpot. Bring to a boil, cover, and reduce heat to low. Simmer for 2 to 3 hours.

2. Strain stock into another pot, discard vegetables, and store in either the refrigerator or freezer in 4-cup containers.

Asian Soup Stock

This delicious and medicinal soup stock can be used as a base for a soup or stew or simply sipped when you have a cold or flu. I like to freeze at least half of this when I make it because you never know when you will need it!

MAKES ABOUT 10 CUPS

12 cups water
1 large onion, skins left on and cut into chunks
1 head garlic, cut in half crosswise
one 2-inch piece fresh ginger, sliced
3 stalks celery, chopped
2 carrots, chopped
3 to 4 cups chopped shiitake mushrooms
one 4-inch piece kombu
1 stalk lemongrass, chopped, optional
½ to 1 teaspoon crushed red chili flakes, optional
1 to 2 teaspoons sea salt

1. Place all ingredients into an 8-quart stockpot. Bring to a boil, cover, and reduce heat to low. Simmer for 2 to 3 hours.

2. Place a strainer into a large bowl or pot and pour the stock through it. You can discard the vegetables, though the shiitake mushrooms are especially good to nibble on!

3. Stock may be frozen for later use or stored in glass quart jars in the refrigerator for 5 to 7 days.

Fall Pinto Bean and Yam Soup

This soup is a celebration of the flavors of autumn and the abundant harvest that this season has to offer. While your beans are cooking bake a fresh loaf of whole wheat or brown rice bread to go along with your finished soup. Serve this soup with the Autumn Harvest Salad on page 178. If you do not want to cook your own beans then use 3 cans of organic beans. Just add them to the soup where you would add the freshly cooked beans.

SERVES 6 TO 8

> 2 cups dry pinto beans, soaked overnight
> 6 to 8 cups water
> 4 cloves garlic, peeled
> one 2-inch piece kombu seaweed
>
> 2 tablespoons extra virgin olive oil
> 1 large onion, chopped
> 5 cloves garlic, crushed
> 1 to 2 jalapeño peppers, seeded and chopped
> 2 small yams, peeled and diced
> 3 carrots, cut into rounds
> 1 tablespoon ground cumin
> 1 teaspoon paprika
> ½ teaspoon chipotle chili powder
> 8 cups bean cooking liquid and/or water
> one 28-ounce can diced fire roasted tomatoes
> 2 to 3 ears fresh corn, corn cut off cob
> 1 small bunch black kale, finely chopped
> 1 cup chopped cilantro
> ½ lime, juiced
> 2 to 3 teaspoons sea salt or Herbamare

1. Rinse and drain soaked beans, place into a 6-quart pot with the water, garlic, and kombu; bring to a boil, then reduce heat to a gentle simmer and cook for approximately 1 hour, or until beans are soft and mash easily. Remove pot from heat. Drain beans and reserve the cooking liquid.

2. To make the soup, heat olive oil in a large 8-quart pot over medium heat. Add chopped onion and sauté for about 5 minutes.

3. Then add the garlic, jalapeño peppers, yams, carrots, cumin, paprika, and chipotle chili powder. Sauté and stir for another 5 minutes then add water. Mix well to remove any spices that have stuck to the bottom of the pan.

4. Add the cooked beans, bean cooking liquid or water, tomatoes, and cut corn, mix well. If the soup needs more liquid, then add more water.

5. Cover pot and simmer until vegetables are tender, about 20 to 25 minutes. Then add chopped kale, chopped cilantro, lime juice, and sea salt or Herbamare. Simmer for about 5 minutes more. Taste and adjust salt and lime juice if needed.

Fragrant Lentil Soup

Garam masala is an Indian spice blend that can be found in the bulk spice section of your local co-op or health food store. It is the secret ingredient in this great tasting soup! Serve this easy-to-make soup with the Winter Quinoa Salad, page 236, and the Pumpkin Spice Bread on page 127, for a festive winter meal.

SERVES 6 TO 8

> 1 tablespoon extra virgin olive oil
> 1 large onion, chopped
> 4 cloves garlic, crushed
> 3 large carrots, diced
> 1 tablespoon dried thyme
> 1 teaspoon garam masala
> 2 cups green lentils, rinsed and drained
> 8 cups water or vegetable stock
> 2 cups chopped tomatoes
> 4 cups baby spinach leaves
> 1 to 2 teaspoons sea salt or Herbamare
> 2 tablespoons red wine vinegar

1. Heat olive oil in a large pot over medium heat. Add chopped onion and sauté for about 5 minutes or until onion begins to get soft.

2. Add crushed garlic, diced carrots, dried thyme, and garam masala; sauté for another 5 to 7 minutes.

3. Add the lentils and water; cover pot and simmer for about 35 to 40 minutes.

4. Add chopped tomatoes, spinach, sea salt, and red wine vinegar and simmer for another 10 minutes more.

French Lentil Soup

French lentils, also called Le Puy lentils, are named after Le Puy in Auvergne, a volcanic area in the center of France with ideal soil and climate for the growth of the lentils. French lentils have a delicate taste and a fine green skin with steel blue speckles. They usually can be found in the bulk section of your local co-op or health food store.

SERVES 6 TO 8

1 tablespoon extra virgin olive oil
1 medium onion, chopped
3 cloves garlic, crushed
2 stalks celery, diced
2 large carrots, diced
3 small red potatoes, diced
1 teaspoon dried thyme
2 teaspoons paprika
1 teaspoon Italian seasoning
2 cups French lentils, rinsed and drained
8 cups water
2 cups chopped tomatoes
1 tablespoon red wine vinegar
2 to 3 teaspoons sea salt or Herbamare
½ cup chopped fresh basil
½ cup chopped fresh parsley

1. In a large 8-quart pot heat olive oil over medium heat, add chopped onions and sauté for about 5 minutes, add crushed garlic and sauté 2 minutes more.

2. Add celery, carrots, potatoes, thyme, paprika, and Italian seasoning, sauté for another 5 minutes stirring frequently.

3. Add French lentils and water, cover, and simmer over low heat for 25 minutes.

4. After lentils are cooked and vegetables are tender add chopped tomatoes, red wine vinegar, salt, and fresh herbs; mix well and simmer uncovered for another 5 minutes.

Lemon and Lentil Soup

This soup is a great dish to prepare when you don't have a lot of time; we use a food processor for all of the chopping which cuts the preparation time in half. Serve this soup over cooked brown jasmine or basmati rice, page 214. This soup also freezes well for later use.

SERVES 4 TO 6

> 1 small onion
> 5 cloves garlic
> 2 tablespoons extra virgin olive oil
> 2 cups red lentils, rinsed and drained
> 8 cups vegetable stock or water
> 4 to 5 cups baby spinach
> 1 small handful fresh parsley
> ½ cup freshly squeezed lemon juice
> 1 to 2 teaspoons sea salt or Herbamare

1. Peel and cut ends off of the onion and place into a food processor fitted with the "s" blade. Peel the garlic and place it into the food processor along with the onion. Pulse the onions and garlic until finely chopped.

2. Heat olive oil in a 6-quart pot. Add onions and garlic and sauté for about 5 minutes or until soft.

3. Add the red lentils and the vegetable broth or water. Cover pot and simmer for about 25 minutes or until lentils are very soft and cooked though.

4. While the lentils are cooking, place the spinach and parsley into the food processor and pulse until minced.

5. Add minced parsley and spinach to the cooked lentils along with the lemon juice and sea salt. Simmer on low for another 3 to 5 minutes. Taste and add more salt or lemon juice if desired. Serve over cooked brown jasmine or brown basmati rice.

Lily's Lemongrass Soup

Our daughter, Lily, created this recipe when she was 4 ½ years old. She has been cooking in the kitchen with me ever since she was a baby and is now beginning to create recipes of her own. She did all of the cutting and preparing for this soup, adding all ingredients of her choice, with no input from me. Our younger daughter, Grace, was standing next to Lily on a stool while she was cooking this and decided to add some cooked rice to the soup. After refining the recipe I added the soup stock, garlic, and kaffir lime leaves. This soup has now become a regular part of our family's meal plans.

SERVES 4 TO 6

6 cups Asian Soup Stock *(recipe page 145)*
2 stalks fresh lemongrass, cut into 3-inch pieces
3 to 4 kaffir lime leaves
3 carrots, chopped
3 to 4 celery stalks, chopped
3 to 4 cloves garlic, crushed
1 teaspoon freshly grated ginger
sea salt or Herbamare, to taste
1 to 2 cups cooked brown jasmine rice, optional
4 to 5 green onions, sliced
½ cup chopped cilantro
crushed red chili flakes

1. Place the stock, lemongrass, kaffir lime leaves into a 6-quart stockpot. Cover and simmer for about 35 minutes.

2. Then add the carrots, celery, garlic, ginger, and salt. Simmer for another 7 to 10 minutes or until the vegetables are crisp-tender.

3. Remove lemongrass and lime leaves from soup. Add cooked rice, if using, green onions, and cilantro. Taste and adjust salt and seasonings if necessary.

4. Garnish each bowl with a pinch or two of crushed red chili flakes.

Minestrone Soup

This is a simple, classic soup that everyone will enjoy. This soup can be made in large batches and then frozen into serving-sized containers. The addition of the large amount of fresh herbs really makes this recipe stand out from others.

SERVES 6 TO 8

1 tablespoon extra virgin olive oil
1 medium onion, finely chopped
8 cloves garlic, crushed
3 stalks celery chopped
2 large carrots, peeled and diced
½ teaspoon dried crushed rosemary
½ teaspoon freshly ground pepper
½ cup chopped fresh basil
¼ cup chopped fresh oregano
2 tablespoons chopped fresh thyme
6 to 8 cups vegetable or chicken stock
4 cups chopped tomatoes or one 28-ounce can diced tomatoes
¼ cup tomato paste
½ pound green beans, ends trimmed and cut into pieces
2 medium zucchini, diced
2 cups cooked kidney beans, or 1 can
2 cups cooked garbanzo beans, or 1 can
1 cup chopped flat-leaf parsley
1 teaspoon sea salt or Herbamare, or to taste

1. Heat olive oil in an 8-quart stock pot over medium heat. Add chopped onion, sauté for about 5 minutes or until soft.

2. Add crushed garlic, celery, carrots, crushed rosemary, black pepper, basil, oregano, and thyme. Sauté for another 5 minutes, stirring frequently.

3. Add chicken or vegetable stock, chopped tomatoes, and tomato paste, stir well. Cover, and cook for about 7 to 10 minutes or until carrots are slightly tender but not cooked all the way through.

4. Add green beans, zucchini, and beans, cover and simmer until all vegetable are tender, about another 7 minutes. Remove from heat and add parsley and sea salt to taste. You can add some cooked semolina or brown rice pasta if desired.

Moroccan Chickpea and Potato Soup

This soup is a favorite among children and adults alike, making it a very family-friendly meal. It is flavorful yet simple to please many tastes. This soup is delicious served with freshly cooked quinoa, olives, and steamed chard. Remember to plan ahead for this recipe and soak the beans before you go to bed the night before.

SERVES 6 TO 8

    2 tablespoons extra virgin olive oil
    1 large onion, chopped
    6 cloves garlic, crushed
    1 teaspoon curry powder
    1 teaspoon ground cardamom
    ½ teaspoon turmeric
    ½ teaspoon freshly ground black pepper
    1 ½ cups dried chickpeas (garbanzo beans), soaked overnight
    10 to 12 cups water
    one 3-inch piece kombu
    4 large carrots, diced
    4 to 5 red or yellow potatoes, diced
    ¼ cup tomato paste
    ¼ cup freshly squeezed lemon juice
    1 to 2 teaspoons sea salt
    ½ cup chopped fresh parsley

1. Heat olive oil in an 8-quart stockpot; add onions and sauté for about 4 to 5 minutes. Then add garlic and spices, sauté a minute more.

2. Drain soaking water from beans and rinse well. Add beans and the fresh 10 to 12 cups of water to pot. Bring to a boil, then reduce heat to low, and simmer, partially covered, for about 35 minutes.

3. After about 35 minutes, add the carrots and potatoes to the pot. Simmer for about 15 to 20 minutes more or until vegetables are tender and beans are completely cooked.

4. Remove kombu from pot. Then add the tomato paste, lemon juice, sea salt, and parsley. Stir well and simmer for a few minutes more. Taste and adjust salt and seasonings if desired.

Red Lentil Dal

Dal is an Indian stew made with lentils and spices which is usually served over rice. It is very easy to make and portions can be frozen for later use. Serve this hearty dal with Indian Fried Rice on page 222 and the Cabbage Salad with Cilantro Vinaigrette on page 181.

SERVES 6 TO 8

> 2 tablespoons virgin coconut oil or extra virgin olive oil
> 1 ½ teaspoons black mustard seeds
> 1 ½ teaspoons cumin seeds
> 1 large onion, diced
> 3 cloves garlic, crushed
> 2 teaspoons turmeric
> 2 teaspoons ground cumin
> ¼ teaspoon cayenne pepper, or to taste
> 2 large carrots, peeled and diced
> 3 medium red potatoes, cubed
> 2 ½ cups red lentils, rinsed and drained
> 6 cups water
> 1 can coconut milk
> 2 cups chopped tomatoes or one 14-ounce can diced tomatoes
> 2 teaspoons sea salt or Herbamare, or to taste

1. In a large 8-quart pot heat olive oil over medium heat, then add cumin seeds and black mustard seeds. Sauté until they begin to pop. Quickly add onions and garlic and sauté until soft, about 5 minutes.

2. Add turmeric, ground cumin, cayenne, carrots, and potatoes, sauté a few minutes more.

3. Add red lentils, water, coconut milk, and chopped tomatoes. Stir well. Bring to a boil, then let simmer, covered, for about 45 minutes. Add salt to taste and serve.

Spicy Black Bean Soup

Not only are black beans high in the nutrients molybdenum, folate, fiber, protein, and manganese, they are also high in antioxidant compounds called anthocyanins. These compounds work synergistically with other compounds found in whole foods to protect against cancer and other diseases. This soup can be made with less spice if you leave out the jalapeño pepper. Serve this soup with some cooked brown rice and a fresh green salad for a balanced meal.

SERVES 6

1 tablespoon extra virgin olive oil
1 medium onion, chopped
¼ teaspoon sea salt
1 medium red bell pepper, diced
1 large carrot, diced
1 small jalapeno chili pepper, seeded and chopped
1 teaspoon cumin powder
1 ½ teaspoons oregano
½ teaspoon chili powder
¼ teaspoon chipotle pepper
1 teaspoon paprika
pinch cayenne
2 to 3 cups water
6 cups cooked black beans, or 3 cans
2 cups chopped fresh tomatoes or one 14-ounce can
1 cup fresh or frozen corn kernels
½ cup chopped cilantro
2 teaspoons sea salt or Herbamare, or to taste
1 tablespoon apple cider vinegar

1. Heat olive oil in a large soup pot over medium heat; add chopped onion and sea salt. Sauté until slightly golden, then add red pepper, carrot, jalapeño pepper; sauté-stir a few minutes more. Add spices and stir to coat.

2. Add water, black beans, tomatoes, and corn, add more water if necessary. Turn heat to medium-low and simmer until vegetables are fork tender, about 20 to 25 minutes.

3. Remove pot from heat and add cilantro. Add Herbamare or sea salt to taste. Add apple cider vinegar. Taste and adjust salt and seasonings if necessary.

Split Pea Soup with Fresh Vegetables and Herbs

Split peas are an excellent source of molybdenum, soluble fiber, protein, and B vitamins. The fiber in peas helps to stabilize blood sugar levels and reduce cholesterol. If you don't have any homemade vegetable stock on hand try using Imagine's No-Chicken Broth from your local co-op or health food store. Serve this soup with a green salad and a cooked whole grain for a balanced meal.

SERVES 6

> 2 cups split peas, rinsed and drained
> 5 cups water
> 3 bay leaves
>
> 1 tablespoon extra virgin olive oil
> 1 medium onion, diced
> 4 cloves garlic, crushed
> 2 medium carrots, diced
> 2 stalks celery, diced
> 1 medium red bell pepper, diced
> 1 tablespoon dried thyme
> 1 teaspoon dried rosemary, ground
> 1 teaspoon sea salt
> 2 to 3 cups vegetable stock
> ¼ cup fresh basil, chopped
> ½ cup Italian parsley, chopped
> 1 tablespoon white wine vinegar
> ½ teaspoon fresh ground black pepper

1. Place the split peas in a pot with the water and bay leaves. Cover, and simmer on medium-low heat for 45 minutes, stirring occasionally. Add more water if needed.

2. In a large skillet heat the olive oil over medium heat. Add the onion and garlic and cook until it begins to soften, about 3 to 5 minutes. Add the carrots, celery, and red bell pepper. Sauté-stir for a minute then add the dried thyme, rosemary, and sea salt; sauté about 3 to 5 minutes more.

3. Add vegetables to cooked split peas. Then add the vegetable stock, stir well, and simmer over medium-low heat until the vegetables are tender. Add the fresh basil, parsley, white wine vinegar, and black pepper. Adjust salt and seasonings if necessary.

Summer Vegetable Soup

This colorful soup celebrates the bounty of the summer harvest. You can really get creative here and use whatever vegetables you have growing in your garden. Try adding fresh corn off the cob, different dark leafy greens, or even a combination of different types of tomatoes.

SERVES 6 TO 8

2 tablespoons extra virgin olive oil
1 medium onion, diced
3 to 4 cloves garlic, crushed
2 to 3 large carrots, diced
½ pound green or yellow beans, ends trimmed and cut into 1-inch pieces
2 to 3 cups diced fresh tomatoes
6 to 8 cups vegetable stock, chicken stock, or water
2 zucchini, diced
4 cups thinly sliced greens (kale, chard, collards, cabbage)
¼ cup finely chopped fresh herbs (basil, oregano, chives, marjoram)
2 cups cooked beans (cranberry, baby lima, garbanzo), optional
1 to 2 teaspoons sea salt or Herbamare
freshly ground black pepper

1. Heat olive oil in a 6-quart pot over medium heat. Add the onions and sauté for about 5 minutes or until soft. Add garlic and carrots; sauté a few minutes more.

2. Then add green beans, tomatoes, and stock. Simmer, covered, for about 10 to 15 minutes or until vegetables are tender but not all the way cooked.

3. Then add zucchini, greens, fresh herbs and beans; simmer for an additional 5 to 7 minutes or until zucchini is cooked. Season with sea salt and freshly ground black pepper to taste.

Three Bean Chili

Serve this warming soup with Easy Polenta, page 240, and Apple Spiced Collard Greens on page 195. Freeze portions in serving-sized containers for later use.

SERVES 6 TO 8

1 cup pinto beans
1 cup kidney beans
1 cup black beans
8 to 10 cups water
one 3-inch strip kombu

1 tablespoon extra virgin olive oil
1 large onion, chopped
4 to 5 cloves garlic, crushed
4 large carrots, peeled and sliced
1 large green bell pepper, chopped
1 tablespoon ground cumin
1 tablespoon chili powder
2 teaspoons dried oregano
one 28-ounce can diced tomatoes
one 14-ounce can tomato sauce
4 to 5 cups bean cooking liquid or water
2 teaspoons Herbamare or sea salt, or to taste

1. Rinse the beans and place them into a large bowl. Add at least twice as much water as there are beans and soak overnight or for 6 to 8 hours.

2. Drain off all of the soaking water from the beans, rinse well, and place into an 8-quart pot with the water and kombu. Simmer for about 1 to 1 ½ hours (or pressure cook, *pages 142 to 143*) or until beans are tender and cooked, set aside.

3. Heat a large 8-quart stockpot over medium heat. Add olive oil and onions; sauté for about 5 minutes or until onions are soft. Then add the crushed garlic, sliced carrots, chopped green bell pepper, cumin, chili powder, and oregano; sauté for another 3 minutes or so.

4. Then add the diced tomatoes, tomato sauce, bean cooking liquid, and cooked beans. Simmer for about 20 to 25 minutes or until vegetables are tender. Add sea salt or Herbamare to taste.

Vegetarian Chipotle Chili

This recipe is very fast and easy to prepare and makes a great weeknight meal. Serve with Sticky Brown Rice, page 214, and the Arugula Salad with Lime Vinaigrette, page 177, for a complete meal.

SERVES 6 TO 8

1 tablespoon extra virgin olive oil
1 large onion, chopped
3 cloves garlic, crushed
2 large carrots, diced
2 medium zucchini, diced
1 medium red bell pepper, diced
2 teaspoons sea salt or Herbamare
2 teaspoons ground cumin
6 to 8 cups cooked kidney beans, or 4 cans
one 28-ounce can fire roasted crushed tomatoes
one 15-ounce can fire roasted diced tomatoes
1 to 2 teaspoons chili powder
¾ teaspoon chipotle chili powder
2 cups water, add more if needed
1 cup chopped cilantro

1. Heat olive oil in a large 8-quart pot over medium heat. Add the chopped onion and sauté until onion softens. Add the crushed garlic and carrots, stir to coat with olive oil and sauté for a few minutes more.

2. Then add the diced zucchini, red bell pepper, sea salt, and ground cumin, stir, and sauté for about one minute.

3. Add the kidney beans, tomatoes, chili powder, and chipotle chili powder to the pot. Add the water, a little at a time, to desired consistency.

4. Simmer covered for 15 to 20 minutes, or until vegetables are tender. Add chopped cilantro and stir. Adjust salt and spices if necessary.

Winter Vegetable and White Bean Soup

Navy beans or great northern beans work very well in this soup. If you are pinched for time use two cans of organic beans instead of cooking your own. Serve this warming soup in the winter with a loaf of freshly baked Honey Whole Grain Bread, page 124, and the Braised Kale with Garlic and Ginger, page 196.

SERVES 6 TO 8

¼ cup extra virgin olive oil
1 large onion, diced
2 teaspoons sea salt
2 stalks celery, diced
2 large carrots, diced
6 to 8 cloves garlic, crushed
2 shallots, minced
1 tablespoon chopped fresh rosemary
1 teaspoon dried thyme
8 cups vegetable or chicken stock
one 28-ounce can crushed tomatoes
2 medium yellow potatoes, diced
1 small rutabaga, peeled and diced
1 small yam, peeled and diced
1 small delicata squash, peeled and diced
4 cups cooked white beans
2 cups Savoy cabbage, chopped

1. Heat olive oil in a large 8-quart stock pot over medium heat; add diced onion and sea salt and sauté until softened, about 5 minutes.

2. Then add celery, carrots, garlic, shallots, rosemary, and thyme. Sauté for about 5 minutes.

3. Then add vegetable or chicken broth, crushed tomatoes, potatoes, rutabaga, yams, squash, and cooked white beans. Cover and turn heat to low; simmer for about 20 to 25 minutes or until vegetables are tender.

4. Stir in Savoy cabbage. Simmer for 5 minutes more. Taste, adjust salt and herbs if necessary.

Creamy Butternut Squash Soup

This is a wonderful warming fall soup. If you like a little less spice then try adding half the amount of chili flakes. This soup freezes very well, so stock your freezer while squash is in season!

SERVES 6 TO 8

> 2 tablespoons extra virgin olive oil
> 1 large onion, chopped
> 6 cloves garlic, crushed
> 1 teaspoon crushed red chili flakes
> one 4 to 5 pound butternut squash, peeled and cubed
> 3 to 4 cups chopped tomatoes or one 28-ounce can
> 2 cans coconut milk
> 4 cups vegetable stock
> ½ cup chopped cilantro
> 2 teaspoons sea salt or Herbamare, or to taste

1. Cut the squash in half. Scoop out the seeds. Peel the squash with a sharp knife then cut into cubes. Instead of peeling and cubing the squash, you could also bake the squash in the oven, then scoop out the cooked flesh and add it to step #3 below.

2. In a large 8-quart stock pot heat olive oil over medium heat, add onion and sauté for about 5 minutes. Then add garlic and chili flakes, sauté for 1 to 2 minutes more, stirring frequently so the garlic doesn't burn.

3. Add the squash, tomatoes, coconut milk, and vegetable stock; cover and simmer over low heat for about 30 minutes or until squash is very tender.

4. When squash is cooked, add cilantro and stir. Ladle some of the soup into the blender and blend on high until very smooth and creamy, transfer to a clean pot. Continue to blend soup in batches until all of the soup has been pureed. If you like your soup a little chunky, then puree only half of it. Add sea salt or Herbamare to taste.

Creamy Cauliflower Soup

When purchasing cauliflower, make sure the tops are white. If the floret has begun to spot brown or purple, it is past its nutritional peak. Cauliflower is an excellent source of the disease fighting nutrients indole-3-carbinol and sulforaphane. These two nutrients act together in the body to destroy and sweep out cancerous cells.

SERVES 6

2 tablespoons extra virgin olive oil
1 leek, chopped
2 cloves garlic, crushed
2 stalks celery, chopped
2 teaspoons Herbamare
¼ teaspoon white pepper
2 teaspoons dried thyme
1 large cauliflower head, cut into chunks
6 cups water
½ cup raw cashews
¼ cup fresh tarragon, chopped
½ cup chopped parsley

> *Going Dairy-Free Tip*
>
> Raw cashews blended with water can easily replace cream in any creamed soup recipe.

1. In a large soup pot heat olive oil over medium heat. Add the sliced leeks and stir to coat with oil. Continue stirring for two minutes, being careful not to let the leeks brown.

2. Add the crushed garlic and chopped celery and stir. Cook for another 3 minutes or until the celery begins to soften. Add the sea salt, white pepper, and thyme. Then add the cauliflower and stir to coat with oil and spices.

3. Add water, if water is insufficient to cover the cauliflower then add more water, a little at a time until the water is about a ½ inch above the vegetables. Cook covered over medium-low heat for about 20 to 25 minutes, or until cauliflower is soft.

4. When cauliflower is soft, add the fresh tarragon and parsley and stir. Remove 1 cup of the broth from the pot and add it to the blender with the raw cashews. Blend on high until the mixture resembles a smooth cream. Add some of the soup and puree until smooth. Pour out pureed mixture into a clean pot. Continue to puree the soup in batches, until it is all blended. Stir to combine the cashew cream with the rest of the soup. Add more water for a thinner soup. Taste and adjust salt and spices if needed.

5. Gently reheat soup over low heat and serve.

Gingered Carrot Soup

Ginger lovers will enjoy this light and creamy soup. Serve this soup with the Spiced Citrus Salmon on page 275, and a mixed green salad for a colorful, nutrient-rich meal.

SERVES 6

1 tablespoon virgin coconut oil
1 medium onion, chopped
3 cloves garlic, crushed
2 tablespoons grated ginger
½ to 1 teaspoon cumin
½ teaspoon cinnamon
¼ teaspoon allspice
2 pounds carrots, peeled and chopped
6 cups water or vegetable broth
2 to 3 tablespoons freshly squeezed lemon juice
1 to 2 teaspoons sea salt or Herbamare, or to taste
coconut milk, for garnish

> ### Going Dairy-Free Tip
>
> Canned organic coconut milk can easily replace heavy cream in any recipe, especially a recipe with a lot of spice.

1. Heat coconut oil in a large 6-quart pot over medium heat; add onions and sauté until soft, about 5 minutes. Add garlic, ginger, and spices; continue to sauté for another 1 minute.

2. Add chopped carrots and stir to coat with oil and spices, cook 3 to 4 minutes. Then add water or broth, cover and simmer until carrots are soft, about 30 minutes. Stir in lemon juice.

3. Transfer soup to a blender and blend on high until pureed. Pour into a clean pot. Work in batches until all of the soup is pureed. Add sea salt to taste.

4. For added taste and appearance, serve with a swirl of coconut milk if desired.

Roasted Red Pepper Soup

This is a very easy soup to make that freezes well. This soup has a medium rating for spiciness, if you like it mild add ½ teaspoon less of the crushed red chili flakes or ½ teaspoon more for a hotter soup. Use Imagine Organic No-Chicken broth if using store bought broth. If you do not want to take the time to roast your own bell peppers, then try buying a 15-ounce jar of organic roasted red peppers by the company, Mediterranean Organic. This recipe was inspired by something I tasted at the Bellingham Community Food Co-op deli.

SERVES 6

> 2 tablespoons virgin coconut oil or extra virgin olive oil
> 1 large onion, diced
> 2 tablespoons chopped garlic
> ½ to 1 teaspoon crushed red chili pepper flakes
> 1 teaspoon sea salt or Herbamare
> 4 to 5 red bell peppers, roasted (*see page 87 for instructions*)
> 4 cups chopped tomatoes, or one 28-ounce can
> 2 cans coconut milk
> 4 cups vegetable or chicken stock
> ¼ cup minced parsley
> ¼ cup minced fresh basil

1. In a large 6-quart pot sauté onions, garlic, crushed chili pepper, and sea salt in oil over medium heat until tender.

2. Next add coconut milk, vegetable stock, red peppers, and tomatoes to pot; simmer for 20 minutes, covered, stirring occasionally.

3. Puree the soup in blender in batches then return to pot. Cook on low heat for about 5 minutes. Then add the minced parsley and basil, cook for an additional 5 minutes, stirring often. Taste, adjust salt and spices if necessary.

Thai Coconut Vegetable Soup

I love the flavors of Thai food. This recipe embodies those flavors without being too difficult to prepare. The Asian Soup Stock on page 145 is especially delicious in this soup, though any vegetable or chicken stock will do. Fish, chicken, shrimp, or tofu can easily be added to this soup if you desire. Unlike most soups which improve with age, this soup tastes best immediately after it is made.

SERVES 4

2 cups vegetable or chicken stock
1 can coconut milk
1 teaspoon crushed red chili flakes
6 to 8 cloves garlic, crushed
1 small onion, cut into half moons
2 to 3 carrots, peeled and cut into matchsticks
1 red bell pepper, cut into strips
1 medium zucchini, cut in half lengthwise then sliced
2 cups thinly sliced bok choy leaves or cabbage leaves
½ cup chopped cilantro
sea salt or Herbamare, to taste

1. Place the vegetable or chicken stock into a 4-quart pot. Add the coconut milk, red chili flakes, crushed garlic, onion, carrots, and red bell pepper. Simmer for 15 minutes, covered, or until the vegetables are just tender.

2. Add the zucchini and simmer 5 minutes more. Remove pot from heat and add the sliced bok choy leaves, cilantro, and salt. Garnish with extra red chili flaks if desired.

Chicken Noodle and Vegetable Soup

Soup is a great way to make use of the whole chicken. By simmering the chicken with vegetables, water, and herbs, vital nutrients from the bone marrow are released into the broth. Don't skip the fresh rosemary! It is the secret ingredient to this great tasting soup.

SERVES 6 TO 8

To make the broth:
1 whole organic chicken, about 4 pounds
1 large onion, cut into quarters with skins on
1 head garlic, cut in half crosswise
3 stalks celery, cut into large pieces
1 large carrot, cut into large chunks
2 bay leaves
one 4-inch strip kombu
2 teaspoons whole black peppercorns
½ bunch parsley, chopped
4 sprigs fresh rosemary
3 sprigs fresh marjoram
3 sprigs fresh thyme
1 sprig fresh savory
1 tablespoon sea salt or Herbamare
water to cover, about 10 to 12 cups

> ### Ingredient Tip
>
> Quinoa noodles typically contain corn. If you have a corn allergy, simply replace the noodles with either cooked brown rice or brown rice noodles.

To make the soup:
1 large onion, diced
3 large carrots, peeled and sliced into rounds
3 stalks celery, chopped
3 to 4 red potatoes, cut into cubes
½ bunch parsley, chopped
1 to 2 tablespoons finely chopped fresh rosemary
1 teaspoon dried thyme
½ package quinoa noodles
4 cups chopped kale
sea salt or Herbamare and black pepper to taste

1. Rinse the chicken and place into a large 8-quart stockpot. Add the remaining ingredients for the broth (onion through water) into the stockpot. Place pot over medium-high heat and bring to a boil, reduce heat to a simmer and cover with a lid. Simmer for 1 ½ to 2 hours or until chicken easily falls off the bone.

2. Next, place a large strainer over a clean large pot; pour the contents of the broth through the strainer to separate the broth from the vegetables and chicken. Remove the chicken and place on a plate to cool. Discard vegetables and herbs.

3. Now, to make the soup, place the pot of broth back on the stove over medium heat; add the chopped onion, sliced carrots, celery, cubed potatoes, and herbs.

4. Remove chicken meat from the bones, cut into pieces if necessary, and place into the soup. When vegetables are tender add ½ package of quinoa noodles into the simmering soup. Cook until tender (just a few minutes).

5. Take off heat and stir the kale into soup. Add Herbamare and black pepper to taste.

Turkey and Wild Rice Soup

This soup makes a wonderful fall or winter soup. Serve with the Spinach Salad with Pecans and Dried Cherries on page 187. Soup freezes well for later use.

SERVES 6 TO 8

To Make the Broth:
2 to 3 pounds organic turkey breast, with bone and skin
1 large onion, chopped with skin on
1 large carrot, cut into large chunks
3 stalks celery, cut into large chunks
½ bunch parsley, chopped
2 sprigs fresh rosemary
3 sprigs fresh thyme
5 whole black peppercorns
1 tablespoon sea salt
8 cups water

To Make the Rice:
1 cup wild rice
2 ½ cups water

To Make the Soup:
2 tablespoons extra virgin olive oil
1 large leek, sliced
2 large carrots, diced
4 stalks celery, diced
2 teaspoons dried thyme
1 teaspoon dried sage
5 ounces fresh baby spinach
½ bunch fresh parsley, chopped

1. To make the broth, place the first 10 ingredients into a large 8-quart stockpot and bring to a boil. Cover, reduce heat to a simmer and cook for about 2 hours or until meat easily falls off the bone.

2. Rinse and drain the wild rice. Place into a medium saucepan with 2 ½ cups of water. Bring to a boil then reduce heat to a simmer and cook for about 45 minutes. Set aside.

3. After the turkey is cooked, place a large strainer over a large clean pot and strain broth into it. Take turkey breast out of the strainer and place on a plate to cool. Discard vegetables.

4. In a clean 6 or 8-quart pot, heat the olive oil over medium heat. Add the leeks and sauté a few minutes until tender. Add the carrots, celery, thyme, and sage. Add the broth to the vegetable mixture; simmer over medium-low heat for 10 minutes or until vegetable are tender.

5. While vegetables are simmering, remove the skin from the turkey and pull the meat from the bone. Cut meat into pieces and then place it into the pot of simmering vegetables and herbs.

6. Then add the cooked wild rice, baby spinach, and chopped parsley. Stir well. Remove from heat and season with sea salt or Herbamare to taste. Soup freezes well for later use.

Fresh Salads and Vegetables

"The ultimate value of life depends upon awareness and the power of contemplation rather than upon mere survival."

~*Aristotle*

V egetables offer us a wide variety of potent antioxidants, anti-cancer agents, phytochemicals, vitamins, minerals, and more. Let your eyes guide you when choosing vegetables from the store or market. The beautiful array of colors offered by our vegetable friends give us the chemicals we need to maintain optimal health. Chances are, that the colors you are most attracted to are the chemicals that your body needs most at that moment. Not only do these plants give us all of the potent nutrients we need, they also offer our taste buds a wide variety of wonderful flavors.

A diet high in fresh organic vegetables has been associated with a decrease in almost every disease. At the same time, a diet low in fresh vegetables has been associated with a higher risk for almost every disease. Try to make vegetables and greens a regular part of every meal. Not only will the flavors be very satisfying to your tastes, but the bright rainbow of colors will satisfy you on a deeper level.

Tips for Adding More Vegetables to Your Diet:

- **Prepare a raw vegetable platter** each day or as often as you like. Choose vegetables like celery, carrots, bell peppers, cucumbers, summer squash, sugar snap peas, cauliflower, even romaine lettuce. It is fun to create a beautiful design on a plate or platter that you will be attracted to. Leave it on the counter at home so everyone can munch throughout the day. Set a bowl of bean dip beside the vegetables and your beautiful platter will disappear in no time.

- **Add spinach, bell peppers, onions, and zucchini to your** eggs or tofu in the morning. You can even add some fresh herbs for added flavor and nutrients.

- **Top a plate of mixed greens with chopped raw vegetables** and drizzle with your favorite salad dressing.

- **Use pureed vegetables** to add to muffins and breads. You can also make many exciting soups using pureed vegetables, spices, and broths.

- **Make a variety of soups and stews** to which you can add almost an endless amount of chopped vegetables.

- **Make vegetable juices** with a variety of vegetables and fruits. Experiment and find a combination that you like best. One of my favorite combinations is pear, pineapple, beet, fennel, carrot, and parsley.

- **Create tantalizing smoothies** with different greens, vegetables, and fruits. Try a combination of 50 to 60% fruit and 40 to 50% greens. You can use kale, lettuce, dandelion greens, carrot tops, radish greens, spinach, cabbage, and more. See *pages 97 to 99* for green smoothie recipes.

How to Select and Store Fresh Produce:

Whenever possible, we prefer to purchase organic vegetables and fruits from our local Farmers Market. Buying locally supports the local economy and benefits small farmers. It is also wonderful to connect with the farmers who grow your food. Chances are, if you have a health food store or food co-op in town, their produce is grown locally. Purchase fresh, organic produce frequently from a store that has a rapid turnover. If possible, make more frequent trips to the store and buy smaller amounts of produce.

- **Choose vibrant, brightly colored vegetables and fruits.** Dull-looking or wilted vegetables have been sitting on the shelf too long. Choose crisp, colorful produce that is free of any discolored areas and slime.

- **Buy only the produce that you plan on using within the next few days.** Longer storage time can not only cause the produce to spoil, but also significantly reduce nutrient levels and flavor. Delicate produce such as leafy greens, fresh herbs, broccoli, summer squash, and soft, ripe fruits are best used within a few days. Though other produce, such as winter squash, onions, garlic, and root vegetables can be stored for longer periods of time without leading to spoilage or significantly reducing nutrient levels.

- **Choose local, seasonal fruits and vegetables.** When you purchase in-season produce, it is much fresher, the nutritional value is significantly higher, and the flavors are far superior to food that has traveled thousands of miles. Imagine the difference in flavor and texture from a just-picked local organic strawberry compared to a strawberry that has traveled across the country to get to your grocery store. Buying local, organic produce also reduces carbon emissions from transport, thus reducing the impact on global warming.

- **Don't wash vegetables before storing.** Wash your vegetables before you use them, not before you store them. They need to be stored dry. If you are purchasing your vegetables at a grocery store, they are usually sprayed with cold water throughout the day. This keeps them fresh and crisp in the store, but at home in a plastic bag they may mold rather quickly. Make sure you dry them well. Wrap leafy greens with a cloth or paper towel and then place them in a plastic bag in the crisper drawer in your refrigerator. Berries can quickly degrade if they are wet, be sure to eat them, freeze them, or cook with them very soon after purchasing. Other vegetables that are damp can simply be dried off before storing.

- **Store fresh produce according to their type.** Place root vegetables, such as potatoes and yams, in a cool, dark place. Exposure to light can cause potatoes to turn green. The green pigment contains the toxic alkaloid, solanine. Green sections of potatoes should be removed before cooking. Pumpkins and other winter squashes can be stored in a dry place for 2 to 3 months. Onions and garlic should be stored in a separate basket that allows for plenty of air flow.

Root vegetables such as carrots, parsnips, and beets can be stored in the refrigerator for several weeks. Cut the leaves from root vegetables before storing as the flow of sap continues to the leaves at the expense of the root. Cabbage can be kept in the refrigerator for several weeks also. Store other vegetables in the refrigerator crisper drawer for up to a week.

Apples, berries, and cherries are best kept in the refrigerator while other fruits can be kept on the counter in a well-ventilated container until ripe. Ripe fruits can be stored in the refrigerator in an open plastic bag until ready to use. Tropical and citrus fruits, as well as avocados and tomatoes, are best kept at room temperature.

Cultured Vegetables

Cultured vegetables are sauerkraut, from the Austrian sauer (sour) and kraut (greens or plants). Cultured vegetables are rich in lactobacilli and enzymes, are alkaline-forming, full of vitamins, especially vitamin C. The taste is very tangy and delicious. Cultured vegetables help to reestablish a healthy inner ecosystem, improve digestion, control cravings for sweets, and stimulate the liver. Try your own combinations of cabbage and vegetables; you can even add sea vegetables and fresh or dried herbs. You can also buy raw cultured vegetables at your local co-op or health food store from the company, Rejuvenative Foods. I began eating and making cultured vegetables when I followed The Body Ecology Diet, by Donna Gates.

MAKES ABOUT 2 QUARTS

> **3 to 4 heads green or red cabbage**
> **fresh vegetables (carrots, beets, garlic, radish, celery, red bell pepper)**
> **herbs (dill, thyme, rosemary, basil)**
> **¾ to 1 cup freshly squeezed lemon juice**

1. Grind cabbage, vegetables, and herbs in a food processor or run them through a Champion juicer using the blank plastic piece.

2. If using a food processor, then place the processed vegetables into a large stainless steel bowl and pound them with a blunt object until their juices are released.

3. Add the lemon juice.

4. Place them into a large glass bowl or ceramic crock, but don't fill to the top. Top with cabbage leaves, completely covering the ground vegetables.

5. Place a large plate on top of the cabbage leaves. Place a clean towel over the plate. Place a weight over the towel and plate (a jar filled with water works well).

6. Let the vegetables sit undisturbed for 5 to 7 days at 60 to 70 degrees F.

7. After the 5 to 7 days, discard the cabbage leaves and any moldy or discolored vegetables. Store your raw cultured vegetables in a glass jar in the refrigerator.

Raw Sauerkraut

Here is a recipe for raw sauerkraut, which is very different from the pasteurized sauerkraut you would find at the store. Raw sauerkraut is rich in live enzymes, vitamins, and beneficial bacteria which, when pasteurized, are lost. This recipe is very easy to make and totally delicious every time.

MAKES ABOUT 1 QUART

1 large head green or red cabbage
1 tablespoon sea salt

1. Remove outer cabbage leaves and reserve. Cut the cabbage into chunks, removing the hard, inner core. You can thinly slice the chunks of cabbage with a very sharp knife or run them through your food processor with the slicing disk in place.

2. Place the sliced cabbage and sea salt into a large bowl and toss together. Using a blunt object, pound the cabbage until the natural juices are released and the volume has reduced. This will take about 5 to 8 minutes.

3. Place cabbage and juices into a wide-mouth quart jar. Tear up the reserved cabbage leaves and place on top of sliced cabbage. Press down so juices rise above cabbage. Cover jar.

4. Place jar in a cool spot, away from heat or light. Your kitchen pantry or a cabinet is a good spot. Let jar sit for 3 to 5 days. Taste it occasionally. Once it has a tangy, fermented flavor and the sliced cabbage is translucent, the sauerkraut is done. Remove the cabbage leaves on top, cover, and place jar in the refrigerator.

Arugula Salad *with Lime Vinaigrette*

This is a light and zesty salad the pairs well with a spicy black bean dish or any dish with Mexican flair. Fresh organic sweet corn cut off the cob is another delicious addition to this salad.

SERVES 4 TO 6

Salad:
6 cups arugula leaves
2 cups mixed greens
½ cup pumpkin seeds, toasted
1 small red bell pepper, sliced into rounds
1 avocado, cubed
3 to 4 green onions, sliced

Dressing:
¼ cup extra virgin olive oil
¼ cup freshly squeezed lime juice
1 tablespoon brown rice vinegar or apple cider vinegar
1 to 2 teaspoons lime zest
1 clove garlic, crushed
¼ teaspoon sea salt
¼ teaspoon ground cumin
pinch ground cardamom

1. Rinse the greens to remove any dirt or sand. Bunched arugula can sometimes have quite a bit of dirt on it. Spin dry with a salad spinner and place the greens into a large salad bowl.

2. In a skillet, toast the pumpkin seeds over medium-low heat until you hear a "pop." Place the seeds into a small bowl to cool.

3. Place the pumpkin seeds, roasted red pepper strips, avocado cubes, and green onion slices in the salad bowl with the greens.

4. Place all ingredients for the dressing into a small bowl and whisk. Pour the dressing over the salad and serve.

Autumn Harvest Salad *with Balsamic Vinaigrette*

This is an excellent salad to serve in early autumn when the fall harvest of greens is available and the green apples and fresh figs are in season. Make a double batch of the dressing to have on hand for a quick salad of mixed greens. Store dressing in a jar in the refrigerator. Dried figs can easily replace the fresh figs in this recipe.

SERVES 4 TO 6

Salad:
8 cups mixed greens
1 to 2 cups finely sliced red cabbage
1 green apple, diced
3 to 4 fresh black mission figs, cut into wedges
½ cup Zante currants
2 to 3 green onions, sliced
½ cup raw walnuts, lightly roasted
½ cup raw pumpkin seeds, toasted

Dressing:
4 tablespoons extra virgin olive oil
3 tablespoons balsamic vinegar
1 tablespoon maple syrup
2 teaspoons Dijon mustard
1 teaspoon wheat-free tamari or ¼ teaspoon sea salt

1. Preheat oven to 350 degrees F. Rinse and dry greens. Place into a large bowl with the chopped cabbage, diced apple, chopped figs, Zante currants, and green onions. Toss gently.

2. Place the walnuts into a small glass baking dish and place into the preheated oven. Lightly roast for about 8 to 10 minutes. Remove from heat, cool slightly then chop. Add them to the salad.

3. Heat a skillet over medium heat. Place the pumpkin seeds in and keep them moving in the pan until they begin to "pop". Remove from heat, let cool slightly and place on top of salad.

4. Prepare the dressing by placing ingredients into a jar with a tight fitting lid, and shake well. To serve, pour dressing over salad, gently toss, and serve immediately.

Beet and Fennel Salad *with Orange Vinaigrette*

This salad is great served with the Balsamic Tempeh Stir-Fry on page 193. Fennel bulb is an excellent source of fiber, vitamin C, folate, potassium, and the phytonutrient anethole. Anethole helps to reduce inflammation and works to prevent the occurrence of cancer.

SERVES 4 TO 6

Salad:
8 cups mixed greens
3 small beets, peeled and cubed
1 small fennel bulb, sliced
1 cup raw walnuts, lightly roasted
1 avocado, cubed
4 green onions, sliced
½ cup chopped basil

Dressing:
¼ cup orange juice
3 tablespoons extra virgin olive oil
1 tablespoon balsamic vinegar
1 tablespoon chopped fresh fennel tops
1 teaspoon orange zest
¼ teaspoon sea salt
¼ teaspoon cinnamon

1. Preheat oven to 350 degrees F. Place walnuts in a glass baking dish and place in preheated oven, bake for 10 minutes or until walnuts give off a nutty aroma. Let cool.

2. Steam cubed beets for 10 to 15 minutes or until tender. Place in a dish to cool completely. Place all ingredients for dressing into a small bowl and whisk together.

3. In a large bowl, place mixed greens, beets, walnuts, fennel, avocado, green onions, and basil; top with dressing and serve immediately.

Berry Hazelnut Salad *with Honey Poppy Seed Vinaigrette*

This northwest inspired salad utilizes fresh greens, hazelnuts, and whatever combination of berries you desire.

Salad:
8 cups mixed greens
2 cups mixed fresh berries (strawberries, blueberries, blackberries, salmonberries, thimbleberries, raspberries)
½ cup hazelnuts, roasted
3 to 4 green onions, sliced into rounds

Dressing:
¼ cup extra virgin olive oil
3 tablespoons red wine vinegar
1 to 2 tablespoons honey
1 tablespoon poppy seeds
¼ teaspoon sea salt

1. Rinse and dry the greens, place into a large salad bowl. Rinse and dry the berries. If using strawberries then slice. Place berries atop the greens. Chop the hazelnuts and add them to the salad along with the green onions.

2. To make the dressing, place all ingredients into a glass jar, and shake well. Pour over the salad just before serving.

*Note: To roast hazelnuts, preheat oven to 350 degrees F. Place nuts into a shallow baking dish. Roast in the oven for about 10 minutes. Remove and let cool on a plate before chopping.

Cabbage Salad *with Cilantro Vinaigrette*

Cabbage is a rich source of powerful phytochemicals that fight against cancer. Raw cabbage is also very detoxifying to the body, improving digestion and elimination, while killing harmful bacteria and viruses in the gut. This salad is delicious served with the Lemon Millet Patties, page 237, and the Navy Beans in a Homemade Barbecue Sauce, page 262.

SERVES 4

Salad:
4 to 6 cups chopped Napa or Savoy cabbage
4 green onions, finely sliced
1 large carrot, grated
½ cup sunflower seeds, toasted

Dressing:
¼ cup chopped cilantro
4 tablespoons extra virgin olive oil
3 tablespoons brown rice vinegar
¼ teaspoon sea salt
pinch cayenne pepper

1. Place cabbage, green onions, grated carrot, and toasted sunflower seeds into a large bowl.

2. Place ingredients for dressing into a blender and blend until smooth. Pour dressing over salad and toss well. Serve immediately.

Fresh Garden Salad *with Herbal Vinaigrette*

This salad is rich in heart-healthy fiber. Fiber binds to bile salts in the colon and removes them from the body. The body then makes more bile which is helpful because it must break down cholesterol to do so. This is just one way in which fiber is able to lower high cholesterol levels. This salad is perfect to include in an evening summer meal when the tomatoes, cucumbers, lettuce, and fresh herbs are sweet and bountiful.

SERVES 4 TO 6

Salad:
1 head green leaf lettuce, rinsed, dried and torn into pieces
1 large ripe tomato, chopped
1 small cucumber, sliced
1 large carrot, shredded
2 green onions, sliced
½ cup raw sunflower seeds, toasted
fresh sprouts

Dressing:
1 small lemon, juiced
⅓ cup extra virgin olive oil
2 tablespoons balsamic vinegar
2 teaspoons Dijon mustard
1 tablespoon maple syrup
3 tablespoons chopped fresh basil
2 tablespoons chopped fresh chives
1 tablespoon chopped fresh oregano
½ teaspoon sea salt

1. Place ingredients for salad into a large bowl.

2. In a smaller separate bowl whisk together the ingredients for the dressing. Pour over salad when ready to serve.

Lettuce and Cabbage Salad *with Creamy Ginger Dressing*

Ginger contains compounds called gingerols. These compounds act as a powerful anti-inflammatory, reducing pain in people with arthritis. This delicious salad dressing will keep you coming back for more. It can also be drizzled over steamed vegetables or cooked whole grains. Store dressing in a glass jar in the refrigerator for up to 10 days. When ready to use place jar under running hot water to "thin out" the olive oil. Dressing recipe inspired by something served at the Silence-Heart-Nest Restaurant in Seattle, Washington.

SERVES 4 TO 6

Salad:
1 head red leaf lettuce, rinsed and torn into pieces
½ head red cabbage, chopped
2 large carrots, shredded
4 green onions, sliced
1 cup chopped cilantro

Dressing:
⅓ cup sesame seeds, toasted
½ cup chopped celery
3 to 4 tablespoons chopped ginger
½ cup extra virgin olive oil
3 tablespoons brown rice vinegar
3 tablespoons wheat-free tamari
2 tablespoons water
1 tablespoon maple syrup or agave nectar
1 to 2 teaspoons organic ketchup or tomato paste
⅛ teaspoon white pepper
⅛ teaspoon celery seed

1. Place the ingredients for the salad into a large bowl and set aside.

2. To prepare the dressing, heat a skillet over medium-low heat; add sesame seeds and dry toast for about 2 minutes. Be sure to keep seeds moving in the pan to prevent burning. Remove from heat and place seeds into a blender with the remaining dressing ingredients, blend on high until very smooth and creamy. When ready to serve pour dressing over salad and serve immediately.

Italian Greens Salad *with Red Wine Vinaigrette*

This crisp, refreshing salad can be served with any dish that has Italian flavors. Try it with some cooked brown rice pasta and a homemade marinara sauce, page 309, or with a chicken or fish dish.

SERVES 4 TO 6

Salad:
1 small head of romaine lettuce, rinsed and dried
1 small red onion, sliced thin
½ small red bell pepper, cut into rings
½ cup kalamata olives, pitted
¼ cup Italian parsley, chopped
3 Roma tomatoes, sliced
5 pepperoncini peppers, chopped
½ cup grated organic parmesan cheese, optional

Dressing:
¼ cup extra virgin olive oil
¼ cup red wine vinegar
1 teaspoon Dijon mustard
1 teaspoon maple syrup or agave nectar
½ teaspoon sea salt
1 teaspoon Italian seasoning
1 teaspoon paprika
1 clove garlic, crushed

1. Chop the lettuce leaves into pieces. Place the chopped greens in a salad bowl.

2. Gently toss in the red onions, red bell peppers, kalamata olives, Italian parsley, Roma tomatoes, and pepperoncini peppers. Sprinkle on the grated parmesan cheese if using.

3. To make the dressing, place all ingredients in a jar with a tight fitting lid and shake. Pour over salad and serve immediately. Leftover dressing will keep in the refrigerator for up to 10 days.

Pear and Hazelnut Salad *with Creamy Cranberry Dressing*

Serve this salad when cranberries, pears, and hazelnuts are in season in autumn. It is also delicious served at a festive holiday meal.

SERVES 4 TO 6

Salad:
1 head red leaf lettuce, rinsed and torn into pieces
1 firm ripe pear, cored and sliced thin
½ small red onion, sliced into thin rounds
1 cup raw hazelnuts, roasted
½ cup crumbled organic feta cheese, optional

Dressing:
2 teaspoons extra virgin olive oil
2 shallots, peeled and thinly sliced
1 cup fresh cranberries
¼ cup freshly squeezed orange juice
¼ cup extra virgin olive oil
3 tablespoons balsamic vinegar
3 to 4 tablespoons maple syrup
1 teaspoon orange zest
½ teaspoon sea salt or Herbamare

1. Place all of the ingredients for the salad in a large bowl.

2. To make the dressing, heat a small skillet over medium heat and add the 2 teaspoons olive oil and sliced shallots. Sauté shallots for 3 to 5 minutes or until soft. Add fresh cranberries and continue to sauté until the cranberries are soft and have "popped."

3. Place shallot and cranberry mixture into a blender with the orange juice, olive oil, balsamic vinegar, orange zest, and sea salt. Blend on high until creamy. Add a few tablespoons of water for a thinner consistency and blend again.

4. Drizzle dressing over salad and serve immediately. Extra dressing can be stored in a glass jar in the refrigerator for up to 10 days.

*Note: To roast hazelnuts, preheat oven to 350 degrees F. Place nuts into a shallow baking dish. Roast in the oven for about 10 minutes. Remove and let cool on a plate before chopping.

Steamed Salmon, Spinach, and Fennel Salad

Steaming is a great way to prepare salmon. It is fast, easy, and helps to retain much of the essential fatty acids. Serve this salad as part of a weekend brunch in the springtime or for a light evening meal. This delicious salad recipe has been adapted from Bastyr University instructor, Mary Shaw.

SERVES 4 TO 6

Salad:
1 large fennel bulb
½ to 1 pound wild Alaskan salmon fillet
1 bunch spinach, washed and torn into pieces
½ red onion, cut into thin rounds
½ cup finely chopped fresh basil

Dressing:
¼ cup extra virgin olive oil
2 to 3 tablespoons apple cider vinegar
2 to 3 tablespoons freshly squeezed orange juice
1 teaspoon orange zest
½ teaspoon cinnamon
¼ teaspoon sea salt

1. Cut the green stalks from the fennel bulb and place them into a 10-inch skillet. Fill the pan with water until it reaches the tops of the fennel, about ½ to 1 inch of water. Place the salmon fillet over the top of the fennel. Cover the skillet and steam fish over medium heat for about 10 to 15 minutes or until salmon is cooked through.

2. While the salmon is cooking, trim the ends off of the fennel bulb and thinly slice it into small strips. Place the sliced fennel, spinach, red onion, and basil into a large bowl and gently toss.

3. In a small bowl, combine the ingredients for the dressing and mix well.

4. After salmon is cooked, remove the skin and discard along with the used fennel tops. Break the flesh into small pieces and place into the bowl with the spinach. Drizzle the dressing over the salad and gently toss. Serve immediately. Extra dressing can be stored in a glass jar in the refrigerator for later use.

Spinach Salad *with Pecans and Dried Cherries*

Spinach can protect you against osteoporosis, heart disease, colon cancer, arthritis, and other diseases all at the same time. Spinach is a rich source of vitamin K and is very high in different flavonoid compounds which function as antioxidants and as anti-cancer agents in the body. In addition, spinach contains a special carotenoid, called neoxanthin, which has shown to be helpful in the treatment of prostate cancer.

SERVES 4 TO 6

Pecans:
1 cup pecans
1 tablespoon extra virgin olive oil
2 tablespoons maple syrup
1 teaspoon Dijon mustard
pinch sea salt

Salad:
8 ounces spinach leaves, washed and dried
½ small red onion, sliced into thin rounds
½ cup dried organic cherries

Dressing:
3 Tablespoons extra virgin olive oil
2 tablespoons balsamic vinegar
1 tablespoon maple syrup
1 teaspoon Dijon mustard
¼ teaspoon sea salt
¼ teaspoon fresh ground pepper

1. Preheat oven to 375 degrees F. Place pecans, olive oil, maple syrup, Dijon mustard, and the pinch of sea salt into a pie plate and mix together. Bake in the oven for about 10 to 12 minutes. Let cool slightly, and then remove from pie plate and place on a plate to cool.

2. Place spinach into a salad bowl. Add pecans, cherries, and sliced red onion.

3. Place all dressing ingredients into a small jar with a tight fitting lid and shake well. Dress salad just before serving.

Whole Meal Salad *with Lemon Tahini Dressing*

This delightful, nutrient-dense salad makes a great energizing lunch, which is how we often eat it. The diverse array of flavors and textures are a delight to the taste buds! I often like to add some steamed cubed beets which add even another dimension of color and flavor. Any dressing will work here, but the Lemon Tahini Dressing below is especially luscious.

SERVES 2

Salad:
4 to 6 cups torn lettuce (green, red, or butter leaf lettuce), rinsed
4 to 6 pieces sautéed tofu
1 handful soaked raw almonds
1 small avocado, cubed
1 carrot, chopped
2 green onions, sliced

Lemon Tahini Dressing:
¼ cup sesame tahini
¼ cup freshly squeezed lemon juice
2 tablespoons water
2 tablespoons extra virgin olive oil
1 clove garlic, crushed
2 to 3 teaspoons lemon zest
¼ teaspoon sea salt, or to taste

Optional Additions:
alfalfa sprouts
steamed cubed beets
cherry tomatoes
chopped celery

1. Evenly distribute the lettuce between two large salad bowls. Place tofu pieces on top of lettuce. Top with soaked almonds, cubed avocado, chopped carrot, sliced green onions, and any other optional additions you might want to add.

2. Place all of the ingredients for the dressing into a small bowl and whisk together. Taste and add more sea salt or garlic if desired. Pour desired amount of dressing over each salad. Store extra dressing in a glass jar in the refrigerator. Dressing will keep for up to 10 days.

Beet, Kale, and Walnut Salad

Beets are a nutrient dense food; particularly rich in folic acid that protects us from heart disease, birth defects, and certain cancers. Kale is a powerful anti-cancer food rich in organosulfur compounds. Walnuts are very high in omega-3 fatty acids which reduce inflammation, protect against cardiovascular disease, and improve cognitive function. Serve this dish with the Wild Salmon with Lemon, Garlic, & Thyme, page 277.

SERVES 4 TO 6

3 to 4 beets, peeled and cubed
1 bunch kale, rinsed and chopped
1 cup raw walnuts, lightly roasted
½ cup organic feta cheese, optional

Dressing:
3 tablespoons extra virgin olive oil
2 tablespoons balsamic vinegar
1 tablespoon maple syrup
2 tablespoons finely chopped basil, optional
1 teaspoon wheat-free tamari or ¼ teaspoon sea salt

1. Preheat oven to 350 degrees F. Place the cubed beets into a steamer basket. Steam for about 15 to 20 minutes or until tender, place into a bowl to cool. Place chopped kale into the steamer basket and steam for 5 to 10 minutes until tender but still bright green. Place into bowl with beets.

2. Place walnuts into a small glass baking dish and roast in the oven for 10 to 12 minutes; watch carefully so they don't burn! Let cool completely. Place into the bowl with the beets and kale.

3. In a small bowl, whisk together the ingredients for the dressing. Pour over beets, kale, and walnuts, and toss. Top with feta cheese and freshly ground black pepper if desired.

Carrot Hijiki Salad *with Sweet Miso Dressing*

Serve this mineral-rich salad at your next potluck. Or, try serving it with the Shiitake Tofu, page 245, and some brown rice noodles for an evening meal. This recipe was inspired by something I tasted at the Bastyr University cafeteria.

SERVES 4 TO 6

¼ cup hijiki
1 pound carrots, grated (about 4 cups)
4 green onions, sliced into thin rounds
½ cup chopped cilantro
¼ cup sesame seeds, toasted

Dressing:
3 tablespoons toasted sesame oil
3 tablespoons brown rice syrup
2 tablespoons gluten-free miso
2 tablespoons brown rice vinegar
1 tablespoon wheat-free tamari
1 to 2 teaspoons hot pepper sesame oil
1 teaspoon grated ginger
1 clove garlic, crushed

1. Place the hijiki into a small saucepan and fill with about 2 cups water. Let soak for about 5 minutes then place pot onto stove and simmer for about 25 minutes or until hijiki is tender. Drain off water.

2. Place the hijiki into a large bowl with the grated carrots, sliced green onions, chopped cilantro, and toasted sesame seeds.

3. In a small bowl whisk together the ingredients for the dressing. Pour the dressing over the carrot mixture and toss well. Serve immediately or store in the refrigerator for up to 3 days. Salad is best served the day it is made.

Cucumber, Tomato, Basil Salad

The skin of cucumbers contains the minerals silica, magnesium, and, potassium. Silica is an essential component to healthy connective tissue. The flesh of cucumbers contains good amounts of vitamin C. Eating cucumbers regularly can improve the look and feel of your skin and hair. Cucumbers, tomatoes, and basil are abundant during the summer months. This salad is easy and quick to prepare. Serve it as part of a summer picnic or as a simple late afternoon snack.

SERVES 2 TO 4

2 medium slicing cucumbers, cut into thin slices
3 to 4 firm tomatoes, quartered, then sliced
½ cup thinly sliced fresh basil
1 to 2 cloves garlic, finely chopped
2 tablespoons extra virgin olive oil
2 tablespoons red wine vinegar
sea salt and freshly ground black pepper, to taste

1. Place the sliced cucumbers and tomatoes into a shallow serving dish. Add thinly sliced basil, chopped garlic, olive oil, and red wine vinegar.

2. Gently toss; add sea salt and freshly ground black pepper to taste. Toss again and serve.

Green Beans *with Garlic Dressing*

Serve these scrumptious green beans as a side dish to the Sunny Sunflower Seed Burgers, page 212, or as a side dish to any baked fish or chicken dish. Green beans are an excellent source of beta-carotene and vitamin C.

SERVES 4 TO 6

2 pounds green beans, ends trimmed
½ cup sliced or chopped almonds
1 tablespoon chopped fresh thyme

Dressing:
2 tablespoons extra virgin olive oil
1 tablespoon fresh lemon juice
1 teaspoon Dijon mustard
2 cloves garlic, crushed
½ teaspoon lemon zest
½ teaspoon sea salt
¼ teaspoon freshly ground black pepper

1. To prepare the beans, blanch beans in a large pot of boiling water for 4 minutes or until crisp-tender. Drain well.

2. Combine all ingredients for dressing in a small bowl, and stir with a wire whisk.

3. Place beans, almonds, and thyme in a large bowl, add dressing and toss well to coat.

Picnic Potato Salad

Olives are an excellent source of vitamin E and monounsaturated fats. The anti-inflammatory actions of the monounsaturated fats and vitamin E in olives may help to reduce the severity of asthma, osteoarthritis, and rheumatoid arthritis, three conditions where most of the damage is caused by high levels of free radicals. This recipe was inspired by something I tasted at the Bellingham Community Food Co-op's deli. Serve this dish as part of a summer meal or try it with the Lemon Millet Patties, page 237, and the Navy Beans in a Homemade Barbecue Sauce, page 262.

SERVES 4 TO 6

5 medium red potatoes, cut into chunks
1 pint cherry tomatoes
1 cup kalamata olives
1 small leek, sliced in half lengthwise then chopped
1 cup chopped parsley
½ teaspoon sea salt
½ teaspoon freshly ground black pepper
3 tablespoons red wine vinegar
3 tablespoons extra virgin olive oil

1. Place potato chunks into a steamer basket and steam until tender but not mushy. Remove from heat and let cool.

2. Place cooled potatoes into a large bowl with the cherry tomatoes, kalamata olives, chopped leek, chopped parsley, sea salt, and black pepper. Gently toss.

3. Drizzle the red wine vinegar and olive oil over the potato mixture and gently toss.

Summer Squash and Cannelini Bean Salad

This vegetable dish makes a great addition to any summer picnic. Summer squash include patty pan, crookneck, and zucchini. Cannelini beans are a traditional white Italian bean, sometimes known as the white kidney bean. They have a very smooth texture with an elusive nutty flavor. Please refer to page 140 for how to cook beans.

SERVES 4 TO 6

> 6 small summer squash, diced
> 1 small red onion, finely chopped
> 3 cups cooked Cannelini beans
> ¾ cup chopped sun-dried tomatoes (olive oil-packed)
> 1 cup chopped fresh parsley
>
> *Dressing:*
> ⅓ cup extra virgin olive oil
> ¼ cup red wine vinegar
> 2 teaspoons Dijon mustard
> 1 tablespoon chopped fresh rosemary
> 1 tablespoon minced shallots
> ½ teaspoon sea salt or Herbamare
> freshly ground black pepper

1. In a large bowl, place diced squash, chopped red onion, cooked Cannelini beans, chopped sun-dried tomatoes, and chopped fresh parsley.

2. To make the dressing, place the olive oil, red wine vinegar, Dijon mustard, chopped rosemary, minced shallots, sea salt, and black pepper into a small bowl and whisk well. Alternatively, you could place all dressing ingredients in a blender and blend until smooth and creamy.

3. When ready to serve, pour dressing over salad and toss.

Apple Spiced Collard Greens

Cooked greens are a warming way to eat your greens in the fall and winter when the weather can be a bit chilly to eat a fresh salad. These greens are great served with the Spicy Black-Eyed Pea Stew on page 269 or with the Three Bean Chili on page 158.

SERVES 2 TO 4

> **2 to 3 bunches collard greens, rinsed and chopped**
> **1 tablespoon extra virgin olive oil**
> **4 to 6 cloves garlic, crushed**
> **¼ to 1 teaspoon dried chili flakes**
> **¼ to ½ cup organic apple cider or apple juice**
> **1 to 2 tablespoons raw apple cider vinegar**
> **½ teaspoon sea salt, or to taste**

1. Heat oil in a large pot over medium heat. Add garlic and sauté 30 seconds; then add the chili flakes, chopped greens, and apple cider or juice and continue to stir.

2. After about 4 to 6 minutes, or when the greens are tender, remove from heat. Add apple cider vinegar and sea salt. Toss gently and serve.

Braised Kale *with Garlic and Ginger*

Kale is powerful anti-cancer food. It is rich in glucosinolates, which are a group of phytonutrients that lessen the occurrence of a wide variety of cancers. A study published in the September 2004 issue of the Journal of Nutrition shows sulforaphane helps to stop the proliferation of breast cancer cells, even in the later stages of their growth. Serve these scrumptious greens as part of a fall or winter meal, when kale is at its peak.

SERVES 2 TO 4

1 tablespoon extra virgin olive oil or virgin coconut oil
4 to 6 cloves garlic, crushed
1 teaspoon grated ginger
2 to 3 bunches kale, rinsed and chopped
¼ to ½ cup water or Asian Soup Stock, *page 145*

Optional Seasonings:
brown rice vinegar
ume plum vinegar
freshly squeezed lemon juice
wheat-free tamari
sea salt
toasted sesame seeds

1. Heat oil in a large pot over medium heat. Add garlic and ginger and sauté about 15 to 30 seconds. Quickly add the chopped greens and water or stock and continue to stir.

2. After about 4 to 6 minutes, or when the greens are tender, remove from heat. Sprinkle with your favorite garnishes, to taste. Our favorite combination is brown rice vinegar and tamari. Toss gently and serve.

Garlic and Sesame Spinach

The combination of spinach, garlic, and sesame is truly delightful. This recipe is very easy to prepare and cooks up in a snap! Serve it with a cooked whole grain and the Tofu with Garlic Ginger Kudzu Sauce on page 253.

SERVES 2 TO 4

1 tablespoon toasted sesame oil
¼ cup sesame seeds
4 to 5 cloves garlic, crushed
8 cups baby spinach leaves
2 to 3 teaspoons brown rice vinegar
2 to 3 teaspoons wheat-free tamari

1. Heat a large pot over medium heat; add sesame oil. Add sesame seeds and stir for about 1 to 2 minutes.

2. Add garlic; sauté 30 seconds, then add baby spinach leaves and sauté until wilted but still bright green adding any water if needed; about 2 to 3 minutes.

3. Remove from heat and add brown rice vinegar and tamari to taste.

Mediterranean Chard

This quick and easy greens dish is wonderful served with the White Bean Stew on page 270, and cooked brown basmati rice. Or serve it with baked halibut or salmon.

1 tablespoon extra virgin olive oil
½ cup pine nuts
4 to 5 cloves garlic, crushed
2 bunches chard, rinsed and chopped
1 lemon, juiced
¼ to ½ cup kalamata olives, pitted and chopped
¼ teaspoon sea salt, or to taste

1. Heat olive oil in a large pot or skillet over medium heat. Add pine nuts and sauté until slightly golden, about 3 to 5 minutes. Add garlic and sauté 30 seconds more.

2. Then add wet greens and sauté until wilted and bright green, making sure all greens reach the heat, about 3 to 4 minutes.

3. Remove from heat and add the lemon juice, olives, and sea salt. Serve immediately.

Steamed Greens *with a Spicy Peanut Curry Sauce*

I love the flavor of curry spices and peanut butter. This is a special treat because we rarely eat peanut butter. In fact, you can easily substitute the peanut butter for cashew butter, which is equally delicious. Try using a single green or a combination of a few. Kale, collards, mustard, chard or spinach all work well; though our favorite always seems to be black kale.

SERVES 4 TO 6

6 to 8 cups finely chopped greens

Sauce:
1 tablespoon virgin coconut oil
1 to 2 small shallots, minced
4 to 5 cloves garlic, minced
1 teaspoon freshly grated ginger
½ teaspoon cumin
½ teaspoon coriander
1 ½ teaspoons curry powder
¼ teaspoon cayenne, or to taste
½ cup organic unsalted peanut butter
¾ to 1 cup water or coconut milk
1 to 2 tablespoons wheat-free tamari
1 tablespoon brown rice vinegar

1. Place the greens in a steamer basket in a 2 or 3-quart pot filled with about 2 inches of water. Steam for bout 7 to 10 minutes or until greens are very tender.

2. While greens are steaming, heat a small saucepan over medium heat. Add the coconut oil, shallots, garlic, and ginger; sauté for about 5 minutes, being careful not to brown. Add the spices and mix well. Then add the peanut butter, water, tamari, and brown rice vinegar; whisk together and simmer over low heat for a few minutes until thickened. Add more water or coconut milk for a thinner sauce. For a smoother sauce try blending it in a blender before serving.

3. Place the cooked greens into a serving bowl and pour the sauce over them. Serve immediately.

Quick Cruciferous Stir-Fry

This stir-fry, rich in cruciferous vegetables, offers significant cancer protection. The anti-cancer effects of these vegetables comes from the phytochemicals sulforaphane and the indoles. These chemicals not only suppress tumor growth, but also cancer cell metastasis. You can add some diced marinated tofu to this stir-fry if desired. Serve with brown basmati rice, page 214.

SERVES 4 TO 6

> 1 tablespoon organic virgin coconut oil
> 1 medium onion, chopped large
> 2 carrots, peeled and cut into ¼ inch thick diagonals
> 2 to 3 cloves garlic, crushed
> 2 teaspoons minced fresh ginger
> 1 head broccoli, cut into florets
> 2 cups chopped baby bok choy
> 3 to 4 cups chopped Napa or Savoy cabbage
> ¼ to ½ cup water
> ½ tablespoon kudzu mixed with a few tablespoons water
> wheat-free tamari and brown rice vinegar, to taste

1. Heat coconut oil in a large stainless steel skillet or wok over medium-high heat. Add chopped onion and sauté for about 3 minutes, being careful not to brown.

2. Add carrots and sauté 2 to 3 minutes more. Add garlic, ginger, and broccoli and sauté for a few minutes more. Add a few tablespoons water to prevent burning.

3. Keep the vegetables moving in the pan. Add the baby bok choy, cabbage, and ¼ cup water, mix well then put a lid on the pan and cook for just a couple of minutes longer or until the vegetables are crisp-tender and still brightly colored.

4. Turn heat to the lowest possible setting and add the kudzu water mixture and tamari and rice vinegar to taste. Gently stir for about 30 seconds or until the liquid is clear. Add any additional water if necessary.

Sautéed Asparagus *with Garlic and Lemon*

Asparagus is a great source for vitamin K, folic acid, vitamin C, beta-carotene, and potassium. Asparagus also contains a large amount of inulin which is a carbohydrate that our bodies cannot digest. The health-promoting friendly bacteria in our large intestine, such as Bifidobacteria and Lactobacilli, do digest it though. When we feed the friendly bacteria in our gut, their growth increases which shields out the more harmful bacteria that can have negative effects on our health. Serve this wonderful springtime dish with fish, tempeh, or over cooked quinoa.

SERVES 2 TO 4

> **1 to 1 ½ pounds asparagus**
> **1 tablespoon extra virgin olive oil**
> **3 cloves garlic, crushed**
> **1 tablespoon lemon juice**
> **¼ teaspoon sea salt**

1. Trim the bottom ends off of the asparagus. The ends are usually too tough and woody for consumption. Cut into 3-inch pieces.

2. Heat olive oil in a large skillet over medium heat. Add crushed garlic and sauté 30 seconds.

3. Add asparagus and sauté for 5 to 6 minutes or until crisp-tender.

4. Remove from heat and add lemon juice and sea salt; stir well and serve immediately.

Sautéed Patty Pan Squash *with Lemon and Capers*

Summer squash is an excellent source for manganese and vitamin C. This dish is best made in the summer when patty pan squash is in season. Serve with Lemon Garlic Tempeh, page 244, and cooked quinoa for a simple summer meal.

SERVES 2 TO 4

> 1 tablespoon extra virgin olive oil
> 2 cloves garlic, crushed
> 4 to 5 medium patty pan squash, chopped
> ¼ cup chopped fresh parsley
> 2 tablespoons fresh lemon juice
> 3 tablespoons capers
> Herbamare or sea salt to taste

1. In a large skillet, heat olive oil over medium heat. Add the garlic and chopped squash and sauté for about one minute. Cover and cook until tender, stirring occasionally, about 3 to 4 minutes.

2. Transfer to a bowl and add parsley, capers, lemon, and salt. Toss to coat. Serve immediately.

Curried Vegetables

Turmeric, one of the ingredients in this dish, acts as an excellent anti-inflammatory. Turmeric is especially effective in arthritis sufferers where it acts not only as an anti-inflammatory but also as an antioxidant to neutralize some of the free radicals that are causing the joint pain. Serve this dish with a lentil dal and brown jasmine rice for a simple, flavorful meal.

SERVES 4 TO 6

1 tablespoon extra virgin olive oil or virgin coconut oil
1 large onion, chopped large
1 teaspoon ground coriander
1 teaspoon ground cumin
1 ½ teaspoons curry powder
½ teaspoon turmeric
¼ teaspoon cinnamon
pinch cayenne pepper
4 to 5 cloves garlic, crushed
3 large carrots, sliced diagonally
2 small yams, peeled and sliced diagonally
2 cups diced tomatoes, or one 14-ounce can
½ cup water
1 large red bell pepper, cut into large pieces
2 medium zucchini, sliced diagonally
1 tablespoon arrowroot powder mixed with ½ cup cold water
1 teaspoon sea salt
1 cup chopped cilantro

1. In a large skillet or pot, heat oil over medium heat. Add chopped onion and sauté until soft, about 5 minutes. Add coriander, cumin, curry powder, turmeric, cinnamon, and cayenne, sauté for a minute more.

2. Add garlic, carrots, and yams. Gently mix to coat with oil and spices. Add diced tomatoes and water, cook for 5 to 10 minutes with the lid on, stirring frequently, adding any additional water to prevent sticking or burning.

3. When vegetables are beginning to get tender, add the red bell pepper and zucchini and gently mix. Cover and cook until zucchini and other vegetables are tender but not mushy.

4. Add arrowroot mixture and simmer for another minute more. Remove from heat and add salt and cilantro, gently mix.

Steamed Vegetables *with Lemon Garlic Dressing*

Lightly steaming your vegetables is a great way to lock in nutrients while increasing digestibility. You can vary the vegetables to what is in season.

SERVES 4

    2 carrots, cut into thin strips
    1 medium zucchini, cut into thin strips
    1 yellow squash, cut into thin strips
    1 small red bell pepper, cut into thin strips
    ¼ cup finely chopped fresh parsley, for garnish

    Dressing:
    ½ lemon, juiced
    2 tablespoons extra virgin olive oil
    1 clove garlic, crushed
    ½ teaspoon lemon zest
    ¼ teaspoon Herbamare, or to taste

1. Place the cut vegetables in a steamer basket over about 2 inches of water in a 2 or 3-quart stock pot. Place a lid on the pot and cook over medium heat. Steam for about 5 to 7 minutes or until crisp tender. Remove from steamer basket and place into a bowl.

2. In a small bowl, whisk together the ingredients for the dressing. Pour dressing over steamed vegetables, add chopped parsley and toss. Add more Herbamare or sea salt if desired.

Oven Fries

This recipe is a favorite for children. Serve with the Sunny Sunflower Seed Burgers, page 263, and organic ketchup for a healthy, kid-friendly meal. These fries are delicious on their own or with the optional spices below.

SERVES 3 TO 4

    4 medium organic russet potatoes or sweet potatoes
    ¼ cup extra virgin olive oil
    ½ teaspoon Herbamare or sea salt
    freshly ground black pepper

    Optional Spices:
    ½ teaspoon turmeric
    1 to 2 teaspoons garlic powder
    1 tablespoon paprika

1. Preheat oven to 425 degrees F.

2. Scrub potatoes well and remove any eyes or discolored areas. Leave the peels on. Cut into wedges and place into a large bowl.

3. Sprinkle with olive oil and Herbamare or sea salt and freshly ground black pepper; toss to coat. Add optional spices if desired.

4. Arrange potatoes in a single layer in a 9 x 13-inch glass baking dish. Bake until golden and fork tender, about 30 minutes.

Balsamic Roasted Beets

Serve these delicate and flavorful beets as an appetizer dipped in plain organic yogurt or as a side dish to your evening meal. They are also wonderful on salads drizzled with a balsamic vinaigrette.

SERVES 4 TO 6

> **1 bunch beets, trimmed and peeled**
> **2 to 3 tablespoons balsamic vinegar**
> **2 tablespoons extra virgin olive oil**
> **½ teaspoon sea salt**

1. Preheat oven to 400 degrees F.

2. Cut beets into quarters and then slice about ¼ inch thin. Place beet slices into a 9 x 13-inch pan and toss with balsamic vinegar, olive oil, and sea salt.

3. Roast for 40 to 45 minutes or until beets are tender when pierced with a fork.

Roasted Butternut Squash *with Shallots and Golden Raisins*

Winter squash is a rich source of the carotenoid, beta-cryptoxanthin, which, when consumed, may lower your risk of developing lung cancer. Serve this dish with Tempeh and Mushroom Stroganoff on page 250, and some steamed kale for a warming winter meal.

SERVES ABOUT 4

1 medium butternut squash, peeled, seeded, and diced
6 small shallots, sliced into halves
½ cup golden raisins
3 tablespoons extra virgin olive oil
¼ teaspoon ground cardamom
½ teaspoon sea salt

1. Preheat oven to 400 degrees F.

2. Place all ingredients into a large baking dish, and stir to coat with olive oil.

3. Roast for 35 to 40 minutes or until squash is tender.

Roasted Yams *with Rosemary*

Yams, which in the United States are actually sweet potatoes, are an excellent source of beta-carotene, vitamin C, and Vitamin B6. Beta-carotene is a powerful antioxidant, which works in the body to eliminate free radicals. Vitamin B6 is needed to convert homocysteine into other benign molecules. High homocysteine levels are associated with an increased risk of heart attack and stroke. I like to serve this dish with the Wild Salmon with Ginger Lime Marinade on page 276.

SERVES 4

2 large yams, peeled and cubed
½ to 1 tablespoon finely chopped fresh rosemary
2 tablespoons extra virgin olive oil
½ teaspoon sea salt

1. Preheat oven to 425 degrees F.

2. Place yam cubes, rosemary, olive oil, and sea salt into a large baking dish. Mix well to coat the yams with the olive oil.

3. Place into a preheated oven. Bake uncovered for 35 to 45 minutes or until yams are very tender.

Roasted Root Vegetables *with Fresh Herbs*

Serve this dish during the bounty of the autumn harvest. It can be served with baked chicken or fish or a bean stew and a wild green salad. You can vary the vegetables in this dish to what you have on hand.

SERVES 4 TO 6

2 to 3 red potatoes, cut into chunks
1 yam, peeled and cut into chunks
2 to 3 Jerusalem artichokes, cut into chunks
2 to 3 carrots, cut into chunks
1 to 2 beets, peeled and cut into chunks
½ teaspoon sea salt or Herbamare
2 to 3 tablespoons fresh herbs (rosemary, thyme, savory)
2 to 3 tablespoons extra virgin olive oil
fresh chopped parsley for garnish

1. Preheat the oven to 400 degrees F.

2. Place the cut vegetables, salt, herbs, and olive oil into a 9 x 13-inch glass baking dish; toss well.

3. Place, uncovered, into the preheated oven and roast for 35 to 45 minutes or until vegetables are tender.

4. Garnish with chopped fresh parsley and serve.

Baked Winter Squash

The autumn harvest brings many varieties of winter squash including, acorn, butternut, buttercup, delicata, golden turban, hubbard, kabocha, spaghetti, and pie pumpkins. Each has its own unique flavor and an incredible sweetness. Winter squash is an excellent source of beta-carotene, which has very powerful anti-oxidant and anti-inflammatory properties. Beta-carotene prevents the oxidation of cholesterol in the body. Oxidized cholesterol is the type the builds up on blood vessel walls and contributes to the risk for heart attack or a stroke. Winter squash is also a good source of vitamin C, potassium, and manganese. Try serving baked winter squash with a drizzle of extra virgin olive oil and a few dashes of cinnamon.

SERVES 1 TO 6

1 winter squash

1. Preheat the oven to 350 degrees F.

2. Cut squash in half using a strong, sharp knife. Scoop out the pith and seeds. Set seeds aside to roast if desired.

3. Place the squash flesh side down into a baking pan, and add about ¼ to ½ inch of water.

4. Bake until tender. Smaller squashes may take up to 35 minutes while larger ones, including pie pumpkins, may take 45 to 90 minutes. Test by inserting a fork; it should slide in easily and feel soft.

Whole Grains

"You gain strength, courage and confidence by every experience in which you really stop to look fear in the face."

~Eleanor Roosevelt

Whole grains are so versatile that they can be used to make casseroles, salads, pilafs, even meatless burgers. A pot of grains may never turn out the same way twice. The amount of time it takes for the grain to cook, how much water it will absorb, and how fluffy your end product is depends on many factors, including the age of the grain, the conditions under which it was stored, and the temperature in which you cooked it.

The following pages contain information on how to cook whole grains including basic recipes for each whole grain. Hopefully you will learn to love the flavor and diversity whole grains can bring to your dinner table.

How to Cook Whole Grains:

Sort through your grains for tiny rocks. Quinoa often has small stones, as can millet and amaranth too. Remove them from the rest of the grains before cooking. You can do this by pouring ½ cup grain at a time onto a plate. Simply sort through them with your fingers and pick out the rocks. This can be very exciting for young children to participate with.

Some grains need to be washed prior to cooking to remove chaff, dust, or other debris. These include millet, quinoa, amaranth, and sometimes brown rice. Quinoa also has a coating called saponin that repels insects and birds. If not washed off, it can cause some digestive upset when consumed. To wash grains, place them in a fine strainer and run warm water through them until the water runs clear. You may also place them into a pot with water and swirl the grains with your hand. Then pour off the water through a fine strainer.

To cook a whole grain you will need to first bring the pot of grain and water to a boil. Once boiling, immediately lower the heat to a simmer. Grains that have been boiled for too long may turn out to be very tough and chewy. If your grains turn out too mushy or clumped together, you may have added too much water or not brought the heat to a high enough temperature initially. It is also very important to use the proper cookware when cooking whole grains. A stainless steel pot with a thick bottom that contains an aluminum core will distribute the heat evenly and prevent the bottom layer of grains from getting burned.

Remember to never stir a pot of cooking grains. Whole grains create their own steam holes so the top layer of grains cooks as evenly as the bottom layer of grains. When you stir a pot of cooking whole grains, the steam holes are destroyed, which causes some of your grain to never fully cook.

A pinch of sea salt brings out the sweetness in grains and helps the grain to open up. Grains cooked without salt will taste flat. Some grains should not be cooked with salt as the salt will inhibit proper absorption of water. These include amaranth, wheat berries, kamut berries, and spelt berries.

The following pages contain basic cooking instructions for each grain. The following grains are all **gluten-free**, which include amaranth, brown rice, wild rice, buckwheat, millet, and quinoa. Oats are gluten-free only if they are certified gluten-free. Wheat, barley, rye, spelt, and kamut all contain gluten and are not safe for someone with celiac disease or who is gluten sensitive.

Many grains that are purchased in bulk bins have a potential for being cross-contaminated with flour dust from nearby bins, scoops used for gluten products, or gluten grains that were previously stored in that bin. Some stores respond well to requests to separate gluten-containing grains and flours from the non-gluten products by moving the bins to a different location altogether and being conscious of these cross-contamination issues. Packaged grain products must be labeled gluten-free and produced in a dedicated facility to be considered truly gluten-free.

Whether or not oats can be consumed by gluten sensitive people is quite controversial. Research indicates that the majority of oat samples tested in both Europe and the US are cross-contaminated wit gluten. Thankfully there are certified gluten-free manufacturers of rolled oats and oat products. However, there are still a good number of gluten sensitive people that react to the *avenin protein* in oats. Many people who are gluten sensitive benefit from leaving oats out of their diet until they can be challenged during an elimination diet (*see page 381*).

Basic Amaranth:

Amaranth is an ancient Aztec grain that is rich in protein and calcium. Amaranth releases a lot of starch while it is cooking, creating a soupier cooked grain than a fluffy one. It is best not add salt to amaranth while it is cooking or it will not absorb enough water to become tender.

MAKES 2 CUPS

> **1 cup amaranth**
> **2 ½ cups water**

1. Place amaranth and water in a 2-quart pot with a tight-fitting lid.

2. Bring to a boil then reduce heat to low and simmer for 20 to 25 minutes or until most of the liquid has been absorbed.

Basic Brown Rice:

Rice with just the hull removed is brown rice. Rice with the hull, bran, and germ removed is white rice. There is a wide variety of brown rice to choose from: short grain, long grain, sweet, jasmine, and basmati are a few.

MAKES ABOUT 3 CUPS

> **1 cup brown rice**
> **1 ¾ to 2 cups water**
> **pinch sea salt**

1. Place rice, water, and sea salt into a medium pot with a tight-fitting lid.

2. Bring to a boil, then turn heat to a low simmer and cook for about 45 minutes or until all of the water has been absorbed. Remember to never stir the rice while it is cooking.

3. Remove rice from heat source and let stand in the pot for about 10 minutes.

Basic Sticky Brown Rice:

Serve this rice with a hearty bean soup or use it to make sushi rolls. You may want to make a half batch of this recipe if serving for only a small number of people.

MAKES ABOUT 8 CUPS

> **2 cups sweet brown rice**
> **1 cup short grain brown rice**
> **6 cups water**
> **pinch sea salt**

1. Place the rice, water, and sea salt in a medium stainless steel pot.

2. Place pot over medium-high heat and bring to a boil. Cover, reduce heat to low and simmer for about 45 minutes.

3. Let stand for at least 10 minutes before serving.

Basic Wild Rice:

Wild rice is a grass that grows in small lakes and slow-flowing streams and is native to North America. Native Americans harvested wild rice by canoeing into a stand of plants and bending the ripe grain heads with wooden sticks, called knockers, to get the rice into the canoe. Wild rice is closely related to true rice as both share the same tribe, Oryzeae. Wild rice is higher in protein than regular brown rice and contains a high amount of zinc. Cooked wild rice can be added to soups or made into grain pilafs or stuffed into cooked squash.

MAKES 3 ½ TO 4 CUPS

1 cup wild rice
2 ½ to 3 cups water
pinch sea salt

1. Rinse the wild rice in a fine strainer and place into a medium pot with the water and sea salt.

2. Put a lid on the pot and bring to a boil, reduce heat to low and simmer for approximately 50 to 55 minutes.

3. Remove pot from heat and let stand 10 minutes.

Basic Buckwheat:

Buckwheat can either be found raw or roasted at your local co-op or health food store. The roasted version of buckwheat is called Kasha. Both have a strong and hearty flavor that lends well for cold weather eating.

MAKES ABOUT 2 CUPS

1 ½ cups water
¼ teaspoon sea salt
1 cup buckwheat groats

1. In a medium-sized pot, bring water and salt to a boil.

2. Add buckwheat and cover the pan. Reduce heat to low and simmer for 15 to 20 minutes.

Basic Millet:

Millet is a small, round, yellow grain with a sweet, earthy taste. It is one of the oldest known foods to humans. Millet is easily digested and is also one of the least allergenic grains. When consumed, it helps to destroy harmful yeasts and bacteria in the gut.

MAKES ABOUT 3 ½ CUPS

> 1 cup millet
> 2 to 2 ½ cups water
> pinch sea salt

1. Wash millet and drain through a fine strainer. Place millet, water, and sea salt into a medium pot with a tight-fitting lid. Use less water for a fluffy grain, or more water for a creamier grain.

2. Bring to a boil, then turn heat to low and simmer for 30 to 35 minutes or until all of the water has been absorbed.

Basic Oat Groats:

Oats, or Avena Sativa, originated in Asia and have been cultivated throughout the world for two thousand years. Oat groats are simply the hulled version of oats. Oats contain a specific fiber known as beta-glucan which can significantly lower cholesterol levels and help to prevent heart disease. Oats contain antioxidant compounds called avenanthramides, which help to prevent free radicals from damaging LDL cholesterol, thus reducing the risk of heart disease. If you are gluten-sensitive, be sure to purchase Certified Gluten-Free Oats.

MAKES 2 TO 2 ½ CUPS

> 1 cup oat groats
> 2 ¼ cups water
> pinch sea salt

1. Place oats, water, and sea salt into a medium pot with a tight-fitting lid.

2. Bring to a boil then reduce heat to low and simmer for about 1 hour or until most of the water has been absorbed. Let stand for 10 minutes.

Basic Quinoa:

Quinoa, pronounced KEEN-WAH, comes from the Andes Mountains in South America where it was once a staple food for the Incas. Quinoa contains all eight essential amino acids and has a delicious, light nutty flavor. Quinoa makes wonderful grain salads or is great served with a vegetable and bean stew.

MAKES ABOUT 3 CUPS

> 1 cup quinoa
> 1 ¾ cups water
> pinch sea salt

1. Rinse quinoa well with warm water and drain through a fine strainer. Quinoa has a natural saponin coating that repels insects and birds. It has a bitter taste and can cause some digestive upset when consumed. Rinsing with warm water removes the saponin.

2. Place rinsed quinoa, water, and sea salt into a medium pot with a tight-fitting lid. Bring to a boil, reduce heat to low and simmer for 15 to 20 minutes or until all of the water has been absorbed. Fluff with a fork before serving.

Basic Teff:

Teff is a very tiny grain that is available in three colors—white, red, or brown—each with its own distinct flavor. Teff originated in Africa where it was once a foraged wild grass before it was cultivated as a staple grain for the Ethiopians. It is now grown in the Snake River Valley of Idaho. Teff is very high in minerals, namely iron. It can be purchased at your local health food store or online at **www.teffco.com**.

MAKES ABOUT 3 ½ CUPS

> 3 cups water
> pinch sea salt
> 1 cup teff grain

1. In a medium pot, bring water and sea salt to a boil. Add teff and stir a little. Cook for 15 to 20 minutes, covered. Towards the end of cooking time, stir occasionally.

Buckwheat Soba Noodle Salad

Buckwheat does not contain any gluten even though the name implies so. Though if you are gluten-sensitive, it is difficult to find a brand of noodles that doesn't also process wheat in the same facility. Brown rice noodles can easily replace the buckwheat noodles for a true gluten-free salad. This dish is great taken to work or school or served at a potluck. People are always attracted to this dish because of the beautiful array of colors it contains.

SERVES 4

1 package buckwheat soba noodles

2 tablespoons hijiki
1 cup grated carrots
1 cup thinly sliced red cabbage
3 green onions, sliced into thin rounds
½ cup chopped cilantro
¼ cup sesame seeds, toasted

Dressing:
3 tablespoons toasted sesame oil
2 tablespoons wheat-free tamari
2 tablespoons brown rice vinegar
1 tablespoon maple syrup
1 to 2 teaspoons hot pepper sesame oil
1 to 2 teaspoons grated fresh ginger
2 to 3 cloves garlic, crushed

1. Cook the buckwheat noodles according to the directions on the package. When the noodles are cooked, drain and rinse with cool water and set aside.

2. While the noodles are cooking, place the hijiki in a small saucepan with about 1 cup of cold water. Let soak for about 5 minutes. Place pot of hijiki on the stove and simmer over medium heat for about 20 to 25 minutes. Pour hijiki through a fine mesh strainer to drain the water off, set aside.

3. Place the cooked noodles, cooked hijiki, shredded carrots, shredded red cabbage, sliced green onions, chopped cilantro, and toasted sesame seeds into a large bowl.

4. In a separate bowl, whisk together the ingredients for the dressing. Pour the dressing over the salad and toss well.

Rice Noodles and Red Cabbage *in a Spicy Cashew Sauce*

Serve this easy-to-make dish with some sautéed tofu or tempeh and steamed broccoli for a complete meal. Brown rice noodles come in a variety of shapes and sizes, any of which can be used in this recipe. You can easily substitute the cashew butter in the sauce for organic unsalted peanut butter if you wish.

SERVES 4

1 package brown rice noodles

1 ½ cups finely sliced red cabbage
4 green onions, sliced into rounds
½ cup finely chopped cilantro

Sauce:
2 teaspoons virgin coconut oil
4 to 5 cloves garlic, crushed
1 teaspoon freshly grated ginger
½ cup cashew butter
1 cup water
2 tablespoons wheat-free tamari
1 tablespoon brown rice vinegar
1 tablespoon agave nectar or maple syrup
1 to 2 teaspoons hot pepper sesame oil

1. Cook rice noodles according to directions.

2. While noodles are cooking prepare the sauce. Heat a small saucepan over medium heat. Add the coconut oil, garlic, and ginger and sauté 30 seconds. Add cashew butter, water, tamari, brown rice vinegar, agave nectar, and hot pepper sesame oil. Whisk mixture together while it simmers. Cook until thickened; add more water if necessary.

3. Place warm noodles, red cabbage, green onions, and cilantro into a large serving bowl. Pour the cashew sauce over the noodle and cabbage mixture and gently toss. Serve warm.

Buckwheat, Potato, and Spinach Pilaf

The roasted form of buckwheat is called kasha. Look for kasha in bulk at your local health food store or food co-op. Leftover pilaf is delicious served as a quick breakfast.

SERVES 4

> 1 ½ cups water
> ¼ teaspoon sea salt
> 1 cup roasted buckwheat
>
> 3 to 4 medium red potatoes, cut into small cubes
> 2 tablespoons extra virgin olive oil
> ⅓ cup pine nuts
> ½ teaspoon sea salt or Herbamare
> ½ teaspoon freshly ground black pepper
> 1 teaspoon dried oregano
> 3 to 4 cloves garlic, crushed
> 1 bunch green onions, cut into 1 inch diagonals
> 4 to 6 cups coarsely chopped spinach
>
> *Garnish:*
> 1 lemon, cut into wedges
> ½ cup finely chopped fresh basil

1. Place water and sea salt into a small 1 ½-quart pot, bring to a boil. Add roasted buckwheat, cover, and simmer for 15 to 20 minutes or until all of the water is absorbed. Remove pot from heat and let stand about 10 minutes.

2. While the buckwheat is cooking, place the potatoes into a steamer basket in a pot filled with about 2 inches of water, cover, and place over medium high heat. Steam until just tender, but not all the way cooked, about 6 to 7 minutes.

3. In a large 11-inch skillet, heat the olive oil over medium heat. Add the pine nuts and sauté until golden, about 1 minute. Quickly add the steamed potatoes, sea salt, black pepper, oregano, garlic, and green onions and gently sauté for another 1 to 2 minutes. Add the spinach and sauté until spinach is wilted but still bright green. Add more olive oil if needed.

4. Place the potato spinach mixture in a large bowl with the buckwheat and gently mix together. Garnish with fresh lemon wedges and chopped basil. Serve warm.

Nori Rolls *with Vegetables, Tofu, and Sticky Brown Rice*

Nori is a sea vegetable that has been dried and made into flat thin sheets. It is what is used to make sushi. Nori can also be crumbled and sprinkled onto salads, cooked vegetables, or soups. It is rich in minerals and lignans. Lignans are compounds that are cancer-protective. Nori rolls typically contain raw fish and white rice, but they can also be made with sautéed tofu and sticky brown rice. A variety of thinly sliced vegetables are usually put into the center, including carrot, green onion, avocado, daikon radish, and red cabbage. These are then rolled together and sliced. They can be served with tamari, wasabi, and pickled ginger if you like.

SERVES 4 TO 8

2 cups sweet brown rice
1 cup short grain brown rice
pinch sea salt
6 cups water

one 16-ounce package firm tofu, cut into 3-inch strips
3 tablespoons wheat-free tamari
1 tablespoon seasoned brown rice vinegar
virgin coconut oil for sautéing

carrots, sliced thin
avocado, sliced thin
green onions, sliced thin

seasoned brown rice vinegar for cooked rice
toasted nori sheets

1. Place rice into a pot with water and sea salt. Cover, bring to a boil, then reduce heat to low and simmer for 45 minutes. Remove from heat and let rice stand for 20 minutes. Place half of the rice into a bowl and drizzle with brown rice vinegar. Mix well.

2. Cut tofu into strips, place into a dish and drizzle with tamari and brown rice vinegar; marinate for 20 minutes. Heat a skillet over medium heat, add coconut oil, then tofu. Sauté for a few minutes or until lightly browned.

3. Place a sheet of nori, shiny side down, on a clean surface. Spread a thin layer of rice to 2 inches below the top of the sheet. Place tofu and vegetables at the bottom of the sheet. Tightly roll from the vegetable end. The nori can be sealed by running your finger with a little water along the seam side. Repeat this process until you have the desired amount of rolls. Slice nori rolls with a serrated knife that has been dipped in water.

Indian Fried Rice

This tasty rice dish is delicious served with the Curried Vegetables on page 203, and Red Lentil Dal on page 154. If you cannot find brown jasmine rice in your area, then use brown basmati rice instead.

SERVES 4 TO 6

2 cups brown jasmine rice
3 ½ cups water
pinch sea salt

2 tablespoons virgin coconut oil
½ cup raw cashews
¼ teaspoon sea salt
1 teaspoon ground cumin
1 teaspoon black mustard seeds
1 ½ teaspoons ground coriander
1 bunch green onions, sliced diagonally into ½-inch pieces
¼ cup Zante currants
½ cup chopped cilantro

1. Place rice, water, and sea salt into a medium pot with a tight-fitting lid. Bring to a boil then turn down heat and simmer for about 40 minutes. Remove pot from heat and let rice stand and cool for about 25 minutes.

2. In a large skillet, heat coconut oil over medium heat, add cashews, sea salt, and spices and sauté-stir for about one minute. After the cashews have begun to turn golden and you smell a rich fragrance, add the green onions and Zante currants. Add the rice while you are stirring and keep the mixture moving until all of the rice is well combined with the cashew-spice mixture.

3. Add the chopped cilantro, stir, and serve.

Lentil and Rice Salad *with Lemon and Olives*

Serve this dish as part of a light summer meal or for a simple lunch. If you can not find French lentils you may substitute green or brown lentils instead. This salad will keep in a covered container in the refrigerator for up to 5 days.

SERVES 6

6 cups water
1 ½ cups French lentils, rinsed and drained

1 cup brown basmati rice
1 ¾ cup water
pinch sea salt

2 medium carrots, diced
1 pint cherry tomatoes
1 cup kalamata olives, pitted and chopped
1 cup chopped fresh parsley
1 small bunch green onions, chopped
½ cup chopped fresh basil

Dressing:
6 tablespoons fresh lemon juice
4 tablespoons extra virgin olive oil
2 cloves garlic, crushed
2 teaspoons lemon zest
1 tablespoon chopped fresh oregano
½ teaspoon sea salt
½ teaspoon freshly ground black pepper

1. In a medium pot, place the 6 cups of water and the rinsed lentils. Bring to a boil, cover, reduce heat and simmer for about 20 to 25 minutes or until lentils are tender. Once the lentils are cooked, drain off cooking liquid.

2. To make the rice, place the rice, water and sea salt into a small pot. Bring to a boil then reduce heat to low and cook, covered, for about 45 minutes. Remove from heat and let stand at least 20 minutes.

3. Place lentils and rice in a large bowl and add carrots, tomatoes, olives, parsley, green onions, and basil. Mix together in a separate bowl the ingredients for the dressing, then pour over the lentil mixture; toss to coat.

Pine Nut Studded Rice

This rice dish will be sure to delight Mediterranean food lovers. Serve with the Poached Halibut with Tomatoes and Fresh Herbs, page 278.

SERVES 4 TO 6

2 cups brown basmati rice
3 ½ cups water
pinch sea salt

1 tablespoon extra virgin olive oil
¼ to ½ cup pine nuts
4 green onions, sliced diagonally into ½-inch pieces
⅓ cup Zante currants
4 cups baby spinach leaves
1 tablespoon chopped fresh oregano
½ teaspoon fresh ground black pepper
2 to 3 tablespoons fresh lemon juice
¼ teaspoon sea salt or Herbamare

1. To cook rice, place rice, water, and sea salt in a medium pot with a tight fitting lid. Bring to a boil, then reduce heat and simmer for about 40 minutes. Remove pot from heat and let rice stand and cool for about 25 minutes.

2. In a separate large skillet or pot, heat olive oil over medium heat, add pine nuts and green onions, sauté a minute or two until pine nuts begin to change color. Quickly add the Zante currants and spinach and continue to stir. Add rice and gently stir mixture together. Add oregano, black pepper, lemon juice, and sea salt. Stir to evenly coat. Remove from heat and serve.

Spanish Rice

Serve this grain dish with the Sensuous Vegan Vegetable and Bean Enchiladas, page 266, for a gourmet vegetarian meal or simply serve with some cooked black beans and a fresh green salad for an easy flavorful meal.

SERVES 4 TO 6

    2 tablespoons extra virgin olive oil
    1 medium onion, diced small
    3 cloves garlic, crushed
    1 teaspoon sea salt
    1 teaspoon ground cumin
    ½ teaspoon chili powder
    1 jalapeno chili pepper, seeded and finely diced
    1 small red bell pepper, seeded and diced
    2 cups brown basmati rice
    3 ¾ cups water
    1 cup tomato sauce or 2 to 3 tablespoons tomato paste

1. Heat olive oil in a medium saucepan, add diced onion and crushed garlic, sauté until soft, about 5 minutes. Next add sea salt, cumin, chili powder, diced jalapeno pepper, and diced red bell pepper; stir and sauté 2 minutes more.

2. Add brown basmati rice, stir, then add water and tomato sauce or paste. Bring to a boil, then reduce heat to low and simmer, covered, until all of the liquid has been absorbed, about 45 to 50 minutes.

Thai Fried Rice

This dish is a fun way to dress up plain brown rice. You may even want to cook the rice a day ahead of time to have on hand for a quick side dish to an evening meal. Use brown basmati rice if you cannot find brown jasmine rice.

SERVES 4 TO 6

2 cups brown jasmine rice
3 ½ cups water
pinch sea salt

1 tablespoon virgin coconut oil
1 bunch green onions, sliced diagonally ½-inch thick
½ cup raw cashews
5 cloves garlic, crushed
¼ teaspoon white pepper
¼ cup raisins
1 medium firm tomato, diced
1 tablespoon whole cane sugar or agave nectar
1 to 2 tablespoons wheat-free tamari
½ cup chopped cilantro

1. Place rice, water, and salt into a medium pot with a tight-fitting lid. Bring to a boil, then turn heat to a low simmer and cook for about 40 minutes or until done. Remove pot from heat and let stand at least 20 minutes.

2. In a large skillet, preferably cast iron, heat coconut oil over medium heat, then add green onions and cashews; cook a minute or two or until cashews are lightly toasted, stirring frequently. Add crushed garlic and white pepper and continue stirring. Add raisins and stir to coat with oil.

3. Add cooked rice and continue stirring. Add more coconut oil if needed. Add chopped tomato, sugar, and tamari, cook a few minutes more while stirring. Take off heat and add chopped cilantro.

Wehani Rice and Pecan Pilaf

Wehani rice is a light clay-colored aromatic brown rice that has a popcorn-like fragrance when cooked. It splits slightly during cooking much like wild rice does. You can buy it in the bulk section of most health food stores and food co-ops. Serve this rice dish in the fall or winter or as part of a holiday meal. It also makes a great stuffing for turkey, chicken, or baked winter squash.

SERVES 4 TO 6

2 cups wehani rice
4 cups water
pinch sea salt

2 tablespoons extra virgin olive oil or organic butter
1 medium red or yellow onion, diced
3 to 4 cloves garlic crushed
1 teaspoon dried thyme
1 cup coarsely chopped pecans
½ cup dried cranberries or dried cherries
¼ cup freshly squeezed orange juice
½ cup finely chopped parsley
½ teaspoon Herbamare or sea salt, or to taste

1. Place rice, water, and sea salt into a medium pot with a tight-fitting lid. Bring to a boil, then turn heat down to low and simmer for about 45 minutes. Remove from heat and let stand for 10 to 15 minutes.

2. Heat olive oil or butter in a large 11-inch skillet over medium heat. Add diced onion and sauté for 5 minutes or until soft. Add garlic, thyme, and pecans; continue to sauté for about 2 to 3 minutes more.

3. Then add dried cranberries and cooked rice; stir to coat with oil. Next add the orange juice, parsley, and Herbamare; gently mix and continue to cook about a minute more. Remove from heat, taste, and adjust salt and seasonings if necessary.

Wild Rice and Kale Salad

This zesty grain salad is very easy to prepare. The combination of the raw kale and red pepper with the cooked wild rice create a nice flavor and texture combination. This dish was inspired by something I tasted at the Bellingham Community Food Co-op's deli.

SERVES 4 TO 6

1 ½ cups wild rice
3 ¾ cups water
pinch sea salt

4 to 5 curly green kale leaves, rinsed and chopped
1 small red bell pepper, diced small
1 bunch green onions, cut into thin rounds
½ cup freshly squeezed lemon juice
¼ cup extra virgin olive oil
sea salt and freshly ground black pepper to taste

1. Place the rice, water, and sea salt into a 3-quart pot. Cover and bring to a boil, then reduce heat to low and simmer for 50 to 55 minutes, remove from heat and let stand at least 30 to minutes to cool.

2. Place chopped kale, diced red bell pepper, sliced green onions, lemon juice, and olive oil into a large bowl and gently toss. Add cooked rice and sea salt and freshly ground black pepper to taste. Toss again and serve.

3. Store extra rice salad in a glass container in the refrigerator for up to 5 days.

Wild Rice Stuffed Squash

This recipe is great for Holiday gatherings or as a warm autumn meal. Try adding some sautéed organic turkey sausage to the rice mixture for a little extra flavor.

SERVES 6

3 small acorn squash, cut in half crosswise

½ cup wild rice
½ cup long grain brown rice
2 cups water
pinch of sea salt

1 tablespoon olive oil
1 leek, chopped
3 cloves garlic, crushed
2 celery stalks, chopped
1 teaspoon dried sage
1 teaspoon dried thyme
½ teaspoon Herbamare
½ cup chopped fresh parsley
½ cup organic dried cranberries (fruit juice sweetened)
¾ cup pecans, chopped

1. Preheat oven to 400 degrees F. Scoop out seeds and pith from squash and place squash halves flesh side down in a glass baking dish filled with ¼ inch of water. Bake uncovered for 40 minutes or until the squash is fork tender.

2. While squash is cooking, prepare the rice. Place wild rice and long grain brown rice in a heavy bottomed two quart pot. Add water and sea salt. Cover and bring to a boil. Reduce to low and simmer for 45 minutes or until all the water is absorbed. Remove pot from heat and let stand while preparing other ingredients.

3. Heat a 10-inch skillet over medium heat. Add olive oil and leeks. Sauté about 3 minutes. Add crushed garlic, chopped celery, dried herbs, and sea salt. Sauté for 5 to 6 minutes more. Place the leek-celery mixture into a bowl. Add parsley, dried cranberries, pecans, and cooked rice. Mix well. Taste and adjust salt and seasonings as desired.

4. Take squash halves and evenly distribute mixture into the center of each. Place stuffed squash back into the pan and into the oven for 10 to 20 minutes, or until heated all the way through.

Coconut Quinoa Pilaf

This yummy Thai style quinoa dish is delicious served on its own or with some sautéed tofu or chicken and steamed broccoli for a balanced meal.

SERVES 4

> **2 cups quinoa**
> **1 can coconut milk**
> **2 cups water**
> **1 bunch green onions, sliced**
> **1 medium red bell pepper, diced small**
> **3 to 4 cloves garlic, crushed**
> **¾ teaspoon sea salt**
> **½ to 1 teaspoon crushed red chili flakes**
> **½ cup chopped cilantro**

1. Rinse the dry quinoa in a fine mesh strainer under warm running water. Quinoa has a natural saponin coating that repels insects and birds and can create a bitter taste. Rinsing the quinoa with warm water removes the saponin.

2. Place rinsed quinoa into a medium saucepan with the coconut milk, water, sliced green onions, diced red bell pepper, garlic, sea salt, and chili flakes. Cover and bring to a boil, then turn heat to a low simmer and cook for about 20 minutes.

3. Remove pot from heat and let pilaf cool in the pot for about 10 minutes. Then add chopped cilantro and gently fluff with a fork. Serve hot.

Quinoa and Pea Pilaf *with Fresh Garden Herbs*

This easy-to-make pilaf is great for spring dining when the fresh herbs are just beginning to pop up in your garden. Serve with the Tempeh and Nettle Stir-Fry on page 251 and a fresh green salad for a complete meal.

SERVES 4 TO 6

1 tablespoon extra virgin olive oil
1 small red or yellow onion, or 1 leek, diced small
2 to 3 cloves garlic, crushed
2 cups quinoa, rinsed
3 ½ cups water or vegetable broth
½ to 1 teaspoon Herbamare or sea salt
1 to 1 ½ cups fresh or frozen peas
¼ cup snipped fresh chives
2 to 3 tablespoons fresh snipped herbs (thyme, oregano, marjoram)
lemon wedges, for garnish

1. Heat olive oil in a 3-quart pot over medium heat. Add onion or leek and lightly sauté for a few minutes. Add the garlic and sauté a minute more. Then add the quinoa, water, and Herbamare. Cook for about 15 minutes.

2. Then gently add the peas to the cooking quinoa, but do not stir them in. Cook for an additional 5 minutes.

3. Remove from heat and let stand about 10 minutes. Add the fresh herbs and fluff with a fork, stirring in the peas as you go. Serve with fresh lemon wedges.

Composed Salad of Quinoa, Chickpeas, *and Tomatoes*

This grain salad makes for an elegant lunch or evening meal. We like to use organic heirloom tomatoes here, which are in season during the summer. We also like to use the bright green, round castelvetrano olives in the recipe, though any high quality olive will do. Often times we will steam a large amount of fresh greens, such as chard or kale, and add it to this meal.

SERVES 4 TO 6

2 cups quinoa
3 ½ cups water
pinch sea salt

2 to 3 cups cooked chickpeas (garbanzo beans)
2 to 3 tomatoes, chopped
1 small red onion, finely diced
1 cup chopped fresh parsley
1 cup (or more) of your favorite variety of olives

Lemon Tahini Dressing:
½ cup sesame tahini
½ cup freshly squeezed lemon juice
¼ cup extra virgin olive oil
3 tablespoons water
2 cloves garlic, crushed
1 tablespoon lemon zest
½ to 1 teaspoon sea salt, or to taste

1. Rinse the dry quinoa in a fine mesh strainer under warm running water. Place rinsed quinoa into a medium saucepan with the water and sea salt. Cover and bring to a boil, then turn heat to a low simmer and cook for about 20 minutes. Remove pot from heat and let quinoa cool in the pot.

2. Arrange quinoa, chickpeas, tomatoes, red onion, parsley, and olives on a large serving platter or wide bowl. Do not mix the ingredients together; simply let them sit next to each other on the platter. Place a serving spoon on the platter so each person can create their own salad.

3. To make the dressing, place all ingredients into a bowl and whisk together. Pour some of the dressing into a small bowl and set next to or on the platter with a small ladle or spoon. Extra dressing can be stored in a glass jar in the refrigerator for up to 10 days.

Mediterranean Quinoa Salad

This grain dish is best eaten right after it has been made. The pumpkin seeds will begin to loose their "crunch" after a while. You may use any white beans, though we prefer to use Cannelini beans in this dish.

SERVES 4 TO 6

2 cups quinoa
3 ½ cups water
¼ teaspoon sea salt

2 to 3 cups cooked white beans, or 1 to 2 cans
2 medium carrots, chopped
1 can artichoke hearts, cut into quarters
½ to 1 cup kalamata olives, pitted
½ cup chopped sun-dried tomatoes (olive oil-packed)
4 cups fresh baby spinach leaves
½ cup fresh basil, chopped
½ cup pumpkin seeds

Dressing:
⅓ cup extra virgin olive oil
3 tablespoons red wine vinegar
4 tablespoons freshly squeezed lemon juice
2 cloves garlic, crushed
1 teaspoon lemon zest
½ teaspoon sea salt or Herbamare

1. Rinse the dry quinoa in a fine mesh strainer under warm running water. Place rinsed quinoa into a medium saucepan with the water and sea salt. Cover and bring to a boil, then turn heat to a low simmer and cook for about 20 minutes. Remove pot from heat and let quinoa cool in the pot.

2. Toast the pumpkin seeds by placing them into a small skillet and heating them over medium heat. Keep them moving in the pan until you hear a "pop" and they are slightly golden. Remove from pan and let cool in a small bowl.

3. Place cooled quinoa into a large bowl. Add the cooked white beans, chopped carrots, cut artichoke hearts, olives, chopped sun-dried tomatoes, baby spinach, chopped basil, and toasted pumpkin seeds.

4. To make the dressing, place all ingredients into a small bowl and whisk together. Pour the dressing over the quinoa salad and mix thoroughly with a large spoon.

Quinoa and Black Bean Salad

This protein-packed dish will keep you going during those days when you need a boost without the heaviness of a large meal. Serve this dish alone or with some steamed winter squash. I learned how to make a version of this recipe in a cooking class while attending Bastyr University.

SERVES 4 TO 6

2 cups quinoa
3 ½ cups water
pinch sea salt

1 cup chopped cilantro
5 green onions, sliced
1 small jalapeno pepper, seeded and finely diced
1 small red bell pepper, diced small
2 cups cooked black beans

Dressing:
¼ cup extra virgin olive oil
½ cup fresh squeezed lime juice
1 teaspoon ground cumin
1 ½ teaspoons sea salt or Herbamare

1. Rinse quinoa in a fine mesh strainer under warm running water. Place the rinsed quinoa in a medium pot with the water and a pinch of sea salt. Bring to a boil, reduce heat to low, cover, and let simmer for about 20 minutes, or until all the water is absorbed.

2. Remove cooked quinoa from pot, place in a large bowl and let cool.

3. Combine olive oil, lime juice, cumin, and sea salt in a small bowl. Whisk together and pour over cooled quinoa, toss well with a fork.

4. Add cilantro, green onions, jalapeno pepper, red bell pepper, and black beans and toss again.

Summer Vegetable Quinoa Salad

This quinoa salad makes a great addition to any summer picnic. Any fresh summer vegetables that you have on hand work well here. Try adding diced summer squash, fresh shelled peas, or thinly sliced young kale leaves. You can use either leftover cooked sweet corn or raw corn cut right off the cob. They both work great, but I prefer the taste and texture of fresh, raw, organic sweet corn.

SERVES 4 TO 6

2 cups quinoa
3 ½ cups water
pinch sea salt

2 carrots, diced
1 cup sugar plum or cherry tomatoes
2 ears corn, cooked or raw, corn cut from the cob
1 cup chopped fresh parsley
½ cup sunflower seeds, toasted

Dressing:
½ cup freshly squeezed lemon juice
6 tablespoons extra virgin olive oil
2 to 3 cloves garlic, crushed
1 ¼ teaspoons Herbamare or sea salt

1. Rinse the dry quinoa in a fine mesh strainer under warm running water. Place rinsed quinoa into a medium saucepan with the water and sea salt. Cover and bring to a boil, then turn heat to a low simmer and cook for about 20 minutes. Remove pot from heat and let quinoa cool in the pot.

2. Place the cooled quinoa into a large bowl and add the carrots, tomatoes, corn, parsley, and toasted sunflower seeds.

3. Whisk ingredients for dressing in a separate small bowl. Pour over quinoa and vegetables. Toss salad together. Serve immediately or chill for later use.

Winter Quinoa Salad

This flavorful grain salad is perfect for the holidays. It can be made up to a day ahead of time, just wait to add the pecans until ready to serve.

SERVES 4 TO 6

2 cups quinoa, rinsed and drained
3 ½ cups water
pinch sea salt

1 tablespoon extra virgin olive oil
1 medium red onion, finely diced
2 teaspoons dried thyme
¼ teaspoon Herbamare or sea salt
1 cup pecans
½ cup dried cranberries
1 cup chopped parsley
freshly ground black pepper and sea salt

Dressing:
½ cup freshly squeezed orange juice
⅓ cup extra virgin olive oil
1 tablespoon white wine vinegar
1 teaspoon orange zest

1. Preheat oven to 300 degrees F. Rinse quinoa in a fine mesh strainer under running water for a few minutes. Place into a medium sized pot with the water and pinch of sea salt. Cover and bring to a boil, then reduce heat to a simmer; cook for about 20 to 25 minutes or until done. Remove from heat and let pot stand for about 20 minutes.

2. Heat the tablespoon of olive oil in a skillet over medium heat. Add red onions, thyme, and Herbamare. Sauté for 5 to 6 minutes or until onions are soft and are beginning to turn color but not browning.

3. Place pecans in a small pie plate or other oven proof dish and lightly roast for about 10 minutes. Watch carefully as they can burn easily.

4. Place cooked quinoa into a large bowl. Add cooked red onions, toasted pecans, dried cranberries, and chopped parsley to bowl. Mix together. Pour the orange juice, olive oil, orange zest, and white wine vinegar over quinoa mixture, and gently mix. Add sea salt or Herbamare and freshly ground black pepper to taste.

Lemon Millet Patties

You will need a food processor to make these. Sometimes I like to add about 8 ounces of firm tofu to these while pulsing in the food processor. You can make the patties up to 3 days ahead of time and store them in between pieces of waxed paper in a storage container in your refrigerator. Serve with Navy Beans in a Homemade Barbecue Sauce, page 262, and the Cabbage Salad with Cilantro Vinaigrette on page 181.

SERVES 4

> 1 cup millet
> 2 cups water
> pinch sea salt
>
> 2 small carrots, chopped
> 1 to 2 green onions, chopped
> small handful fresh parsley
> 3 to 4 tablespoons fresh lemon juice
> 1 tablespoon lemon zest
> ¼ teaspoon sea salt or Herbamare
> 3 to 4 tablespoons virgin coconut oil for sautéing

1. Rinse dry millet in a fine strainer under warm running water. Place rinsed millet, water, and sea salt into a medium pot with a tight fitting lid. Bring to a boil, then turn down heat to a low simmer and cook for 30 minutes.

2. Place chopped carrot, chopped green onions, fresh parsley, lemon juice, lemon zest, and Herbamare into a food processor and pulse a few times. Add cooked millet and continue to pulse until just mixed.

3. Form millet mixture into patties. Heat coconut oil over medium heat in a large skillet. Lightly sauté patties on both sides.

Tex-Mex Millet and Amaranth Corn Casserole

This dish is great served with some cooked black beans and the Arugula Salad with Lime Vinaigrette on page 177. This recipe is adapted from The Body Ecology Diet by Donna Gates.

SERVES 4 TO 6

2 tablespoons virgin coconut oil
1 large onion, chopped
1 small jalapeno pepper, seeded and finely diced
1 to 2 teaspoons ground cumin
1 tablespoon Mexican Seasoning
1 ½ cups millet, rinsed and drained
¾ cup amaranth, rinsed and drained
2 to 3 teaspoons sea salt or Herbamare
6 ½ cups water
2 cups fresh organic corn kernels or one 10-ounce bag frozen corn
1 large red bell pepper, diced

1. Sauté onion in coconut oil in a large pot over medium heat for about 2 minutes. Add jalapeño pepper and sauté a minute more. Turn down heat to medium-low and add cumin and Mexican seasoning; stir to coat onions and pepper.

2. Rinse grains in a fine mesh strainer and add them to the pot along with the sea salt, water, and corn. Turn up heat and bring to a boil. Then cover, turn heat to a low simmer, and let cook for 30 minutes.

3. Preheat oven to 350 degrees F.

4. Fold in red bell pepper. Adjust salt and seasonings to taste.

5. Coat a 9 x 13-inch baking dish with coconut oil. Pour cooked millet and amaranth mixture in, dot with coconut oil if desired, and bake for 30 minutes or until bubbly.

Millet *with Summer Vegetables*

Serve this tasty dish with the Fresh Garden Salad with Herbal Vinaigrette, page 182, for a simple summer meal.

SERVES 4

1 ½ cups millet
3 cups water
pinch sea salt

2 to 3 tablespoons extra virgin olive oil
1 medium sweet onion, chopped fine
2 cloves garlic, crushed
1 large red bell pepper, diced
2 medium zucchini, diced
2 to 3 ears fresh corn, corn cut off cob
2 tablespoons fresh thyme leaves
¼ cup finely chopped fresh basil
½ to 1 cup chopped fresh parsley
fresh lemon wedges for garnish

> ### Ingredient Tip
>
> Try replacing the millet with wehani rice.
>
> Cook 1 ½ cups rice according to directions for Basic Brown Rice on page 214.

1. Rinse the millet in a fine strainer and place into a 3-quart pot with the water and sea salt. Put a lid on the pot and bring to a boil, reduce heat to low and simmer for approximately 30 minutes. Remove lid and set aside.

2. In a large skillet or pot, heat olive oil over medium heat. Add onions and sauté until soft, about 3 to 5 minutes. Then add garlic, red bell pepper, zucchini, and corn and sauté until vegetables are crisp-tender, about another 5 to 7 minutes, adding water or vegetable broth as necessary to prevent browning.

3. Add cooked millet to vegetable mixture and sauté a minute more. Remove from heat; add fresh herbs and sea salt. Mix well. Taste and adjust salt and seasonings as necessary. Serve with fresh lemon wedges.

Easy Polenta

Polenta is made from coarsely ground cornmeal. It can be served with fish or chicken dishes or simply with a red sauce on top of it. You can also double this batch, pour it into a 9 x 13-inch pan, and then use it as an alternative gluten-free pizza crust. Simply top the polenta with pizza sauce, your favorite sautéed vegetables, and some organic cheese if you wish. Follow the directions for baking below.

SERVES 3 TO 4

> **3 cups water**
> **1 teaspoon sea salt**
> **1 tablespoon extra virgin olive oil, coconut oil, or organic butter**
> **1 cup polenta**

1. Preheat oven to 350 degrees F.

2. In a 3-quart pot, bring 3 cups water to a boil. Add salt and oil. Slowly add polenta, stirring continuously with a whisk. Lower heat and continue to stir for 10 to 15 minutes with a wooden spoon.

3. Pour into an oiled 9-inch pie plate. Bake in the oven for 25 minutes. Let cool for 5 to 10 minutes, and then serve.

Vegetarian Main Dishes

"Within each of us lies the power of our consent to health and sickness, to riches and poverty, to freedom and to slavery. It is we who control these, and not another."

~Richard Bach

*E*ating a whole foods diet can be easy when you have recipes like the ones in this chapter to keep your taste buds happy and your soul fulfilled. Remember that whole foods are very nutrient dense because they are in their whole form and have had no parts removed from them. All living things contain amino acid structures, therefore all living things, including plants, contain protein. When eating a balanced, plant-based diet that contains sufficient calories, you can be assured that you are getting a more than adequate amount of protein.

Eating beans, including soybean foods, as part of your main meal provides a full feeling and an appreciable amount of soluble fiber. Regular intake of soluble fiber keeps cholesterol levels low and the bowel, liver, and gallbladder functioning properly.

Enjoy the following vegetarian main dish recipes on a regular basis and hopefully some of them will become your weekly staples.

Balsamic Tempeh Stir-Fry

For most people, unrefined or minimally processed soy foods can be a very nutritious part of the whole foods diet. Unrefined soy includes foods such as tempeh and miso, and minimally processed soy includes tofu, tamari, and shoyu. Current research has shown that whole soy foods help to lower cholesterol levels, lower blood pressure, stabilize blood sugar levels and protect against many forms of cancer. Serve this easy-to-make tempeh dish with some cooked brown rice noodles and the Beet and Fennel Salad with Orange Vinaigrette on page 179.

SERVES 4

one 8-ounce package tempeh
3 tablespoons balsamic vinegar
2 tablespoons wheat-free tamari
1 clove garlic, crushed
1 teaspoon Italian seasoning
1 teaspoon paprika

2 tablespoons extra virgin olive oil
1 medium red onion, diced into large pieces
2 cups mushrooms, quartered
1 medium zucchini, cut in chunks
1 large carrot, diced large
1 cup artichoke hearts
1 cup cherry tomatoes
1 cup chopped parsley
½ cup chopped basil

1. Cut the tempeh into 2-inch cubes and place in a bowl. Add the balsamic vinegar, tamari, garlic, and Italian seasoning. Marinate for at least 30 minutes. Longer marinating times will produce deeper flavors.

2. In an 11-inch skillet, heat olive oil over medium heat. Add tempeh, and cook for about 5 to 10 minutes, turning frequently. Remove tempeh from pan and place into a bowl, set aside.

3. Add onion and sauté for a few minutes, and then add mushrooms, zucchini, and carrots. Stir-fry until vegetables are just tender.

4. Then add the artichoke hearts, cherry tomatoes, fresh parsley and basil, and cooked tempeh. Stir-fry for about 2 minutes more to let flavors combine. Serve over brown rice or brown rice pasta.

Black Bean and Tempeh Tostadas

A tostada is typically a flat tortilla that has been toasted or deep-fried then topped with refried beans, meat, sour cream, salsa, and thinly sliced lettuce. Our version of a tostada uses a lightly toasted corn tortilla topped with Spanish Rice, cooked black beans, sautéed tempeh, avocado, salsa, cilantro, and thinly sliced romaine lettuce. This is a great healthy dish to serve for a crowd. People will have fun creating their own tostadas.

SERVES 4 TO 6

1 recipe Spanish Rice, *page 225*

one 8-ounce package tempeh, crumbled
1 lime, juiced
2 to 3 tablespoons wheat-free tamari
1 to 2 teaspoons chili powder
2 teaspoons extra virgin olive oil
extra virgin olive oil for sautéing

1 to 2 packages organic corn tortillas, toasted
3 cups cooked black beans, or 2 cans
1 ripe avocado, cut into small cubes
1 cup chopped cilantro
4 cups thinly sliced romaine lettuce
organic salsa

1. Prepare the Spanish Rice.

2. Crumble tempeh into a medium sized bowl. Pour the lime juice, tamari, chili powder and olive oil over the tempeh; mix well. Marinate tempeh for about 30 minutes. Heat a large skillet over medium heat; add about 1 to 2 tablespoons extra virgin olive oil. Place marinated tempeh into pan and sauté for about 5 to 7 minutes. Place cooked tempeh into a bowl.

3. To toast the tortillas, heat a large skillet over medium heat and add about ½ teaspoon olive oil or coconut oil. Place each tortilla into the skillet and cook for about 30 seconds on each side. Keep warm.

4. Place the black beans, avocado, cilantro, romaine lettuce, and salsa into separate bowls. Set bowls and plate of tortillas on the counter or table so people can create their own tostadas. What works well is to lay the tortilla flat onto your plate then add a little Spanish Rice, then black beans, then tempeh, followed by some avocado, cilantro, romaine lettuce, and salsa.

Lemon Garlic Tempeh

This tempeh dish makes a great quick evening meal. Simply serve with some freshly cooked quinoa and steamed broccoli.

SERVES 3 TO 4

> one 8-ounce package tempeh, cubed
> ¼ cup lemon juice
> 2 tablespoons wheat-free tamari
> 1 tablespoon extra virgin olive oil
> 3 cloves garlic, crushed
> ½ teaspoon lemon flavoring or 1 teaspoon lemon zest
> 1 tablespoon extra virgin olive oil, for sautéing

1. Place tempeh into a medium-sized shallow dish. Cover with lemon juice, tamari, olive oil, garlic, and lemon extract; mix well, then marinate for 20 to 30 minutes.

2. Heat the remaining 1 tablespoon of olive oil in a skillet, add marinated tempeh and sauté for about 4 to 5 minutes, being careful not to burn.

Shiitake Tofu

Serve this medicinal dish over some buckwheat soba noodles with a fresh green salad or steamed broccoli on the side. Shiitake mushrooms boost our immune system, protect against and help treat cancer, and help to lower serum cholesterol.

SERVES 4 TO 6

one 16-ounce package firm tofu, cut into cubes
¼ cup wheat-free tamari
2 tablespoons brown rice vinegar

2 tablespoons virgin coconut oil or extra virgin olive oil
1 medium onion, chopped
3 to 4 cloves garlic, crushed
1 tablespoon grated ginger
4 cups thinly sliced shiitake mushrooms, about 5 ounces
2 carrots, cut into thin strips
1 red bell pepper, cut into small strips

Sauce:
1 cup water
1 ½ tablespoons kudzu
1 to 2 tablespoons brown rice vinegar
2 tablespoons wheat-free tamari
1 to 2 teaspoons hot pepper sesame oil

Garnish:
toasted sesame seeds

1. Place the tofu cubes into a shallow dish and marinate with the ¼ cup tamari and 2 tablespoons brown rice vinegar for about 30 minutes. Prepare other ingredients while the tofu is marinating.

2. In a large 11-inch skillet, heat coconut oil or olive oil over medium heat. Sauté onion for about 5 minutes or until soft. Add garlic, ginger, shiitake mushrooms, carrots, and red bell pepper and sauté for about 5 minutes or until vegetables are slightly tender. Move vegetables to the side of the pan and add the tofu, sauté-stir for about 1 minute then stir into vegetable mixture. Sauté for a few more minutes.

3. Place the ingredients for the sauce into a small bowl, whisk thoroughly. Add sauce to the tofu vegetable mixture. Simmer over low heat for about 5 minutes. Adjust seasonings if desired. Garnish with toasted sesame seeds.

Skillet Tempeh Casserole *with Cornbread Topping*

Make this dish in a cast iron skillet if you own one, if not you can sauté the casserole ingredients in a stainless steel skillet and then transfer the mixture to a casserole dish when ready to bake.

SERVES 4 TO 6

1 tablespoon extra virgin olive oil
1 medium onion, diced small
2 large carrots, diced
3 stalks celery, diced
1 small red bell pepper, diced
one 8-ounce package tempeh, cut into small cubes
2 teaspoons dried thyme
½ teaspoon dried oregano
1 to 2 teaspoons sea salt or Herbamare
1 cup vegetable broth
½ cup unsweetened soy milk
1 to 2 tablespoons arrowroot powder
1 cup frozen peas
½ cup chopped parsley
2 to 3 teaspoons red wine vinegar

Cornbread Topping:
1 cup cornmeal
1 cup rolled oats, ground
½ teaspoon sea salt
2 teaspoons baking powder
1 cup soy milk or hemp milk + 1 tablespoon lemon juice
¼ cup melted virgin coconut oil
2 tablespoons maple syrup

> ### Going Gluten-Free Tip
>
> If you are gluten-sensitive then be sure to use Certified Gluten-Free Oats.

1. Preheat oven to 375 degrees F.

2. In a cast iron skillet, heat olive oil over medium heat, add diced onion and sauté until soft, about 5 minutes. Add carrots, celery, red bell pepper, tempeh, thyme, oregano, and salt. Sauté for an additional 5 to 10 minutes or until vegetables are beginning to get tender.

3. While vegetables and tempeh are cooking, prepare the cornbread topping. Place the cornmeal, flour, sea salt, and baking powder into a medium bowl. In a separate bowl whisk together the soy milk, lemon juice, coconut oil, and maple syrup. Set both bowls aside.

4. Measure out vegetable broth and soy milk and place into a small dish with the arrowroot powder. Stir to dissolve powder, then add to skillet with cooking vegetables. Continue to cook until mixture thickens, about 5 minutes. Add the frozen peas and chopped parsley, and stir well. Taste and adjust salt and seasonings if you like.

5. To finish the cornbread topping, add the wet mixture to the dry and gently mix together with the minimum amount of strokes. Gently pour the batter over the tempeh vegetable mixture and evenly spread out. Place into preheated oven and bake for 25 to 30 minutes or until cornbread topping is cooked and casserole is bubbling.

Spinach and Tofu Enchiladas *with Spicy Ancho Chili Sauce*

If you are new to making enchiladas, then this recipe is perfect to begin with. The wonderful thing about it is that the ingredients are so versatile. If you don't have cooked black beans on hand then don't add them; if you are allergic to soy, then replace the tofu with all black beans or cooked shredded chicken; not a spinach fan, then use chopped steamed kale instead. The combinations are endless. The key player in this recipe is the super flavorful Ancho chili sauce—anything tastes great with it!

SERVES 4 TO 6

Sauce:
2 tablespoons extra virgin olive oil
1 small onion, chopped
6 cloves garlic, chopped
1 tablespoon ground cumin
3 dried ancho chilies, seeded and torn into pieces
one 28-ounce can fire roasted tomatoes
½ cup water
1 to 2 teaspoons sea salt, or to taste

Enchiladas:
1 tablespoon extra virgin olive oil
1 medium onion, diced
4 to 6 cloves garlic, crushed
2 teaspoons ground cumin
2 teaspoons chili powder
1 teaspoon sea salt
one 16-ounce package firm tofu
1 medium red bell pepper, diced
2 Anaheim chilies, diced
3 to 4 cups baby spinach leaves
1 to 2 cups cooked black beans
grated raw organic jack cheese, optional
10 to 12 large organic corn tortillas, warmed

1. To make the sauce, heat a 3-quart pot over medium heat. Add the olive oil and onion, gently sauté for a few minutes. Then add the garlic and cumin and sauté a few minutes more. Next add the remaining ingredients (ancho chili pieces, tomatoes, water, and sea salt), cover and simmer over low heat for about 30 minutes. Transfer sauce to a blender and blend until smooth.

2. To make the enchiladas, heat a large 11-inch skillet over medium heat and add olive oil. Then add diced onion and sauté until soft, about 5 minutes. Next, add the crushed garlic, cumin, chili powder, and sea salt; sauté about a minute more.

3. Remove tofu from package and rinse well, hold tofu block over skillet and crumble it with your hands into the onion/spice mixture. Stir together and cook for a few minutes more.

4. Then add the red bell pepper, Anaheim chilies, and baby spinach; sauté for about a minute more. Turn off heat and add cooked black beans, mix together.

5. Preheat the oven to 400 degrees F.

6. To assemble the enchiladas, use a 9 x 13-inch glass baking dish and coat it with olive oil. Grate cheese, if using, and set aside. Hold a warmed tortilla in your hand and place a scoop of filling (about ¼ to ½ cup) along the center, sprinkle with cheese, if using, and then tightly roll the tortilla; place in the dish, seam side down. Repeat this process with the remaining filling and tortillas.

7. Top enchiladas with sauce. You may also sprinkle the top with a little cheese. Cover the dish with foil. Bake in the preheated oven for approximately 40 minutes or until bubbly. Serve with steaming hot brown rice and a large green salad for a complete meal!

Tempeh and Mushroom Stroganoff

This scrumptious tempeh dish can be made with a variety of different mushrooms. Try using button, cremini, oyster, chanterelle, or morel. Serve it atop a whole grain noodle or cooked quinoa. Pair it with a fresh green salad to complete the meal.

SERVES 4

one 8-ounce package tempeh, cut into cubes
3 tablespoons wheat-free tamari
1 tablespoon brown rice vinegar

1 tablespoon extra virgin olive oil
1 medium onion, chopped
2 to 3 cloves garlic, crushed
½ teaspoon dried oregano
1 to 2 teaspoons dried thyme
1 large carrot, diced
4 to 6 cups mushrooms, sliced
1 ½ tablespoons arrowroot powder
1 to 2 tablespoons sherry vinegar or dry red wine
1 to 2 teaspoons Herbamare or sea salt
1 cup unsweetened soy milk, other non-dairy milk, or vegetable broth
freshly ground black pepper
½ cup chopped fresh parsley, for garnish

1. Place tempeh into a small dish; add tamari and brown rice vinegar. Marinate for about 15 to 20 minutes.

2. Heat olive oil in an 11-inch skillet. Add tempeh and sauté for about 2 minutes; remove from pan and set aside.

3. Add onion, garlic, and herbs to the pan. Sauté until onions soften and begin to brown, adding more olive oil if needed. Add carrots and mushrooms. Stir to coat with oil, sauté for about 4 to 5 minutes. Then add tempeh.

4. In a separate bowl, mix the arrowroot, sherry vinegar, salt, and soy milk together. Slowly add this mixture to the vegetables and tempeh in the pan, stirring as you go to make a gravy. Add a little water or broth for a thinner sauce and season with black pepper to taste.

5. Simmer, covered, on low heat for 10 to 15 minutes. Serve over brown rice noodles or cooked quinoa, and garnish with chopped parsley.

Tempeh and Nettle Stir-Fry

Freshly harvested stinging nettles (urtica dioica) have many culinary uses as well as medicinal uses. Rich in minerals and chlorophyll, fresh nettles can be used in soups, stir-fries, smoothies, and my favorite—lasagna. Nettles are picked in the early spring when they are young and tender. Fresh nettles can be stored in a plastic bag in the refrigerator for up to 5 days. Serve this stir-fry atop a freshly cooked whole grain or brown rice noodle. It is also delicious drizzled with the Lemon Tahini Sauce on page 312.

SERVES 4

> **one 8-ounce package tempeh, cut into cubes**
> **2 tablespoons wheat-free tamari**
> **1 tablespoon brown rice vinegar**
>
> **1 to 2 tablespoons extra virgin olive oil**
> **1 large leek, chopped**
> **4 to 5 celery stalks, chopped**
> **2 cloves garlic, crushed**
> **4 to 5 cups fresh nettle leaves**
> **¼ cup fresh snipped chives**
> **sea salt and freshly ground black pepper, to taste**

1. Place tempeh cubes, tamari, and brown rice vinegar in a small bowl and marinate for about 20 minutes.

2. Heat an 11-inch skillet over medium hat. Add olive oil and tempeh; sauté for a few minutes, keeping the tempeh moving in the pan. Then add the leek, celery, and garlic; sauté for another 5 to 7 minutes, or until the celery is just tender. Then add the nettle leaves and sauté until wilted, about 2 minutes.

3. Remove from heat and add the chives and salt and pepper to taste.

Tempeh Fajitas

This Tempeh dish is a favorite of ours and will definitely keep you coming back for more. This recipe is an adapted version of something I learned in a cooking class at Bastyr University. If you are serving this to more than two adults you may want to double the recipe.

SERVES 3 TO 4

one 8-ounce package tempeh, cut into thin strips
1 small lime, juiced
2 tablespoons wheat-free tamari
1 tablespoon Mexican seasoning
1 teaspoon extra virgin olive oil

2 tablespoons extra virgin olive oil, divided
1 medium red onion, cut into strips
2 medium zucchini, cut into strips
1 red bell pepper, cut into strips
2 cloves garlic, chopped

1 ripe avocado, cut into strips
shredded raw organic jack cheese, optional
organic salsa
fresh organic greens, such as arugula
brown rice tortillas

> **Going Gluten-Free Tip**
>
> Instead of using the traditional wheat tortilla for this recipe, try using a brown rice tortilla. Just be sure to warm the tortilla before using, as they tend to fall apart when they are cold. See *page 88* for different warming techniques.

1. Preheat oven to 400 degrees F. Place the tempeh slices in a small dish. In a small bowl, mix together the lime juice, tamari, Mexican seasoning, and 1 teaspoon extra virgin olive oil. Pour this over the tempeh and marinate for at least 30 minutes. Longer marinating times will produce deeper flavors.

2. After the tempeh has been marinated, heat a skillet over medium heat with 1 ½ tablespoons of the extra virgin olive oil. Add the tempeh; sauté on each side for 3 to 4 minutes, being careful not to burn the tempeh.

3. In a 9 x 13-inch baking pan, add the remaining ½ tablespoon of the extra virgin olive oil, red onion, zucchini, red bell pepper, garlic, and a dash of sea salt or Herbamare; mix well. Place pan in oven and cook for 20 to 25 minutes or until vegetables are tender.

4. Fill each tortilla with a few strips of tempeh, some vegetables, a few pieces of avocado, some fresh greens, and about a tablespoon of salsa; roll and enjoy.

Tofu *with Garlic Ginger Kudzu Sauce*

This is a quick and easy tofu recipe that can be served with brown rice and steamed vegetables for a simple meal. Or try it served with the Lemon Millet Patties on page 237 with a fresh salad.

SERVES 3 TO 4

> one 16-ounce package firm or extra firm tofu
> ¼ cup wheat-free tamari
> 2 tablespoons seasoned brown rice vinegar
> virgin coconut oil for sautéing
>
> 1 recipe Garlic Ginger Kudzu Sauce, *page 311*

1. Slice tofu into 1-inch thick squares then slice each square in half to form a triangle. Place tofu triangles into a medium square baking pan. Drizzle with rice vinegar and tamari; gently mix by turning the tofu pieces until they are all covered with the marinade. Marinate on the counter for about 20 minutes.

2. Heat a skillet over medium-high heat, add a few tablespoons of coconut oil, then place each triangle of tofu in the skillet. If your skillet is too small you will have to do this in two batches. Sauté tofu for a few minutes on each side.

3. Remove tofu from skillet and place into a serving dish or plate. Pour Kudzu sauce over tofu triangles and serve immediately.

Black Bean, Rice, and Yam Wraps

If you are new to eating whole foods or would just like a really easy meal to prepare then this one is for you. It is simple, flavorful, and can be made ahead of time for a quick meal on the go.

SERVES 4 TO 6

1 ½ cups short grain brown rice
½ cup sweet brown rice
4 cups water
pinch sea salt

1 large yam, cut into large chunks
3 cups cooked black beans, or 2 cans
1 large avocado, mashed
salsa
mixed greens
brown rice tortillas

> ### Going Gluten-Free Tip
>
> Instead of using the traditional wheat tortilla for this recipe, try using a brown rice tortilla. Just be sure to warm the tortilla before using as they tend to fall apart when they are cold. See *page 88* for different warming techniques.

1. Preheat the oven to 425 degrees F.

2. To cook the rice, place the short grain rice, sweet rice, water, and sea salt into a 2-quart pot, cover, and bring to a boil. Reduce heat and simmer for about 45 minutes. Remove pot from heat and let stand for at least 10 to 15 minutes.

3. While the rice is cooking, place the yam chunks into a small casserole dish, fill with about ½-inch of water, place the lid on the casserole dish and bake in the oven for out 40 to 45 minutes, or until yams are very tender. Remove skins from yams and slightly mash them with a fork.

4. To assemble a wrap, lay a tortilla flat onto a plate and place a small amount of rice in the middle of it, add some cooked black beans, some mashed yam, mashed avocado, salsa, and some mixed greens. Fold the ends in and roll.

Coconut Vegetable Curry *with Chickpeas*

This quick curry can be made in a snap! Serve over brown jasmine rice for an easy weekday meal.

SERVES 4

2 tablespoons virgin coconut oil or extra virgin olive oil
1 tablespoon finely chopped fresh ginger
1 ½ teaspoons cumin seeds
1 teaspoon black mustard seeds
3 small red potatoes, cut into cubes
3 medium carrots, diced
½ teaspoon turmeric
2 teaspoons coriander
1 teaspoon curry powder
1 tablespoon tomato paste
1 can coconut milk
¼ to ½ cup water
2 small zucchini, diced
1 cup frozen peas
2 cups cooked chickpeas (garbanzo beans)
2 teaspoons sea salt
½ cup cilantro

1. In a large pot, heat olive oil over medium heat. Add ginger, cumin seeds, and black mustard seeds; cook for 1 to 2 minutes, or until the seeds begin to "pop".

2. Add potatoes, carrots, turmeric, coriander, and curry powder. Stir well and continue to cook for another minute or so. Add the tomato paste, coconut milk, water; stir well.

3. Simmer, covered, for 5 to 10 minutes until potatoes and carrots are almost done but still a little crisp. Add zucchini, peas, chickpeas, and sea salt; cover the pot and simmer until vegetables are tender, about another 6 to 7 minutes. Remove from heat and stir in chopped cilantro.

Cuban Black Bean and Yam Stew *with Avocado Salsa*

This hearty stew makes a great meal when served atop some freshly cooked long grain brown rice. Add extra cayenne for a spicier stew.

SERVES 6

Soup:
2 cups dry black beans, soaked overnight
6 to 8 cups water
2 bay leaves

1 tablespoon extra virgin olive oil or virgin coconut oil
1 large onion, chopped
6 to 8 cloves garlic, crushed
1 jalapeño pepper, seeded and finely diced
2 teaspoons ground cumin
2 teaspoons dried oregano
1 teaspoon chili powder
pinch cayenne
1 large yam, peeled and diced
2 to 4 tablespoons freshly squeezed lime juice
1 to 2 teaspoons sea salt

Avocado Salsa:
2 large avocados, diced
½ small red onion, finely diced
2 to 3 tablespoons freshly squeezed lime juice
¼ cup chopped cilantro

1. To cook the beans, drain off the soaking water from the beans; rinse well. Place beans, water, and bay leaves into a 6 or 8-quart pot. Bring to a boil, cover, and reduce heat to low; simmer for 1 ½ to 2 hours, or until beans are cooked.

2. When beans are close to being done, begin to prepare the other ingredients for the stew. Heat olive oil in a large skillet over medium heat. Add onions and sauté until soft, about 5 minutes. Then add the garlic, jalapeño pepper, cumin, oregano, chili powder, cayenne, and yams. Sauté a minute or so more. Add onion mixture to the pot of cooked black beans. Simmer for 15 to 20 minutes or until yams and beans are tender. Remove bay leaves from pot and add the lime juice and sea salt. Mix well, taste, and adjust salt and seasonings if necessary.

3. To make the salsa, place all ingredients into a small bowl and gently mix. To serve, ladle stew into serving bowls and top with a few spoonfuls avocado salsa.

Curried Garbanzo Bean and Squash Stew

Serve this flavorful stew over cooked brown jasmine rice for a simple and easy meal. You can vary the recipe by replacing the squash with potatoes for an equally delicious meal.

SERVES 4 TO 6

2 tablespoons virgin coconut oil or extra virgin olive oil
1 medium onion, chopped
4 to 5 cloves garlic, crushed
2 teaspoons curry powder
1 teaspoon ground cumin
1 teaspoon ground coriander
½ teaspoon turmeric
½ teaspoon cinnamon
pinch cayenne pepper
2 delicata squash, peeled, seeded, and cut into chunks
2 cups diced tomatoes, or one 14-ounce can
3 to 4 cups chopped kale or spinach
3 cups cooked garbanzo beans, or 2 cans
1 cup bean cooking liquid or water
1 to 2 teaspoons sea salt or Herbamare

1. Heat an 11-inch skillet or 6-quart pot over medium heat. Add coconut oil then add onions; sauté for about 5 minutes or until soft. Then add the crushed garlic and spices; sauté for a minute more.

2. Next add the delicata squash and tomatoes. Place a lid on the pot and simmer over low to medium-low heat until squash is tender, about 15 minutes.

3. Then add the chopped kale, cooked garbanzo beans, bean cooking liquid, and sea salt; gently stir together and simmer for an additional 5 minutes. Taste and add more salt and seasonings if desired.

Fall Vegetable Stew with Moroccan Spices

This is a wonderful warming dish that celebrates the flavors of autumn. Serve this stew over cooked quinoa with a fresh green salad or steamed broccoli on the side.

SERVES 4 TO 6

2 tablespoons extra virgin olive oil
1 large onion, chopped
6 cloves garlic, minced
2 teaspoons ground cardamom
2 teaspoons curry powder
2 teaspoons sea salt
½ teaspoon freshly ground black pepper
pinch cayenne pepper
3 large carrots, diced
3 medium red potatoes, diced
1 small delicata squash, peeled, seeded, and cut into chunks
½ cup Zante currants
2 cups tomato sauce
2 cups cooked garbanzo beans
1 cup water
½ cup dried figs, chopped
¾ cup almonds, toasted and chopped
fresh mint for garnish

1. Heat a large pot over medium heat, and add the olive oil. Add the onions and sauté until tender, about 3 to 5 minutes.

2. Add crushed garlic, then the cardamom, curry powder, salt, black pepper and cayenne. Sauté and stir a few minutes more.

3. Next add the carrots and potatoes. Stir well to coat with the oil and spices. Sauté-stir until the potatoes and carrots for about 5 minutes, then add the squash and stir. Add the Zante currants, tomato sauce, garbanzo beans, and water. Place a lid on the stew and continue cooking until the vegetables are tender, about 25 to 30 minutes, stirring occasionally and adding more water if necessary.

4. Preheat the oven to 350 degrees F. Place the whole almonds into a glass baking dish. Place into oven and toast for about 10 minutes. Remove from pan and let cool on a plate. Chop almonds when completely cooled.

5. Before serving, sprinkle the figs and almonds on top of the stew. Top with freshly chopped mint.

Lentil and Spinach Dal

Here is a simple, easy recipe that is delicious served over cooked brown basmati rice with a dollop of Raita, page 314, on top.

SERVES 4 TO 6

1 tablespoon virgin coconut oil or extra virgin olive oil
1 medium onion, diced
2 teaspoons freshly grated ginger
1 teaspoon ground cumin
1 teaspoon garam masala
½ teaspoon turmeric
pinch cayenne
2 cups green or brown lentils
5 to 6 cups water
3 to 4 cups chopped fresh spinach
½ to 1 teaspoon sea salt, or to taste

1. Heat a 4 or 6-quart pot over medium heat, add oil. Then add onion and sauté until soft, about 5 minutes. Add freshly grated ginger, ground cumin, garam masala, turmeric, and cayenne; sauté about 30 seconds more.

2. Rinse the lentils in a fine mesh strainer then add them to the onions and spices. Add the water, stir, cover and simmer for about 40 minutes or until lentils are cooked through.

3. Add spinach and sea salt to taste. Add more cayenne for a spicier dal. Simmer for a few minutes more. Serve over cooked brown basmati rice.

Luscious Lentil and Brown Rice Casserole

This is a warming, hearty, and easy to prepare evening meal. Serve with some freshly made Carrot Raisin Buckwheat Muffins, page 134, or Honey Whole Grain Bread, page 124, and a fresh green salad for a complete meal.

SERVES 4

1 tablespoon extra virgin olive oil
1 medium red onion, chopped
1 to 2 cloves garlic, crushed
2 large carrots, diced
1 ½ teaspoons dried thyme
1 teaspoon garam masala
1 teaspoon sea salt
2 cups frozen chopped spinach
2 tablespoons red wine vinegar
¾ cup green lentils
½ cup brown basmati rice
4 cups water

1. Preheat oven to 350 degrees F.

2. In an oven-proof pot, heat olive oil over medium heat. Add chopped red onion and crushed garlic. Sauté for about 3 minutes, stirring frequently. Then add the diced carrots, dried thyme, garam masala, and sea salt; stir to coat with olive oil. Sauté for a few minutes more then add the chopped spinach and stir.

3. Wait until the spinach has thawed and the mixture is sizzling again, then add the red wine vinegar and stir to remove any browned bits. Quickly add the lentils, brown rice, and water; mix well.

4. Place into a covered pot in the preheated oven and bake for 1 hour and 25 minutes.

Mexican Pink Bean Burritos

Pink beans have a smooth creamy texture similar to pinto beans. You can buy pink beans in bulk at your local co-op or health food store.

SERVES 4 TO 6

Beans:
2 cups dry pink beans, soaked overnight
1 tablespoon extra virgin olive oil
1 large onion, chopped
6 cloves garlic, crushed
2 to 3 teaspoons ground cumin
1 tablespoon Mexican seasoning
6 to 8 cups water

Rice:
2 cups short grain brown rice
4 cups water
pinch sea salt

Other Ingredients:
brown rice tortillas
sliced avocado or guacamole
salsa
mixed baby greens or thinly sliced lettuce

> ### Going Gluten-Free Tip
>
> Instead of using the traditional wheat tortilla, try using a brown rice tortilla. Just be sure to warm the tortilla before using as they tend to fall apart when they are cold. See *page 88* for different warming techniques.

1. Place beans in a medium-sized bowl and cover with water, soak overnight at room temperature. When ready to cook, drain beans in a colander and rinse thoroughly. Heat a 6 to 8-quart pot over medium heat; add olive oil and onions, and sauté for about 5 minutes or until tender. Add crushed garlic, cumin, and Mexican seasoning, sauté for another minute or two. Add beans and water; make sure water is about one inch above the beans. Bring to a boil then reduce heat to a simmer. Cook uncovered for about one hour. When beans are cooked, add sea salt to taste. Continue to simmer over low heat until onions fall apart and most of the liquid evaporates, about 15 more minutes.

2. Start the rice just after you have the beans on the stove cooking. Place the rice into a medium 3-quart stainless steel pot. Add water and sea salt, cover and bring to a boil. Reduce heat to low and simmer for about 45 minutes.

3. Place a tortilla on a flat surface. Spread about ½ cup rice down the center of the tortilla, add about ¼ cup beans and your favorite fixings. Fold each end of the tortilla in then roll the burrito away from you creating a firm wrap.

Navy Beans in a Homemade Barbecue Sauce

Serve these scrumptious beans for a summer meal with the Lemon Millet Patties, page 237, and a salad for a balanced meal. If you do not want to cook your own beans for this or are pinched for time, you may use 3 cans of navy beans in place of the dry navy beans, water, and garlic cloves. Recipe adapted from Bastyr University instructor, Mary Shaw.

SERVES 4 TO 6

1 ½ cups dry navy beans, soaked overnight
6 cups water
4 cloves garlic, peeled

Barbecue Sauce:
1 tablespoon extra virgin olive oil
1 small onion, chopped fine
4 cloves garlic, crushed
¼ cup tomato paste
¼ cup apple cider vinegar
¼ cup maple syrup
1 tablespoon blackstrap molasses
1 teaspoon sea salt or Herbamare
¼ to ½ teaspoon chipotle powder, or to taste
½ cup water or bean cooking liquid

1. Soak beans overnight or for about 8 hours. Drain off soaking water and rinse well. Place beans into a 3-quart pot and add the water and garlic cloves, bring to a boil then reduce heat to a simmer. Cook beans for about 1 hour or until beans are soft and cooked through. Remove garlic cloves.

2. Heat the olive oil over medium heat in a 6-quart pot. Add the chopped onion and crushed garlic, sauté until soft, about 5 to 7 minutes.

3. In a small bowl, mix together the tomato paste, cider vinegar, maple syrup, molasses, sea salt, chipotle chili powder, and water.

4. Add the drained beans, tomato mixture, and chipotle pepper to onions: mix thoroughly. Simmer covered for 20 to 25 minutes, stirring occasionally, and adding more water or bean cooking liquid if necessary. Taste and add more sea salt and chipotle pepper if necessary.

Sunny Sunflower Seed Burgers

Serve these tasty meatless burgers with your favorite organic condiments, sliced avocado, lettuce, sliced tomatoes, and gluten-free bread. Serve with Oven Fries, page 205, and a fresh green salad for a balanced meal.

MAKES 6 TO 8 BURGERS

1 cup uncooked short grain brown rice
2 cups water
pinch sea salt

2 cups raw sunflower seeds
1 teaspoon garlic powder
½ teaspoon dried thyme
½ teaspoon dried oregano
½ teaspoon ground cumin
½ teaspoon Herbamare
1 small carrot, coarsely chopped
small handful of fresh parsley
extra virgin olive oil for cooking

1. Place rice into a small pot with a tight-fitting lid. Add water and sea salt, cover and bring to a boil. Turn heat to a low simmer and cook for 45 minutes. Remove from heat and let stand for at least 20 minutes.

2. In a food processor, place the sunflower seeds, garlic powder, thyme, oregano, cumin, and Herbamare and process until finely ground. Add the chopped carrots and parsley and pulse a few times. Then add the rice and pulse a few times to combine all of the ingredients. Be sure not to over process the mixture or it will get very gooey.

3. Form mixture into patties. Uncooked patties can be stored in a glass container in between pieces of waxed paper in the refrigerator for up to a week.

4. When ready to cook, heat a skillet over medium heat and add about one tablespoon extra virgin olive oil. Add burger and cook on both sides for 3 to 5 minutes.

Savory Adzuki Bean and Mushroom Shepherd's Pie

This recipe is easy to make and perfect for a weekday dinner. In fact, it is one of our family's favorite meals. Sometimes I eliminate the mushrooms to please the family members who don't like them, and it still tastes great. You can also replace the adzuki beans with lentils, mung beans, pink beans, kidney beans, or marinated and sautéed tempeh cubes; though our favorite is definitely the adzuki beans. This is a great recipe to make if you are on the Elimination Diet, page 381, just be sure to use the yams instead of potatoes in the topping.

SERVES 4 TO 6

Filling:
2 cups dry adzuki beans, rinsed
6 cups water
one 2-inch strip kombu

1 tablespoon extra virgin olive oil
1 medium onion, diced
1 to 2 teaspoons dried thyme
1 teaspoon dried oregano
3 to 4 carrots, chopped
3 to 4 celery stalks, chopped
2 to 3 cups chopped cremini mushrooms
1 to 2 cups mushroom stock or water
½ cup chopped fresh parsley
sea salt and freshly ground black pepper, to taste

Topping:
3 large baking potatoes or yams, peeled and cut into large chunks
water for cooking
¼ cup extra virgin olive oil or organic butter
sea salt or Herbamare, to taste

1. Rinse the adzuki beans and place them into a 3-quart pot, add the water and kombu. Bring to a boil, then reduce heat to a simmer and cook for approximately one hour, or until done. Remove the kombu.

2. Preheat oven to 375 degrees F. When beans are almost done, heat a large 11-inch skillet over medium heat. Add olive oil and onions and sauté until soft, about 5 minutes. Then add dried herbs, carrots, celery, and mushrooms. Sauté for another 5 to 7 minutes or until vegetables are tender but not soft.

3. Add mushroom stock or water, chopped parsley, and sea salt and black pepper to taste. Add cooked beans and mix well. Simmer for a few minutes and then pour mixture into an oiled casserole dish.

4. While vegetables are sautéing, place potatoes or yams (or a combination of both) into a pot, cover with water and boil for about 7 to 10 minutes, or until potatoes are soft and cooked through. Drain off most of the water, reserving some.

5. Place the potatoes into a glass mixing bowl and add the olive oil and salt; beat with an electric mixer until light and fluffy, adding any of the reserved water if necessary. Spoon the topping onto the bean and vegetable mixture, spreading it out as you go with the back of the spoon.

6. Bake for 30 to 35 minutes. Serve with a large green salad and some whole wheat or brown rice bread for a satisfying, balanced meal.

Sensuous Vegan Vegetable and Bean Enchiladas

This recipe does take some time to prepare but you are rewarded with a large batch of enchiladas that are bursting with flavor. You may also add some fresh or frozen corn to the filling for added color and flavor. The enchiladas can easily be frozen before they are baked for another night's quick meal. Serve with the Arugula Salad with Lime Vinaigrette on page 177 and some freshly cooked brown basmati rice.

SERVES 8 TO 10

Sauce:
2 large dried ancho chilies, seeded
2 small dried chipotle peppers, seeded
1 ½ cups boiling water
¼ cup extra virgin olive oil
6 cloves garlic, crushed
1 small onion, finely diced
2 teaspoons sea salt
2 tablespoons ground cumin
2 tablespoons organic cocoa powder
1 tablespoon whole cane sugar or agave nectar
2 cups organic tomato sauce
½ cup tapioca flour
2 cups cold water

Enchiladas:
1 tablespoon extra virgin olive oil
1 large onion, diced small
4 cloves garlic, crushed
2 teaspoons sea salt
1 tablespoon cumin
2 teaspoons dried oregano
½ teaspoon cinnamon
2 large yams, peeled and diced small
2 medium zucchini, diced small
1 medium red bell pepper, diced small
2 tablespoons fresh lime juice
6 cups cooked black beans, or 4 cans, drained
1 cup bean cooking liquid or water
16 to 20 large organic corn tortillas, warmed *(see page 88)*

1. To make the sauce, place the seeded ancho and chipotle chilies in a small bowl and pour the boiling water over them, let stand for 15 minutes.

2. In a medium saucepan, heat olive oil over medium heat. Add garlic, onions, and sea salt; sauté until tender. Add ground cumin, cocoa powder, and whole cane sugar and sauté a few minutes more. Add tomato sauce and soaked chili peppers with the soaking water. Simmer for about 10 minutes.

3. Place the tapioca flour and cold water into a small bowl and stir to dissolve. Place the sauce mixture and the dissolved tapioca flour into a blender and blend on high until smooth.

4. To make the filling, in a large pot heat the olive oil over medium heat, add the onion and garlic and sauté for a few minutes until tender. Then add the sea salt, cumin, oregano, and cinnamon; sauté stir for one minute.

5. Add the diced yams and sauté for about 5 minutes. Then add the diced zucchini and diced red bell pepper, sauté about 5 minutes more or until the zucchini begins to get tender. Turn off heat and add the fresh lime juice and cooked black beans. Taste and adjust salt and seasonings if necessary.

6. Preheat oven to 400 degrees F.

7. This recipe makes about 16 large enchiladas; enough to fill two 9 x 13-inch baking dishes. You may either bake them all at once in two pans or bake just one pan and freeze the other half of the enchiladas in two 8 x 8-inch plastic storage containers before baking.

8. Coat baking pans and/or plastic storage containers with olive oil. Take a warmed corn tortilla and fill it with the bean and vegetable mixture, roll, and place in the pan with the ends down. Repeat this until all of the filling has been used. Now cover each pan evenly with the sauce.

9. Cover and freeze any of the enchiladas in the plastic storage containers. Place foil over the 9 x 13-inch baking dish and bake enchiladas at 400 degrees F for about 45 to 50 minutes.

*Note: To bake frozen enchiladas, place container under hot running water to release. Then place frozen enchiladas into an appropriate sized, oiled baking dish and bake as directed above. Longer baking time may be required to bake frozen enchiladas.

Smashed Yam and Black Bean Quesadillas

Serve these child-friendly quesadillas with a mild salsa for dipping and a small green salad on the side. Other fun things to serve with these are freshly made guacamole or plain organic yogurt for dipping. Use a pizza cutter to slice into wedges to making dipping easy for little hands.

SERVES 4

1 large yam, peeled and cut into chunks

1 tablespoon extra virgin olive oil
1 small onion, diced small
2 teaspoons ground cumin
½ teaspoon chili powder
2 to 3 cups cooked black beans, well drained
sea salt, to taste

brown rice or corn tortillas
spinach or arugula leaves
grated organic cheese, optional

1. Preheat oven to 400 degrees F. Place yam chunks into a baking dish and add about ¼ inch of water. Cover and bake for about 35 minutes or until very tender.

2. To make the beans, heat a large skillet over medium heat. Add the olive oil then onions; sauté for about 5 to 7 minutes or until onions are very tender.

3. Add cumin, chili powder, black beans, and salt. Using a fork or the back of a spatula, smash the black beans as you heat them with the onions. Continue turning and smashing until the desired consistency has been reached. Set aside in a bowl.

4. In a clean 10-inch skillet, add one tortilla then spread a layer of black beans, spinach leaves, and cheese if desired. Then add a few chunks of yams and smash them with the back of a fork. Top with another tortilla. Heat over medium heat for about 2 minutes then flip the quesadilla and heat the other side for another 2 minutes. The trick to making these is to make sure you don't add too much filling!

5. Transfer to a plate and cut into slices with a pizza cutter.

Spicy Black-Eyed Pea Stew

Black-Eyed Pea stew, often times called Hoppin John, is a typical southern dish. Serve this stew over brown rice or Easy Polenta, page 240, with a side of Apple Spiced Collard Greens, page 195, for some real Southern Flare!

SERVES 4 TO 6

2 cups dry black-eyed peas, rinsed
2 bay leaves
6 cups water

1 tablespoon extra virgin olive oil
1 medium onion, chopped
8 cloves garlic, minced
2 to 3 tablespoons chopped fresh thyme or 1 tablespoon dried
½ teaspoon red chili flakes
¼ teaspoon black pepper
2 large carrots, chopped
2 to 3 celery stalks, chopped
1 medium red bell pepper, diced
1 ½ cups fresh or frozen corn kernels
2 teaspoons Herbamare
2 to 3 tablespoons brown rice vinegar or apple cider vinegar

1. Place the black-eyed peas into a 3-quart stainless steel pot with the bay leaves and water. Bring to a boil, then reduce heat to a simmer and cook for about 45 minutes or until peas are cooked. Drain off bean cooking liquid into a bowl and save to add to the stew if needed.

2. In a large stainless steel pot or skillet, heat olive oil over medium heat, add onions and garlic and sauté for about 5 minutes or until soft. Add fresh thyme, red chili flakes, black pepper, carrots, celery, red bell pepper, and corn kernels. Sauté for another 5 to 7 minutes or until vegetables begin to get tender.

3. Add beans and Herbamare, simmer covered until vegetables are tender, about another 10 minutes, adding a little of the reserved bean cooking liquid if necessary. Finish with brown rice vinegar. Adjust salt and seasonings if desired.

White Bean and Vegetable Stew

Serve this scrumptious stew with the Rosemary Olive Dinner Rolls on page 128, and the Italian Greens salad with Red Wine Vinaigrette on page 184 for a light, balanced meal. If you don't have cannelini beans on hand, try cooking with another white bean such as navy or great northern.

SERVES 6

3 cups dry cannelini beans, soaked overnight
one 3-inch strip kombu
8 cups water

2 tablespoons extra virgin olive oil
1 large onion, chopped
4 to 5 cloves garlic, crushed
1 tablespoon dried thyme
2 teaspoons dried rosemary, crushed
2 teaspoons dried tarragon
3 stalks celery, chopped
3 large carrots, peeled and diced
4 cups water, bean cooking liquid, or vegetable broth
2 medium zucchini, diced
1 to 2 teaspoons sea salt or Herbamare, or to taste
½ cup finely chopped fresh parsley

Optional garnishes:
chopped fresh parsley
sliced kalamata olives
crumbled organic feta cheese

1. Drain and rinse soaked beans then place into a large pot with the kombu and water. Bring to a boil, then reduce heat and simmer for about 1 to 1 ½ hours. Set aside when done.

2. Heat olive oil in a 6-quart pot over medium heat. Add onions and sauté for about 5 minute or until tender. Add crushed garlic, thyme, rosemary, and tarragon and sauté a minute more. Then add celery and carrots and sauté for about 3 more minutes.

3. Next add the cooked beans and water. For a thinner stew add some of the bean cooking liquid. Simmer, covered, for about 15 minutes or until carrots and celery are slightly tender but not completely soft. Add zucchini and continue to simmer until zucchini is tender, about 5 minutes.

4. Add sea salt or Herbamare to taste and stir in chopped parsley. Serve each bowl topped with chopped fresh parsley, kalamata olive slices, and crumbled organic feta cheese.

Fish, Poultry, & Meat

"There is no higher religion than human service.
To work for the common good is the greatest creed."

~Woodrow Wilson

A nimal foods can play a very healthful role in the diet. Be sure to use fish, poultry, and meat as more of a side dish in your meals. Eating the majority of your food from plants, such as vegetables, fruits, beans, and grains, will not only benefit your health but the health of the planet as well. Although Tom is vegan, I tend to eat fish about once a week, poultry a few times per month, and red meat only about twice per year. Try to find a balance that works best for you.

Remember to always purchase *organic* free range chicken, *organic* grass fed meats, and *wild* Alaskan fish to be sure you are getting the safest and most nutritious forms of these foods. For more information on this please refer to *pages 29 through 31.*

Basil Balsamic Wild Salmon *with Plum Tomato Topping*

Serve this flavorful salmon dish with the Balsamic Roasted Beets on page 206 and a fresh green salad. If you are soy sensitive then replace the tamari with about one teaspoon sea salt or Herbamare.

SERVES 3 TO 6

1 to 2 pounds wild Alaskan salmon fillets

Marinade:
1 lemon, juiced
¼ cup olive oil
¼ cup wheat-free tamari or 1 teaspoon sea salt
¼ cup balsamic vinegar
1 cup tightly packed fresh basil leaves
3 cloves garlic, peeled
2 teaspoons lemon zest

Topping:
1 cup chopped fresh plum tomatoes
½ cup kalamata olives, pitted and chopped
½ cup crumbled organic feta cheese, optional
1 tablespoon extra virgin olive oil
2 to 3 tablespoons finely chopped basil

1. Rinse salmon fillets under cool running water and place skin side up in a shallow baking dish. Place all of the ingredients for the marinade into a blender and blend on high until completely pureed and smooth. Pour marinade over salmon fillets, cover, and place into the refrigerator for 1 to 4 hours.

2. Preheat oven to 400 degrees F. Drain off marinade and place the salmon fillets skin side down in a shallow baking dish. Bake salmon at 10 minutes per inch of thickness. Drizzle some of the remaining marinade over the salmon half way through baking.

3. While the salmon is baking prepare the topping. Place all of the ingredients for the topping into a small bowl and gently mix. To serve, let each person spoon a desired amount of topping over their piece of salmon.

Spiced Citrus Salmon

This salmon recipe contains a bouquet of citrus flavors and would pair well with the Steamed Vegetables with Lemon Garlic Dressing on page 204, and some cooked brown jasmine rice or millet. Try topping the baked salmon with the Mango Salsa on page 307.

SERVES 3 TO 6

1 to 2 pounds wild Alaskan salmon fillets

Marinade:
½ cup freshly squeezed orange juice
¼ cup freshly squeezed lime juice
¼ cup freshly squeezed lemon juice
¼ cup extra virgin olive oil
2 tablespoons minced shallots
2 cloves garlic, crushed
1 to 2 teaspoons sea salt
½ to 1 teaspoon crushed red chili flakes

1. Rinse salmon under cool running water and place skin side up in a shallow baking dish. In a separate dish, whisk together all of the ingredients for the marinade. Pour marinade over salmon, cover, and refrigerate for 2 to 4 hours.

2. Preheat oven to 400 degrees F. Pour off marinade and flip salmon so the skin is down. Bake, uncovered, for 10 minutes per inch of salmon thickness. It is best to take salmon out just before it is cooked through because it will continue to cook after you take it out of the oven.

Wild Salmon *with Ginger Lime Marinade*

Wild salmon is a great source of vitamin D, protein, omega 3 fatty acids, selenium, and vitamins B12 and B3. Serve this dish with Roasted yams with Rosemary on page 208, and the Autumn Harvest Salad on page 178.

SERVES 3 TO 6

1 to 2 pounds wild Alaskan salmon fillets

Marinade:
½ cup tamari
1 lime, juiced
2 tablespoons maple syrup or agave nectar
1 teaspoon grated ginger
2 to 4 cloves garlic, crushed
few dashes hot pepper sesame oil

1. Rinse salmon under cool running water and place skin side up in a glass baking dish. Mix all other ingredients in a small bowl and pour over salmon. Cover pan. Marinate for ½ hour to 2 hours in the refrigerator.

2. Preheat oven to 400 degrees F. Drain off marinade. Flip salmon to skin side down. Cook 10 minutes per inch of thickness, about 15 to 25 minutes, or until done.

Wild Salmon *with Lemon, Garlic, and Thyme*

Baking is a great and easy way to prepare salmon. One pound of salmon will serve 2 to 3 people; therefore this recipe can easily be doubled or tripled if cooking for a larger number of people.

SERVES 2 TO 3

> 1 pound wild Alaskan salmon fillet
> ⅛ teaspoon Herbamare or sea salt
> 1 teaspoon dried thyme
> ¼ teaspoon freshly ground black pepper
> 3 cloves garlic, crushed
> 1 tablespoon extra virgin olive oil
> ½ lemon, cut into slices

1. Preheat oven to 400 degrees F.

2. Rinse salmon under cool running water, pat dry. Place salmon skin side down in a glass baking dish. Sprinkle with Herbamare, dried thyme, and black pepper. Rub in the crushed garlic then drizzle with olive oil. Place the lemon slices atop of the salmon.

3. Place dish into the oven and bake at 400 degrees F at 10 minutes per inch of salmon thickness. It is best to take salmon out just before it is cooked through because it will continue to cook after you take it out of the oven.

Poached Halibut *with Tomatoes and Fresh Herbs*

Serve this dish over brown rice noodles or Pine Nut Studded Rice, page 224, and a fresh green salad such as the Italian Greens Salad on page 184. If Halibut is unavailable you may use Wild Salmon instead, it is equally delicious.

SERVES 3 TO 6

1 to 2 pounds fresh halibut fillets, skin removed
4 tablespoons fresh lemon juice
½ teaspoon sea salt

1 tablespoon extra virgin olive oil
1 small red onion, chopped
1 teaspoon Italian seasoning
2 cloves garlic, crushed
2 small zucchini, chopped
½ cup kalamata olives, pitted
2 cups chopped tomatoes or one 14-ounce can diced tomatoes
½ cup chopped fresh basil
2 teaspoons chopped fresh oregano
1 tablespoon sherry vinegar, or to taste

> ### Chef's Tip
> When you purchase your fish at the market, have the fishmonger cut the skin off the fish.

1. Cut skin from halibut with a very sharp knife then place halibut fillet on a plate and cover with lemon juice and sea salt; let fish marinate for about 10 minutes while preparing other ingredients.

2. In a large skillet or pot heat olive oil over medium heat, add the chopped red onion and sauté for about 5 minutes or until it begins to turn golden. Add Italian seasoning, garlic, zucchini, and olives. Sauté 5 minutes more.

3. Move vegetables to the side of the pan and add halibut fillets; cook for 3 minutes then flip. Add tomatoes, fresh basil, and fresh oregano; add a little water if needed. Cover and simmer on low until halibut is done and flakes easily, about 10 minutes. Add the sherry vinegar and serve.

Fish Soft Tacos *with Fresh Tomato Peach Salsa*

These tacos are easy to make and delicious served with the peach salsa. If peaches are out of season or you do not want to take the extra time to prepare the salsa, then try using your favorite organic pre-made variety from your local co-op or health food store.

SERVES 3 TO 4

1 pound fresh wild Alaskan salmon or halibut fillets, skin removed

Marinade:
1 lime, juiced, about 2 to 3 tablespoons
¼ cup wheat-free tamari or 1 teaspoon sea salt
1 tablespoon Mexican Seasoning
virgin coconut oil, for sautéing

Chef's Tip

When you purchase your fish at the market, have the fishmonger cut the skin off the fish.

Other Ingredients:
organic corn or brown rice tortillas, warmed
thinly sliced avocado
thinly sliced Napa cabbage or romaine lettuce
grated organic raw jack cheese, optional

1 recipe Fresh Tomato Peach Salsa, *page 308*

1. Cut the skin off of the fish fillet, and then cut fish into 1-inch cubes. Place the fish into a small bowl or shallow dish and add the ingredients for the marinade. Mix the fish and marinade in the dish gently with a spoon. Let marinate for 30 to 40 minutes in the refrigerator.

2. While fish is marinating, prepare other ingredients.

3. To cook fish, heat a 10-inch skillet over medium heat and add about 1 tablespoon virgin coconut oil. Add cubed fish and gently sauté for 5 to 6 minutes or until fish is cooked through.

4. Immediately serve by taking a tortilla and adding some of the cooked fish, avocado, cabbage, salsa, and the optional cheese. Roll and enjoy!

Chicken Fricassee

A stew made by frying the meat first and then cooking it with vegetables and a liquid is called a Fricassee. There are many different Fricassee recipes using all sorts of different ingredients and herbs. This recipe is made gluten-free by replacing the traditional white flour for dredging with arrowroot powder. Serve this dish over Polenta or Brown Rice Noodles with a green salad on the side.

SERVES 4

¼ cup arrowroot powder
½ teaspoon sea salt or Herbamare
½ teaspoon freshly ground black pepper
1 teaspoon dried thyme
2 large organic boneless chicken breasts, cut into pieces

1 tablespoon extra virgin olive oil
10 to 12 cloves garlic, crushed
2 cups chopped tomatoes or one 14-ounce can diced tomatoes
3 tablespoons white wine vinegar
2 tablespoons tomato paste
¼ to ½ cup water
1 can artichoke hearts, drained and rinsed
½ cup pitted kalamata olives
¼ cup tightly packed chopped fresh basil
3 tablespoons chopped fresh oregano
6 cups baby spinach
Herbamare and freshly ground black pepper to taste
chopped fresh basil and oregano for garnish

1. Place arrowroot powder, Herbamare or sea salt, black pepper, and dried thyme into a shallow dish and gently mix together with a fork. Add the chicken pieces and move chicken around to coat with arrowroot mixture.

2. Heat olive oil in an 11-inch skillet over medium heat. Add chicken pieces and lightly sauté for about 5 minutes, moving the chicken around to cook on all sides. Add the crushed garlic and continue to cook for about another minute, keeping everything moving in the pan. Add the diced tomatoes, white wine vinegar, tomato paste, and water; stir to mix everything together. Then add the artichoke hearts, kalamata olives, basil, and oregano; mix well. Cover and simmer for about 25 to 35 minutes over low heat, stirring occasionally.

3. Then add the spinach, and cook for about another 10 minutes. Remove from heat and add salt and pepper to taste. Garnish with chopped fresh basil and oregano.

Chicken Nuggets

These chicken nuggets make for a great, healthy alternative to conventional nuggets that you would buy at the store. You can serve these with some organic honey mustard for dipping, Oven Fries, page 205, and a steamed or raw vegetable for a quick, nutritious, child-friendly meal.

SERVES 2 TO 4

> **1 or 2 organic chicken breasts**
> **½ cup plain soy milk or hemp milk**
> **1 cup organic corn meal or brown rice flour**
> **1 ½ teaspoons Herbamare**
> **2 to 3 tablespoons virgin coconut oil**

1. Preheat oven to 400 degrees F.

2. Cut chicken breasts into "nugget" sized pieces. Place soy milk or hemp milk into a bowl. Place corn meal or rice flour and Herbamare into another bowl.

3. Take chicken pieces and place them into soy milk, mix them around to get them coated then dredge the chicken pieces into the corn meal mixture until very well coated. Rub the bottom of a 9 x 13-inch glass baking dish with the coconut oil, and then place the nuggets evenly in the pan.

4. Place pan into preheated oven and bake for about 20 minutes. Remove the pan from the oven and cut into the thickest nugget to see if it is still pink. If it is still a little pink then place pan back into oven for some extra cooking time.

*Note: These nuggets can be frozen before baking to make a very quick meal at another time. Simply bake the frozen nuggets as directed above.

Chicken Verde Enchiladas

Sometimes I like to boil a whole chicken and use the broth to make a soup, and the chicken for a variety of other dishes, this one being one of them. Remember to save some of the broth for making this recipe. These enchiladas can easily be frozen into serving sized containers before baking. This way you will have a homemade meal ready to go in the oven for another night. Serve enchiladas with some cooked brown basmati rice and the Cabbage Salad with Cilantro Vinaigrette on page 181.

SERVES 4 TO 6

Sauce:
1 pound fresh tomatillos, husks removed
1 small onion, skins removed and ends trimmed off
4 to 5 cloves garlic, peeled
2 jalapeño chili peppers, seeded
2 to 3 Serrano chilies, seeded
¼ cup tightly packed fresh cilantro
1 tablespoon extra virgin olive oil
1 cup organic chicken broth
sea salt, to taste

Enchiladas:
1 tablespoon extra virgin olive oil
1 small onion, finely diced
3 cloves garlic, crushed
2 teaspoons cumin
½ teaspoon sea salt
2 small zucchini, diced small
2 cups chopped fresh spinach
½ cup chopped cilantro
2 to 3 cups shredded cooked organic chicken
1 cup grated organic pepper jack cheese, optional
organic corn tortillas, warmed
extra grated organic pepper jack cheese for sprinkling on top

1. To make the sauce, place the husked tomatillos, small onion, garlic, seeded chili peppers, and cilantro in a blender and blend on high until smooth. Heat a 3-quart pot over medium heat, add the 1 tablespoon olive oil, then add the blended green sauce; stir the sauce for about 5 minutes or until darkened and thickened. Add the chicken broth and sea salt to taste.

2. To make the enchiladas, heat a large skillet over medium heat, add olive oil and diced onions; sauté for 5 minutes or until soft. Add the garlic, cumin, and sea salt

and sauté another minute more. Remove from heat and place into a large bowl with the diced zucchini, chopped spinach, chopped cilantro, shredded chicken, and optional pepper jack cheese. Mix well.

3. Preheat oven to 375 degrees F. Oil a 9 x 13-inch pan or similar sized casserole dish with a lid.

4. To assemble enchiladas, place about ½ cup filling in a corn tortilla, tightly roll, and place seam side down in the oiled pan. Repeat this process until all of the filling has been used. Pour sauce over enchiladas.

5. You may want to place some enchiladas into a small rectangular plastic freezer container with some sauce on top and freeze for later use.

6. Sprinkle some cheese over the sauce, if desired. Place a lid or foil over the pan and place into the preheated oven. Bake for 45 to 50 minutes or until sauce is bubbly.

Coconut Lime Chicken *with Almond Dipping Sauce*

This quick-to-prepare meal is always a crowd pleaser. Try serving it with brown rice and steamed vegetables for an easy weeknight dinner. The chicken can also be replaced with tofu or tempeh for equally delicious results.

SERVES 4

2 large organic boneless chicken breasts, cut into 1-inch cubes
virgin coconut oil, for sautéing

Marinade:
2 tablespoons coconut milk
2 tablespoons lime juice
2 tablespoons wheat-free tamari

Almond Lime Dipping Sauce:
6 tablespoons almond butter
¼ cup freshly squeezed lime juice
¼ cup coconut milk
1 to 2 tablespoons tamari
1 tablespoon agave nectar
1 to 2 cloves garlic, crushed

1. Place chicken breast pieces into a bowl and cover with the ingredients for the marinade. Stir chicken and marinade together with a spoon to evenly distribute. Let chicken marinate for about 20 to 30 minutes.

2. Heat a 10-inch skillet over medium-high heat. Add about one tablespoon of virgin coconut oil. Then add chicken pieces. Sauté, stirring frequently, for about 3 to 5 minutes, or until chicken is cooked through. Cooking times will vary depending on the size of the chicken pieces.

3. Place all ingredients for dipping sauce into a bowl and whisk together until the mixture is thickened and well combined. Sauce can also be warmed on the stove in a small pot over low heat.

4. To serve, divide dipping sauce into four small serving bowls for each person to dip chicken into.

Home Style Chicken and Vegetable Stew

This hearty stew is great for a chilly evening. It is quick to prepare so it works well for a weeknight dinner. Try serving it with some freshly made brown rice or whole grain bread (pages 122 to 124). A large green salad is also always a nice accompaniment to this meal.

SERVES 4

1 to 2 tablespoons extra virgin olive oil
1 medium onion, diced
3 to 4 cloves garlic, crushed
1 teaspoon dried thyme
2 large organic boneless chicken breasts, cut into chunks
2 to 3 large carrots, diced
3 to 4 celery stalks, diced
2 large red or yellow potatoes, diced
2 ½ to 3 cups vegetable or chicken stock
¼ cup arrowroot powder
1 teaspoon sea salt or Herbamare, or to taste
1 cup fresh or frozen peas
½ cup chopped fresh parsley

1. Heat a large 11-inch skillet over medium heat and add olive oil. Add diced onions and sauté until soft, about 5 minutes. Add garlic, thyme, and chicken breasts; sauté a few minutes more. Then add carrots, celery, potatoes; sauté a minute more.

2. Combine the stock and arrowroot powder and whisk well. Add this mixture to the pan with the sea salt or Herbamare. Cover and simmer for about 20 to 25 minutes.

3. Add peas and parsley, cover and simmer 5 more minutes. Taste and adjust salt and seasonings if necessary.

Indian Chicken Curry

This dinner makes a great easy weeknight meal. Serve over cooked brown jasmine rice with a large green salad on the side. Try eating a spoonful of raw cultured vegetables with this meal to maximize digestion.

SERVES 4

    1 tablespoon extra virgin olive oil
    1 medium onion, diced
    4 cloves garlic, crushed
    2 teaspoons ground cumin
    1 teaspoon ground coriander
    1 teaspoon curry powder
    ½ teaspoon turmeric
    ½ teaspoon cinnamon
    pinch cayenne pepper
    2 large organic boneless chicken breasts, cut into pieces
    3 large carrots, peeled and sliced
    1 can coconut milk
    1 tablespoon tomato paste
    4 cups thinly sliced kale or Swiss chard
    1 to 2 teaspoons Herbamare or sea salt

1. Heat olive oil over medium heat in a large pot. Add diced onions and sauté until soft, about 5 minutes. Add crushed garlic, ground cumin, ground coriander, curry powder, turmeric, cinnamon, and cayenne; sauté for another 2 minutes then add chicken breast pieces.

2. Sauté chicken in spices and onion for another 5 minutes. Add carrots, coconut milk, and tomato paste, stir well then cover and simmer on low heat for 15 to 20 minutes, stirring occasionally.

3. Add sliced kale, stir well then simmer an additional 5 minutes. Turn off heat and add sea salt or Herbamare to taste.

Thai Chicken Curry

This recipe can be prepared up to a day ahead of time and then baked when ready for dinner. Serve with Thai fried Rice, page 226, and steamed organic broccoli for a complete meal. Chicken breasts and sauce can also be frozen in individual containers before baking for a quick, ready-to-go meal. Recipe adapted from Bastyr University instructor, Mary Shaw.

SERVES 4

> **4 organic boneless chicken breasts**
> **5 kaffir lime leaves, optional**

> *Sauce:*
> **1 can coconut milk**
> **4 small shallots, peeled**
> **1 stalk lemon grass, ends trimmed then chopped**
> **6 cloves garlic, peeled**
> **2 tablespoons chopped fresh ginger**
> **2 tablespoons Thai fish sauce**
> **1 tablespoon wheat-free tamari or ½ teaspoon sea salt**
> **3 tablespoons organic unsalted peanut butter or cashew butter**
> **2 tablespoons whole cane sugar or agave nectar**
> **1 tablespoon curry powder**
> **1 teaspoon crushed red chili flakes**
> **1 teaspoon ground coriander**
> **1 teaspoon ground cumin**
> **1 teaspoon turmeric**
> **¼ teaspoon white pepper**

> *Garnish:*
> **½ cup chopped cilantro**

1. Cut chicken into large pieces and place into a 9 x 13-inch baking dish along with the kaffir lime leaves, if using.

2. Place all ingredients for the sauce into a blender. Blend on high until smooth and creamy. Cover the chicken with curry marinade. Cover and refrigerate for 3 to 24 hours.

3. Preheat oven to 400 degrees F. Place pan of chicken and marinade uncovered in the oven and bake for 30 to 35 minutes, or until done. Garnish with chopped cilantro.

Whole Roasted Organic Chicken *with Lemon and Herbs*

You will need to plan in advance in order to roast a chicken because of the long cooking time. Serve roasted chicken with mashed Yukon gold potatoes or baked sweet potatoes, steamed broccoli, and a fresh salad for a complete meal.

SERVES 4 TO 6

1 whole organic chicken, 3 ½ to 5 pounds
1 small onion, chopped
3 cloves garlic, chopped
2 stalks celery, chopped
1 small lemon, cut into chunks
handful fresh parsley, chopped
¼ cup chopped fresh herbs (rosemary, thyme, marjoram)
1 tablespoon extra virgin olive oil
2 teaspoons Herbamare or sea salt

1. Preheat oven to 450 degrees F. Place chicken in a clean sink and rinse, inside and out. Then place in a 9 x 13-inch glass baking dish.

2. In a small bowl, mix together the remaining ingredients. Place some of the mixture into the cavity of the chicken and the rest sprinkled around the chicken on the bottom of the pan. Add about ½ inch of water to bottom of pan. Sprinkle the top of the chicken with some Herbamare or sea salt, freshly ground black pepper, and some extra virgin olive oil.

3. Place chicken into preheated oven and roast at 450 degrees F for 15 minutes; this seals in the juices. Turn down heat to 325 degrees F and continue to roast for 1 to 1 ½ hours or until juices run clear. Baste throughout cooking time to keep moist.

4. To test for doneness, pull the thigh away and check for clear juices. If they are still a little pink, then the chicken needs more time. You can also use a meat thermometer to test for doneness. Insert it at the thickest part of the thigh, it should read about 180 degrees F when fully cooked.

5. When chicken is done, place onto a platter to carve. Pour juices from pan through a strainer and into a small pot. Whisk about 2 tablespoons of arrowroot powder with a little cold water in a small bowl then add to the juices and whisk together. Simmer over low heat while whisking until the gravy thickens. Add salt to taste.

Apricot and Fig Roasted Turkey Breast

Serve this festive dish at your next holiday gathering or for just a comfy home cooked family meal on a chilly evening. Try serving it with some baked winter squash, page 210, and the Pear and Hazelnut Salad with Creamy Cranberry dressing on page 185. Dried figs can replace the fresh ones here; just soak them in water for about 30 minutes before using.

SERVES 4 TO 5

1 organic bone-in turkey breast, about 2 ½ to 3 pounds
¼ cup apricot jam
¼ cup balsamic vinegar
¼ cup water
2 tablespoons extra virgin olive oil
1 tablespoon finely chopped fresh oregano
1 teaspoon sea salt
1 small leek, chopped
8 to 10 fresh black mission figs

1. Rinse the turkey breast and place into a baking dish.

2. In a separate small dish, whisk together the apricot jam, balsamic vinegar, water, extra virgin olive oil, chopped oregano, and sea salt. Pour over turkey breast. Place leeks and figs on the bottom of the pan around the turkey. Cover the pan and refrigerate for one to four hours, or overnight.

3. Preheat oven to 325 degrees F. Place pan of turkey with marinade in preheated oven and roast for approximately 1 ½ to 2 hours, or until juices run clear. A meat thermometer inserted into thickest part of meat should read approximately 170 degrees F. I have also baked this at 200 degrees F for 3 to 4 hours, which makes the meat slightly more tender.

4. To serve, cut the turkey into slices and place the figs, leeks, and juices over the turkey slices.

Beef Stew *with Swiss Chard*

It is best to buy organic grass-fed beef if you are going to eat meat. If you cannot find it locally then you can order it online and have it shipped to you. Serve this stew over cooked quinoa. The juices from the stew will seep down into the quinoa making a luxurious combination.

SERVES 4

2 tablespoons extra virgin olive oil
1 medium onion, chopped
3 shallots, minced
4 cloves garlic, minced
2 teaspoons dried thyme
1 teaspoon dried rosemary, crushed
2 cups cremini mushrooms, quartered
2 large carrots, sliced ½-inch thick
1 pound organic beef stew meat
one 14-ounce can crushed tomatoes
1 cup organic beef stock
4 cups thinly sliced Swiss chard
1 tablespoon red wine vinegar
1 to 2 teaspoons sea salt or Herbamare
freshly ground black pepper to taste

1. In a large skillet or pot, heat olive oil over medium heat. Add onions, shallots, and garlic, sauté for 5 to 7 minutes or until onions are soft and beginning to turn golden.

2. Add dried thyme, dried rosemary, mushrooms, and carrots; sauté for an additional 5 minutes then add beef stew meat. Continue to sauté for about 5 more minutes.

3. Add crushed tomatoes and beef stock, cover and simmer over low heat for 35 to 40 minutes stirring occasionally. Then add Swiss chard, red wine vinegar, sea salt, and freshly ground black pepper. Cover and cook an additional 5 minutes or until the Swiss chard is tender. Taste and adjust salt and seasonings if necessary.

Fall Vegetable Beef Roast

This recipe was passed down to me from my mother and makes a great hearty meal when the weather is beginning to get cold. Serve with a large green salad, or raw sauerkraut, and some freshly made bread for a balanced meal.

SERVES 4 TO 6

> 1 tablespoon extra virgin olive oil
> 2 pounds organic beef roast
> 2 teaspoons dried thyme
> 1 teaspoon freshly ground black pepper
> 1 teaspoon sea salt
> 1 medium onion, chopped large
> 3 cups organic vegetable juice cocktail
> 4 medium carrots, peeled and cut into 3-inch pieces
> 4 small red potatoes, cut into large chunks
> 1 rutabaga or 1 yam, cut into large chunks
> 3 stalks celery, cut into 3-inch pieces

1. Preheat the oven to 325 degrees F.

2. In a large Dutch oven, over medium-high heat, sear the roast in olive oil. Sprinkle with dried thyme, black pepper, and sea salt. Then add the chopped onions and vegetable juice.

3. Place, covered, in the preheated oven. Cook for 2 hours, then remove pot from oven and add the remaining vegetables.

4. Cook for 2 more hours, or until roast begins to fall apart. Season with sea salt or Herbamare to taste.

Dressings, Dips, & Sauces

"Laughter is the tonic, the relief, the surcease for pain."

~Charlie Chaplin

*H*aving fresh salad dressings ready to go in your fridge will be an invaluable asset to your health. Simply drizzle your favorite dressing over some fresh, organic mixed greens and you'll have a vital, nutrient packed snack or meal. Stored in a glass jar, all of the following dressings will keep for 7 to 10 days in the refrigerator. Since the olive oil in these dressings will harden slightly at cold temperatures, simply place the jar under warm running water to thin out before using.

Eating raw vegetables with a bean dip or nut pate is a wonderful way to get more raw vegetables into your diet. Raw vegetables provide the desirable "crunch" that people crave and dips provide a slightly salty flavor and a creamy consistency that we all love.

Sauces are indispensable for spicing up cooked grains, whole grain noodles, or steamed vegetables. Some sauces may also be easily frozen for later use.

Salad Dressings

Balsamic Vinaigrette

    4 tablespoons extra virgin olive oil
    3 tablespoons balsamic vinegar
    1 tablespoon maple syrup
    2 teaspoons Dijon mustard
    1 teaspoon tamari

1. Place all ingredients into a small bowl and whisk.

Orange Vinaigrette

    3 tablespoons extra virgin olive oil
    ¼ cup freshly squeezed orange juice
    2 teaspoons balsamic vinegar
    1 tablespoon chopped fresh fennel tops
    1 teaspoon orange zest
    ¼ teaspoon sea salt
    ¼ teaspoon cinnamon

1. Place all ingredients into a small bowl and whisk.

Honey Poppy Seed Vinaigrette

    ¼ cup extra virgin olive oil
    3 tablespoons red wine vinegar
    1 to 2 tablespoons honey
    1 tablespoon poppy seeds
    ¼ teaspoon sea salt

1. Place all ingredients into a small bowl and whisk.

Cilantro Vinaigrette

    ¼ cup chopped cilantro
    4 tablespoons extra virgin olive oil
    3 tablespoons brown rice vinegar
    ¼ teaspoon sea salt
    pinch cayenne pepper

1. Place ingredients into a blender and blend until smooth.

Herbal Vinaigrette

1 small lemon, juiced
⅓ cup extra virgin olive oil
2 tablespoons balsamic vinegar
2 teaspoons Dijon mustard
2 tablespoons maple syrup
3 tablespoons chopped fresh basil
2 tablespoons chopped fresh chives
1 tablespoon chopped fresh oregano
½ teaspoon sea salt

1. Place all ingredients into a small bowl and whisk.

Red Wine Vinaigrette

¼ cup extra virgin olive oil
¼ cup red wine vinegar
1 teaspoon Dijon mustard
1 teaspoon maple syrup
½ teaspoon sea salt
1 teaspoon Italian seasoning
1 clove garlic, crushed

1. Place all ingredients into a small bowl and whisk.

Lime Vinaigrette

¼ cup extra virgin olive oil
¼ cup freshly squeezed lime juice
1 tablespoon brown rice vinegar or apple cider vinegar
1 to 2 teaspoons lime zest
1 clove garlic, crushed
¼ teaspoon sea salt
¼ teaspoon ground cumin
pinch ground cardamom

1. Place all ingredients into a small bowl and whisk.

Creamy Ginger Dressing

¼ cup sesame seeds, toasted
½ cup chopped celery
3 tablespoons chopped ginger
½ cup extra virgin olive oil
3 tablespoons brown rice vinegar
3 tablespoons tamari
2 tablespoons water
1 tablespoon maple syrup
1 teaspoon organic ketchup
⅛ teaspoon white pepper
⅛ teaspoon celery seed

1. Heat a small skillet over medium-low heat; add sesame seeds and toast for about 3 minutes. Be sure to keep seeds moving in the pan to prevent burning.

2. Remove from heat and place seeds into a blender with the remaining ingredients, blend on high until smooth.

Creamy Cranberry Dressing

2 teaspoons extra virgin olive oil
2 shallots, peeled and thinly sliced
1 cup fresh cranberries, washed
¼ cup freshly squeezed orange juice
¼ cup extra virgin olive oil
¼ cup water
3 tablespoons balsamic vinegar
3 to 4 tablespoons maple syrup
1 teaspoon orange zest
½ teaspoon sea salt or Herbamare

1. Heat a small skillet over medium heat, add 2 teaspoons olive oil and sliced shallots. Sauté shallots for 3 to 5 minutes or until soft.

2. Add fresh cranberries and continue to sauté until the cranberries are soft and have "popped."

3. Place mixture into a blender with remaining ingredients. Blend on high until smooth.

Hummus

Hummus is a traditional Middle-Eastern dish made from garbanzo beans, also called chickpeas, and tahini. It makes an excellent dip for fresh vegetables or a great spread for sandwiches or wraps.

MAKES ABOUT 4 CUPS

> **3 cups cooked garbanzo beans, or 2 cans**
> **½ cup sesame tahini**
> **½ cup freshly squeezed lemon juice**
> **¼ cup extra virgin olive oil**
> **2 teaspoons garlic powder or 2 to 3 cloves, crushed**
> **1 teaspoon ground cumin**
> **1 to 2 teaspoons sea salt or Herbamare, or to taste**
> **¼ cup bean cooking liquid or water to desired consistency**

1. Place all ingredients into a food processor and process until smooth and creamy.

2. You will want to taste the hummus to see if it needs more lemon, tahini, garlic, or salt. Also, add more water for a thinner consistency and process again. Hummus freezes very well.

White Bean and Roasted Red Pepper Dip

This bean dip is a great alternative to Hummus for people with sesame seed allergies. Try putting some into a brown rice tortilla with some chopped cucumbers, tomatoes, olives, and lettuce. If you do not want to take the time to roast your own peppers, you can purchase organic roasted red bell peppers in a jar from your local co-op or health food store.

MAKES ABOUT 4 CUPS

> **3 cups cooked white beans, try navy or great northern**
> **1 small red bell pepper, roasted** *(see page 87 for directions)*
> **½ cup almond butter**
> **¼ cup freshly squeezed lemon juice**
> **3 tablespoons extra virgin olive oil**
> **2 teaspoons garlic powder or 2 cloves, crushed**
> **½ to 1 teaspoon chili powder**
> **1 teaspoon sea salt or Herbamare, or to taste**
> **bean cooking liquid if necessary**

1. Place all ingredients into a food processor and process until smooth and creamy.

2. You will want to taste the bean dip to see if it needs more lemon, red peppers, garlic, or salt. Add bean cooking liquid or water for a thinner consistency and process again.

Spicy Black Bean Dip

Not only are black beans good in soup, they are also wonderful as a dip. If you would like an even spicier dip try adding one additional jalapeño pepper and some crushed red chili flakes. You may freeze some of this dip just as long as you keep the fresh tomato out of the portion you will freeze.

MAKES ABOUT 3 CUPS

1 tablespoon extra virgin olive oil
1 small onion, chopped
1 small jalapeño pepper, chopped
3 cloves garlic, crushed
1 tablespoon ground cumin
1 teaspoon chili powder
3 cups cooked black beans, or 2 cans, drained
1 to 2 tablespoons apple cider vinegar
½ teaspoon sea salt, or to taste
1 to 2 plum tomatoes, diced

1. In a large skillet, heat the olive oil over medium heat. When hot, add the onions, peppers, and garlic, and sauté until the onions are soft, about 5 minutes. Add the cumin and chili powder and sauté 1 minute more, stirring often.

2. Add the cooked beans and mix thoroughly, making sure you scrape up all of the spices from the bottom of the pan.

3. Place bean and spice mixture into a food processor, and process until smooth. Add apple cider vinegar and salt to taste, process again.

4. Remove dip from processor and place into a medium sized bowl, stir in chopped tomatoes. Serve as a dip for chips or vegetables or use as a spread for tortillas.

Guacamole

Guacamole is delicious served with many of the recipes in this cookbook. Try it with the Mexican Pink Bean Burritos on page 261, or on top of the Black Bean and Tempeh Tostadas on page 243, or simply as a dip for corn chips, pita bread, or fresh cucumber slices.

SERVES 2 TO 4

> **2 to 3 ripe avocados**
> **½ lime, juiced**
> **¼ to ½ cup finely diced red onion**
> **1 small plum tomato, diced small**
> **¼ cup finely chopped cilantro**
> **sea salt, to taste**

1. Remove the peels and pits from the avocados. Keep one pit to store any leftover guacamole.

2. Place avocados into a medium bowl and mash with a fork until desired consistency. For a smoother dip you may place avocados into a blender and blend until creamy.

3. Mix mashed or blended avocados with the remaining ingredients in a bowl, taste and add more salt and lime juice if necessary.

4. For a spicier dip, try adding a finely diced jalapeño pepper and some cayenne pepper.

5. If not serving right away, place the reserved pit into center of dip, cover, and refrigerate until ready to serve.

Artichoke and Almond Pate

This delightful pate is wonderful served in a bowl next to a platter of raw vegetables, or try rolling into romaine lettuce leaves for a snack. You may use a can of artichoke hearts for this recipe or you can use about 1 ½ cups freshly cooked artichoke hearts for an even more flavorful pate.

SERVES 4 TO 6

 1 cup raw almonds, soaked overnight
 one 14-ounce can of artichokes, drained and rinsed
 ¼ cup extra virgin olive oil
 ¼ cup freshly squeezed lemon juice
 ½ small red onion, coarsely chopped
 2 tablespoons organic capers
 1 small clove garlic, peeled
 ½ teaspoon sea salt

1. Soak almonds by placing them into a medium sized bowl, then add purified water to cover. Leave on your countertop overnight, or for about 6 to 12 hours. When ready to use drain off soaking water and rinse well.

2. Place all ingredients into a food processor fitted with the "s" blade. Process until mixture is smooth.

Raw Almond and Vegetable Pate

Serve this tasty and nourishing pate with a platter of fresh organic vegetables and crackers. We like to use a gluten-free cracker called Mary's Gone Crackers, which are available at most health food stores and food co-ops. Wakame is a sea vegetable that gives this recipe added flavor while providing an abundance of trace minerals; look for it in the bulk section or macrobiotic section of your local food co-op or health food store.

SERVES 4 TO 6

> 1 ½ cups raw almonds, soaked overnight
> ¼ to ½ cup wakame pieces, soaked
> 1 cup coarsely chopped carrots
> 1 cup coarsely chopped celery
> ½ cup coarsely chopped red bell pepper
> 2 to 3 cloves garlic, chopped
> ½ cup chopped parsley
> 5 medjool dates, pitted
> 1 to 2 tablespoons wheat-free tamari or about 1 teaspoon sea salt

1. Soak almonds by placing them into a medium sized bowl, then add purified water to cover. Leave on your countertop overnight, or for about 6 to 12 hours. When ready to use drain off soaking water and rinse well.

2. Soak the wakame pieces in a small bowl with some purified water for about 10 minutes. After the wakame is soaked, drain off soaking water and place the wakame in a food processor fitted with the "s" blade.

3. Add the soaked almonds, chopped carrots, chopped celery, chopped red bell pepper, chopped garlic, parsley, and medjool dates. Pulse until well combined, being careful not to over-process.

4. Add tamari to taste, and pulse again. Store in the refrigerator until ready to serve.

Olive Tapenade

Olive tapenade is delicious used as a dip with brown rice crackers or as a spread on freshly made Brown Rice Bread, page 122. You can also use it as a garnish for the White Bean Stew on page 270.

MAKES ABOUT 1 ½ CUPS

    1 cup kalamata olives, pitted
    ¼ cup pine nuts
    ¼ cup coarsely chopped roasted red peppers
    ¼ cup tightly packed fresh basil leaves
    ¼ cup fresh parsley
    2 tablespoons capers
    1 tablespoon freshly squeezed lemon juice
    1 to 2 cloves garlic
    ¼ teaspoon freshly ground black pepper
    2 tablespoons extra virgin olive oil

1. Place all ingredients into a food processor fitted with the "s" blade. Pulse a few times. Then while pulsing, slowly add the olive oil.

2. Make sure not to over process, as the mixture can quickly turn into a paste. You will want it to be a rather coarse mixture.

Lemon Basil Pesto

Make this pesto in the summer when fresh basil is in season and freeze in small containers for later use. This pesto is delicious served over cooked brown rice noodles or any whole grain noodle. It also works well atop cooked polenta or tossed with some lightly steamed vegetables.

MAKES ABOUT 1 CUP

½ cup pine nuts
2 to 4 cloves garlic, peeled
1 to 2 teaspoons lemon zest
¼ to ½ teaspoon Herbamare or sea salt
3 cups tightly packed fresh basil leaves
¼ cup extra virgin olive oil
2 to 4 tablespoons fresh lemon juice

1. Place the pine nuts, garlic cloves, lemon zest, and Herbamare in a food processor fitted with the "s" blade. Pulse a few times until mixture is coarsely ground.

2. Add fresh basil leaves. While the food processor is running, slowly add the olive oil and lemon juice through the feed tube. Continue to process until pesto is the desired consistency.

Avocado Salsa

This salsa tastes great atop spicy bean stews, wrapped inside burritos, or as a garnish to any enchilada recipe. It is best eaten the day it is made.

MAKES ABOUT 2 CUPS

    2 large avocados, diced
    ½ small red onion, finely diced
    2 to 3 tablespoons freshly squeezed lime juice
    ¼ cup chopped cilantro
    pinch sea salt, or to taste

1. Place all ingredients into a small bowl and gently mix. Serve immediately or refrigerate for up to 2 hours.

Fresh Tomato Salsa

Serve this fresh salsa with the Mexican Pink Bean Burritos on page 261, or with Black Bean and Tempeh Tostadas on page 243, or simply as a dip for baked corn chips or vegetables.

MAKES ABOUT 2 CUPS

> **4 Roma tomatoes, diced small**
> **½ small red onion, finely diced**
> **¼ cup chopped cilantro**
> **1 small jalapeño pepper, seeded and minced**
> **1 to 2 tablespoons apple cider vinegar**
> **1 small clove garlic, minced**
> **¼ teaspoon sea salt, or to taste**
> **¼ teaspoon cumin**
> **pinch cayenne pepper**

1. Place ingredients into a small bowl and gently mix.

Fresh Mango Salsa

Serve this salsa over the Spiced Citrus Salmon on page 275, or atop fresh baby arugula greens for a light, refreshing salad.

MAKES ABOUT 1 ½ CUPS

2 mangos, peeled and diced small
1 small red onion, finely diced
½ red bell pepper, finely diced
1 small jalapeño pepper, seeded and minced
2 to 3 tablespoons freshly squeezed lime juice, or to taste
sea salt, to taste

1. Place ingredients into a small bowl and gently mix.

Fresh Tomato Peach Salsa

Serve this salsa with the Fish Soft Tacos on page 279, or with your favorite spiced bean and grain combination.

MAKES ABOUT 1 ½ CUPS

2 firm plum tomatoes, diced small
1 ripe firm peach, diced small
½ small red onion, finely diced
1 small jalapeño pepper, seeded and finely diced
½ cup chopped cilantro
1 to 2 tablespoons freshly squeezed lime juice
sea salt, to taste

1. Place ingredients into a small bowl and gently mix.

Fresh Marinara Sauce

This sauce is fun to make; children love to help pick the fresh herbs and stir the sauce. Blending the sauce makes the flavors meld together perfectly, also making it suitable for young children who sometimes like things smoother.

MAKES ABOUT 4 CUPS

2 to 4 tablespoons extra virgin olive oil
1 medium onion, chopped
4 to 5 cloves garlic, crushed
1 teaspoon sea salt or Herbamare
2 to 4 tablespoons fresh herbs (thyme, oregano, parsley, basil, rosemary)
4 to 6 cups fresh chopped tomatoes
¼ cup organic tomato paste
1 tablespoon whole cane sugar or agave nectar
1 to 2 tablespoons red wine vinegar

1. In a large skillet, heat the olive oil over medium heat. Add onions and sauté for about 5 minutes, being careful not to brown. Add the garlic and salt, sauté about 2 minutes more.

2. Add fresh herbs, chopped tomatoes, tomato paste, sugar, and red wine vinegar; simmer uncovered over low heat for 15 to 20 minutes.

3. Spoon sauce mixture into blender and blend on high until smooth. Serve over brown rice pasta or polenta.

Almond Lime Dipping Sauce

This sauce is delicious served with sautéed chicken or tofu for dipping or try it over steamed vegetables or a cooked whole grain. You can also use other nut butters in place of the almond butter. Try cashew butter or peanut butter for a tasty alternative.

MAKES ABOUT 1 CUP

> **6 tablespoons almond butter**
> **¼ cup freshly squeezed lime juice**
> **¼ cup coconut milk**
> **1 to 2 tablespoons wheat-free tamari**
> **1 tablespoon agave nectar**
> **1 to 2 cloves garlic, crushed**

1. Place all ingredients into a bowl and whisk together until the mixture is thickened and well combined. Add water for a thinner consistency.

Garlic Ginger Kudzu Sauce

Serve this sauce over sautéed tofu or tempeh; it is also wonderful served over the Lemon Millet Patties on page 237.

MAKES ABOUT 1 ½ CUPS

1 cup water
2 tablespoons kudzu
3 to 4 tablespoons wheat-free tamari
2 to 3 tablespoons brown rice vinegar
1 tablespoon maple syrup or agave nectar
2 to 3 teaspoons hot pepper sesame oil
1 clove garlic, crushed
1 to 2 teaspoons grated ginger

1. Place all ingredients into a small saucepan. Mix well to dissolve the kudzu.

2. Place pan over medium heat and bring to a gentle simmer, reduce heat to low and simmer for about 5 minutes, stirring constantly, or until the sauce has thickened and is clear.

3. Remove from heat, taste, and adjust ingredients as necessary.

Lemon Tahini Sauce

Tahini is made from ground sesame seeds and is very high in calcium. Serve this creamy and light sauce over steamed vegetables; it is especially good over asparagus. Or try it drizzled over some sautéed tempeh and a cooked grain. You can also add more water and use it as a salad dressing.

MAKES ABOUT 1 ½ CUPS

½ cup sesame tahini
½ cup freshly squeezed lemon juice
¼ cup extra virgin olive oil
3 to 4 tablespoons water
2 cloves garlic, crushed
2 to 3 teaspoons lemon zest
½ to 1 teaspoon sea salt, or to taste

1. Place all ingredients into a small bowl and whisk together with a fork. Taste and add more salt if necessary. Add more water for a thinner consistency.

Miso Sauce

Serve this sauce over some steamed vegetables, or my favorite: sautéed tempeh, onions, and asparagus. The combination is truly delicious!

MAKES ABOUT ¾ CUP

¼ cup gluten-free miso
2 to 3 tablespoons water
2 tablespoons brown rice vinegar
2 tablespoons toasted sesame oil or extra virgin olive oil
1 tablespoon honey or agave nectar
dash hot pepper sesame oil

1. Whisk all of the ingredients in a small bowl. Add more water for a thinner consistency. Spoon over steamed or sautéed vegetables and brown rice.

Raita

Raita, a classic Indian condiment, provides a cooling accompaniment to many spicy dishes. Try serving a dollop of Raita atop a serving of Lentil and Spinach Dal, page 259.

MAKES ABOUT 1 ½ CUPS

> 1 cup organic plain yogurt (cow, goat, or soy)
> 1 small cucumber, seeded and finely diced
> 1 tablespoon finely chopped mint
> ½ teaspoon ground cumin
> sea salt, to taste

1. Combine all ingredients into a small bowl and chill until ready to serve.

Warm Berry Sauce

Serve this scrumptious sauce over pancakes for breakfast or chocolate cake for dessert. Sauce can be made with only one fruit or a combination of a few, you choose.

MAKES ABOUT 2 CUPS

1 to 2 tablespoons kudzu
1 cup apple or berry juice
2 cups fresh or frozen organic berries (blueberries, raspberries, strawberries, blackberries)
2 tablespoons agave nectar, honey, or maple syrup

1. Place the kudzu and juice in a small saucepan to dissolve. Use less kudzu for a thinner sauce and more for a thicker sauce.

2. Blend the berries in a blender until very smooth. If using raspberries or blackberries, you may choose to strain the seeds through a fine mesh strainer. Our preference is not to strain the seeds.

3. Add the puréed berries to the pot along with the sweetener. Whisk together, and then place pot over medium heat. Bring to a simmer, whisking continuously until mixture has thickened and is translucent. Serve warm.

Nutritious Desserts

"Sharing food with another human being
is an intimate act that should not be indulged in lightly."

~M. F. K. Fisher

Removing refined sugar from your diet is a big step towards improving your overall health and vitality. These types of sugars have been stripped of all of their natural vitamins and minerals, which when consumed, leaves the body susceptible to large spikes in blood sugar, mood swings, lowered immunity, and a host of other short and long term health problems. Eating a balanced diet full of vegetables, whole grains, beans and fresh fruits usually eliminates the cravings for refined sweets.

Sweetness is an important flavor to have in the diet and need not be eliminated completely. It balances other flavors in the diet including bitter, salty, pungent, and sour. Your overall diet will be much more satisfying with the occasional consumption of natural sweets. By wisely adding these, you will find that cravings for junk food will wane and bingeing will disappear. The following recipes contain natural sweeteners combined with other wholesome ingredients such as fresh or dried fruit and nuts, whole grain flours and healthy fats to create a satisfying yet nutrient-packed way to round out your meals.

Fresh Strawberries *with Honey Lemon Cashew Sauce*

Serve this dessert in late spring or early summer when the strawberries are in their peak season. In midsummer, try pouring the cashew sauce over a bowlful of fresh raspberries, blueberries, peaches, and apricots for a delicious, seasonal dessert.

SERVES 2 TO 4

1 pound fresh organic strawberries

Cashew Sauce:
1 cup raw cashews
¼ cup lemon juice
¼ cup honey, or maple syrup
1 to 2 tablespoons water, or as needed
1 teaspoon vanilla
½ teaspoon lemon zest
pinch sea salt

1. Wash, dry, and trim the strawberries. Place into a serving bowl.

2. In a blender, place all ingredients for sauce and blend until creamy and smooth, adding more water if necessary.

3. Drizzle cashew sauce over fresh strawberries and serve.

Spring Rhubarb and Ginger Compote

Tart and tangy rhubarb is the quintessential "fruit" of spring. Of course rhubarb is not a fruit, but rather a vegetable, though its culinary use is much like a fruit. In most climates it comes up before any other fruits are available making it the perfect component of a spring dessert. This recipe pairs tangy rhubarb with spicy ginger and sweet agave nectar for a taste sensation! Serve it alone or with the Honey Lemon Cashew Sauce on the previous page.

SERVES 4 TO 6

> 1 ½ pounds fresh rhubarb stalks, cut into 1-inch pieces
> ¼ to ½ cup agave nectar or honey
> 2 tablespoons freshly squeezed orange juice
> 1 tablespoon arrowroot powder
> ½ to 1 teaspoon freshly grated ginger
> 1 teaspoon orange zest
> pinch sea salt

1. Place rhubarb pieces and agave nectar into a 2-quart pot.

2. In a small bowl, whisk together the orange juice and arrowroot powder. Then add it to the pot with the rhubarb. Add the remaining ingredients and gently stir.

3. Place the pot over medium heat on the stove. Simmer, uncovered, for 5 to 6 minutes. Be very careful not to overcook the rhubarb, as it will turn very mushy if cooked for too long.

4. Place compote into a glass bowl and cool in the refrigerator. To serve, spoon chilled compote into small serving bowls, top with Honey Lemon Cashew Sauce, some sliced strawberries, and a sprig of mint if desired.

Cherry Apple Pudding *with Almond Cream*

Serve this easy-to-make pudding at the peak of cherry season when fresh cherries are in abundance. You can also use frozen cherries if fresh are not available. The pudding without the nut topping makes for a wonderfully nutritious and easily digested dessert for older babies and toddlers.

MAKES ABOUT 6 SERVINGS

Pudding:
4 tablespoons kudzu, dissolved in 2 to 3 tablespoons water
1 cup organic apple juice
2 cups fresh or frozen pitted cherries
¼ cup maple syrup or agave nectar

Almond Cream:
1 cup raw cashews
¼ cup agave nectar
2 to 3 tablespoons water
1 teaspoon vanilla
1 to 2 teaspoons almond extract

Garnish:
fresh cherries, stems attached
finely chopped raw almonds

1. To make the pudding, place the kudzu and water in a small pan, stir with a fork, and let stand for 2 to 4 minutes until the kudzu is completely dissolved. Place juice, cherries, and maple syrup into a blender and blend on high until very smooth. Pour cherry juice mixture into pan with kudzu.

2. Place the pan over medium heat and stir continuously with a wire whisk until thick and clear, about 5 to 10 minutes. Take off heat and pour into parfait glasses or small bowls. Place into the refrigerator to set. It will take about 30 minutes to 1 hour for the pudding to set.

3. To make the almond cream, place all of the ingredients into a blender fitted with a sharp blade and blend on high until thick and creamy. Taste and adjust sweetness if necessary.

4. To serve, place a large dollop of almond cream atop each dish of cherry pudding. Place a whole cherry in the middle of the cream and sprinkle with chopped raw almonds if desired.

Lemon Blueberry Pudding

Children will love this rich yet nutritious dessert. Tapioca is the starch from the root of the cassava plant. The cassava plant is a shrubby tropical plant which is grown for its large, tuberous, starchy roots.

MAKES ABOUT 6 SERVINGS

1 ½ cups water
½ cup small pearl tapioca
1 cup raw cashews
1 cup maple syrup
2 cups water
¾ cup lemon juice
½ teaspoon sea salt
1 ½ cups fresh or frozen blueberries
1 tablespoon vanilla
½ teaspoon lemon extract

1. Place the water and tapioca pearls in a 3 or 4-quart pot and let soak 1 hour.

2. Place cashews, maple syrup, water, lemon juice, and sea salt in a blender fitted with a sharp blade. Blend on high for 1 to 2 minutes until smooth and creamy. Next, add blueberries, vanilla, and lemon extract. Blend on high again for another 1 to 2 minutes, or until very smooth and creamy.

3. Add this mixture to the pot of soaked tapioca pearls. Stir well, and then bring to a boil. Turn down heat to a low simmer and stir frequently for about 15 minutes, or until pudding has thickened and tapioca pearls are translucent.

4. Pour into small serving containers and chill in the refrigerator. Pudding will thicken as it cools.

Pumpkin Pudding

This recipe is a version of our Lemon Blueberry Pudding on the previous page. It is delicious served in the fall and wintertime when pumpkins and other winter squash are in abundance. See page 210 for directions on baking pumpkins and other winter squash.

MAKES ABOUT 6 SERVINGS

1 ½ cups water
½ cup small pearl tapioca
1 cup raw cashews
2 cups water
½ cup maple syrup or agave nectar
2 cups baked sugar pie pumpkin or other winter squash
2 tablespoons lemon juice
2 teaspoons vanilla
½ teaspoon sea salt
½ teaspoon cinnamon
¼ teaspoon ground ginger
¼ teaspoon nutmeg
pinch ground cloves

1. Place the water and tapioca pearls in a 3 or 4-quart pot and let soak 1 hour.

2. Place cashews, water, and maple syrup in a blender. Blend on high for 1 to 2 minutes or until smooth and creamy. Add pumpkin, lemon juice, vanilla, sea salt, and spices; blend for another 1 to 2 minutes, or until very smooth and creamy.

3. Add this mixture to the pot of soaked tapioca pearls and whisk together. Bring to a boil while stirring. Then turn heat to low and simmer, stirring frequently for about 15 minutes, or until pudding has thickened and tapioca pearls are translucent.

4. Pour into small serving bowls and chill in the refrigerator. Pudding will thicken as it cools.

Dried Fruit Compote *with Cashew Cream*

This recipe makes for a wonderful winter dessert when fresh fruit is not in season. I like to dehydrate fresh apples, pears, and plums in the fall when they are abundant and falling off of the trees. We store our dried fruit in glass jars in our pantry to use during the winter months.

SERVES 4 TO 6

½ cup dried apricot halves
½ cup dried apples
½ cup dried pear halves
½ cup prunes
¼ cup dried cherries
2 cinnamon sticks
2 cups water
½ cup raisins
¼ cup honey or agave nectar
1 small lemon, juiced
mint leaves, for garnish

Cashew Cream:
½ cup raw cashews
2 to 3 tablespoons maple syrup
1 teaspoon vanilla
2 to 3 tablespoons water

1. Place the dried fruit into a large pot with the cinnamon stick and water. Heat gently until almost boiling, then cover the pan, lower the heat and simmer gently for 12 to 15 minutes, or until fruit has softened.

2. Remove pan from heat. Add the raisins and honey, stir. Cover the pan with the lid and let cool.

3. In a blender fitted with a sharp blade, place the cashews, maple syrup, water, and vanilla; blend until smooth and creamy.

4. Once compote has cooled, remove the cinnamon sticks and stir in the lemon juice. Serve in small containers at room temperature with a dollop of cashew cream. Garnish with fresh mint leaves.

Apricot Fruit Gel

Using agar and fruit juice instead of gelatin, sugar, and artificial flavor and colors makes for a light nutritious dessert or snack that children will love. Try pouring this into parfait glasses with sliced cherries at the bottom. Sprinkle the top with shredded organic coconut for a deliciously simple dessert. You can also substitute any organic fruit juice for the apricot juice for equally delicious results!

SERVES 6 TO 8

4 cups organic apricot juice
2 to 3 tablespoons agar flakes
fresh sliced fruit, optional

1. Place apricot juice and agar flakes into a 2-quart saucepan. Bring to a boil, and then reduce heat to a gentle simmer, stirring constantly. Simmer for about 10 minutes or until agar flakes are completely dissolved.

2. Lightly grease a 9 x 13-inch pan with coconut oil. Place any fresh fruit you would like on the bottom of the pan. Pour agar juice mixture into pan.

3. Chill in the refrigerator for about 1 hour. Before serving let pan sit at room temperature for about 10 to 15 minutes. Store in the refrigerator for up to a week.

Chocolate Truffles

These healthful and easy-to-make little treats are always a crowd pleaser. They can be made a day ahead of time and stored in a covered container in your refrigerator until ready to serve.

MAKES ABOUT 1 ½ DOZEN TRUFFLES

2 cups raw walnuts
1 cup medjool dates, pitted
4 to 6 tablespoons organic cocoa powder

shredded organic coconut

1. Place walnuts into a food processor fitted with the "s" blade and process until very finely ground and pasty.

2. Add dates and cocoa powder and continue to process until well-combined. Add more dates for a sweeter taste and process again.

3. Roll into small balls and place into a bowl of shredded coconut. Make sure each ball gets coated in coconut, then place onto a plate.

Chewy Chocolate Chip Cookies

These gluten-free cookies are very easy to make. Serve with hemp milk or fresh almond milk for a fun treat! You can also vary the recipe by adding cocoa powder and a little extra sugar for chocolate cookies or take out the chocolate chips and add 1 to 2 teaspoons ginger powder and cinnamon each for a ginger spice cookie.

MAKES ABOUT 1 ½ DOZEN COOKIES

> 1 cup medjool dates, pitted
> 1 cup boiling water
> ½ cup melted virgin coconut oil or organic butter
> ¼ cup whole cane sugar
> 2 teaspoons vanilla
> 2 cups brown rice flour
> ½ cup tapioca flour
> 1 teaspoon baking powder
> ½ teaspoon baking soda
> ½ teaspoon xanthan gum
> ¼ teaspoon sea salt
> ½ cup (or more) organic chocolate chips

1. Preheat oven to 350 degrees F.

2. Place pitted medjool dates into a small bowl, cover with boiling water. Let sit for about 15 minutes. Then place soaked dates and water into a blender and puree.

3. Scoop out date puree with a rubber spatula and place into a bowl. Add melted coconut oil, whole cane sugar, and vanilla; whisk together.

4. In a separate bowl, mix together the brown rice flour, tapioca flour, baking powder, baking soda, xanthan gum, and sea salt. Add the wet ingredients to the dry and mix together with a fork or wooden spoon. Fold in chocolate chips.

5. Drop by the spoonful onto a greased cookie sheet. Gently flatten each cookie with the back of a spoon. You don't want to flatten them too much, only slightly.

6. Bake for 10 to 14 minutes. Baking time will depend on what size the cookies are. Larger cookies need a little extra time and smaller cookies a little less. Let cool slightly then enjoy! Store in an airtight container for up to 5 days.

Coconut Cashew Cookies

Not only are these cookies gluten-free but they are also vegan, meaning they contain no dairy or eggs. Try experimenting with different nuts and dried fruit. Or try adding some organic chocolate chips into the dough.

MAKES 1 DOZEN COOKIES

⅓ cup softened virgin coconut oil
¼ cup maple syrup or agave nectar
2 tablespoons whole cane sugar
¼ teaspoon sea salt
2 teaspoons vanilla
1 cup brown rice flour
¼ cup tapioca flour
½ to 1 cup shredded organic coconut
½ cup raw cashews, ground
1 teaspoon baking powder
1 teaspoon xanthan gum
organic chocolate chips, optional

1. Preheat oven to 350 degrees F.

2. Place coconut oil, maple syrup, sugar, sea salt, and vanilla into a medium bowl and blend on high with electric beaters for about 2 minutes.

3. Place cashews into a coffee grinder and grind until finely ground.

4. In a separate bowl, mix together the brown rice flour, tapioca flour, coconut, ground cashews, baking powder, and xanthan gum. Pour the wet ingredients into the dry and mix together with an electric mixer until well combined. Add water, one tablespoon at a time, if mixture seems too dry. Fold in chocolate chips if desired.

5. Grease a cookie sheet with coconut oil. Form dough into balls then gently flatten between the palms of your hands. Place on the cookie sheet. Bake for 12 to 15 minutes. Cool on a wire rack. Cookies will be somewhat crumbly when hot and will harden as they cool.

Double Chocolate Cookies

If you are a chocolate lover, then you are going to enjoy these little gluten-free treats. The ground walnuts are optional. They add a little extra nutrition to these cookies, but don't take anything away from them, in terms of flavor and texture, if you decide not to add them. You can also add some chopped dried organic cherries to the dough for a nice twist.

MAKES 1 DOZEN COOKIES

⅓ cup softened virgin coconut oil
⅓ cup maple syrup or agave nectar
½ cup walnuts, ground (optional)
2 to 4 tablespoons whole cane sugar
¼ teaspoon sea salt
2 teaspoons vanilla
1 teaspoon almond extract
1 cup brown rice flour
½ cup arrowroot powder
⅓ cup organic cocoa powder
1 teaspoon baking powder
1 teaspoon xanthan gum
½ cup organic chocolate chips
whole raw almonds

1. Preheat oven to 350 degrees F.

2. Place coconut oil, maple syrup, ground walnuts, sugar, sea salt, vanilla, and almond extract into a medium bowl and blend on high with an electric mixer for about 2 minutes.

3. In a separate bowl, mix together the brown rice flour, arrowroot powder, cocoa powder, baking powder, and xanthan gum. Pour the wet ingredients into the dry and gently mix together with a fork or wooden spoon until well combined. Fold in chocolate chips.

4. Grease a cookie sheet with coconut oil. Form dough into balls then gently flatten between the palms of your hands. Place on the cookie sheet and press one almond into the center of each cookie. Bake for about 12 minutes. Cool on a wire rack. Cookies will be somewhat crumbly when hot and will harden as they cool.

Gingerbread Cut-Out Cookies

These amazing little gluten-free cookies are fun to make with children. They can help roll out the dough and cut it into shapes using different cookie cutters. Try pumpkins for Halloween, gingerbread people and stars for Christmas, and hearts for Valentines Day.

MAKES 1 ½ TO 2 DOZEN COOKIES

½ cup softened virgin coconut oil or softened organic butter
¼ cup whole cane sugar
¼ cup maple syrup
¼ cup blackstrap molasses
½ cup pumpkin puree
1 tablespoon vanilla
½ teaspoon sea salt
2 cups brown rice flour or sorghum flour
½ cup tapioca flour
2 teaspoons baking powder
1 ½ teaspoons xanthan gum
1 ½ teaspoons cinnamon
1 teaspoon ginger powder
½ teaspoon ground cloves
¼ teaspoon ground nutmeg

1. In a medium sized mixing bowl, whisk together the coconut oil, sugar, maple syrup, molasses, pumpkin puree, vanilla, and sea salt.

2. In a separate bowl, combine the brown rice flour, tapioca flour, baking powder, xanthan gum, and spices. Add the dry ingredients to the wet and mix well with a wooden spoon.

3. Form dough into a ball and wrap in waxed paper; place in the refrigerator to chill for about 20 minutes.

4. Preheat oven to 375 degrees F. Lightly flour a surface for rolling out your dough. Place the dough on the surface and roll until it is about ¼ inch thick. Cut out with your favorite cookie cutters and then place cookies onto an oiled baking sheet.

5. You may decorate the cookies before baking by gently pressing whole nuts and seeds such as almonds, pecans, or pumpkin seeds into the cookies. Bake for about 15 minutes. Then remove from cookie sheet and place onto a rack to cool.

Raw Chocolate Hazelnut Brownies

These brownies are amazingly fast to prepare and no baking required. You will need a food processor for this recipe. A high quality cocoa powder can make all the difference with this recipe; we like to use Dagoba® non-alkalized organic baking cocoa.

MAKES ABOUT 16 SMALL SQUARES

> **1 cup raw hazelnuts**
> **½ cup raw almonds**
> **1 to 1 ½ cups medjool dates, pitted**
> **½ cup raw almond butter**
> **4 to 6 tablespoons organic cocoa powder**
> **3 tablespoons raw shredded organic coconut**

1.   Place hazelnuts and almonds into food processor fitted with the "s" blade and process until finely ground.

2.   Add the pitted dates, raw almond butter, and cocoa powder and process until completely mixed. You can add more or less cocoa powder depending on how rich you would like the brownies.

3.   Firmly press mixture evenly into an 8 x 8-inch square pan. Sprinkle with shredded coconut. Cut into squares when ready to serve. Refrigerate in a covered container for up to a week.

Apple Cranberry Crisp *with Almond Oat Topping*

Apple peels are high in the flavonoid quercitin which has been found to be cardio-protective among other things. So leave your apple peels on when making this dish.

MAKES ABOUT 6 SERVING

4 tart apples, cored and thinly sliced
1 cup fresh or frozen cranberries
¼ cup whole cane sugar
2 tablespoons fresh lemon juice
2 tablespoons arrowroot powder
2 teaspoons cinnamon
¼ teaspoon nutmeg

Going Gluten-Free Tip

If you are gluten sensitive then use Certified Gluten-Free Oats.

Topping:
1 cup rolled oats
¼ cup brown rice flour or sorghum flour
¼ cup arrowroot powder
¼ cup whole cane sugar
¼ cup softened virgin coconut oil or organic butter
½ cup sliced or chopped almonds (optional)
1 teaspoon cinnamon
¼ teaspoon ground cardamom

1. Preheat oven to 375 degrees F. Place the thinly sliced apples, cranberries, sugar, lemon, juice, arrowroot, cinnamon, and nutmeg into a medium sized bowl and gently mix to combine all of the ingredients. Set aside while preparing topping.

2. To make the topping, place all ingredients into a medium sized bowl and mix well until crumbly. Place the apple mixture into a 9 x 13-inch pan and sprinkle it evenly with the topping.

3. Bake in a preheated oven for 25 to 30 minutes, or until bubbly.

Fresh Berry Tart *with Nutty Oat Crust*

Serve this light dessert in mid summer at the peak of berry season. Berries are not only bursting with flavor but also antioxidants that protect your body from free radical damage and many diseases.

SERVES 6 TO 8

Crust:
1 cup raw pecans
1 cup rolled oats
1 cup medjool dates, pitted
¼ cup raw almond butter
½ teaspoon cinnamon
¼ teaspoon cardamom

Berry Filling:
1 ½ cups organic berry juice
2 tablespoons kudzu
2 tablespoons maple syrup or agave nectar
2 cups fresh organic berries, such as raspberries, blueberries, and strawberries

1. To make the crust, place the pecans and rolled oats in a food processor fitted with the "s" blade. Process until ground, then add the pitted medjool dates, raw almond butter, and spices and process until well combined.

2. Place into an 8 x 8-inch square baking dish and firmly press evenly into the bottom of the pan. Place into the refrigerator to chill while you are making the filling.

3. To make the filling, place the berry juice, kudzu, and maple syrup into a small saucepan. Let the kudzu dissolve for about 5 minutes then place pan over medium heat. Bring mixture to a simmer, stirring frequently. Turn heat down and cook until mixture is thick and clear, stirring frequently, for about 10 minutes.

4. Remove pan from heat and let cool for about 5 minutes. Wash and dry berries and spread evenly over crust, then pour kudzu mixture over the top of the berries.

5. Chill for about 20 minutes before serving. Tart will keep covered in the refrigerator for up to 3 days.

Zesty Lemon Tart

I love making this dessert in the springtime and garnishing it with fresh sliced strawberries. Recipe has been adapted from Bastyr University instructor, Mary Shaw.

SERVES 6 TO 8

Crust:
1 ¼ cups rolled oats
¼ cup almonds, ground
¼ cup walnuts, ground
2 tablespoons brown rice flour
2 tablespoons arrowroot powder
¼ teaspoon xanthan gum
pinch sea salt
¼ cup maple syrup
¼ cup melted virgin coconut oil

Lemon Filling:
2 tablespoons agar flakes
1 cup rice milk or other non-dairy milk
½ cup brown rice syrup
2 to 4 tablespoons whole cane sugar
pinch turmeric
pinch sea salt
2 tablespoons kudzu mixed with ¼ cup water
½ cup fresh lemon juice
1 teaspoon vanilla extract
1 teaspoon lemon zest or 1 teaspoon lemon flavoring

> ### Going Gluten-Free Tip
>
> If you are gluten sensitive then use Certified Gluten-Free Oats.

1. Preheat oven to 350 degrees F. Combine the oats, ground nuts, rice flour, arrowroot powder, xanthan gum, and salt in a mixing bowl. Add syrup and oil, mix well. Press the mixture into the bottom of an 8 x 8-inch pan with wet hands. Bake for 10 to 12 minutes. Remove from oven and let cool completely.

2. Mix the agar, rice milk, rice syrup, sugar, turmeric, and salt in a pot. Simmer until agar melts, about 5 minutes.

3. Mix kudzu and water together in a separate bowl until kudzu is dissolved. Add the kudzu-water mixture to the simmering ingredients in the pot. Cook until thickened and translucent, stirring frequently, about 10 to 15 minutes.

4. Remove from heat and add lemon juice, vanilla, and lemon zest. Mix well and pour into cooled crust. Chill for 30 minutes in the refrigerator or until firm.

Blueberry Fruit Pie *with Raw Nut Crust*

Don't be fooled by the long list of ingredients. This lively fruit pie is relatively easy and fast to prepare and perfect for a summer picnic when fresh fruit is in season.

MAKES ABOUT 8 SERVINGS

Crust:
1 cup raw pecans
1 cup raw almonds
½ teaspoon cinnamon
¼ teaspoon ground cardamom
¼ teaspoon ginger powder
1 cup medjool dates, pitted

Blueberry Filling:
6 tablespoons kudzu, dissolved in 2 to 3 tablespoons water
1 ½ cups organic berry juice, such as Santa Cruz Organic Berry Nectar
2 cups fresh or frozen blueberries
2 tablespoons pure maple syrup

Cashew Cream:
1 cup raw cashews
¼ cup pure maple syrup
2 to 3 tablespoons water
2 teaspoons vanilla

Fruit Topping:
1 large ripe mango, peeled and thinly sliced
1 large ripe peach, thinly sliced
1 kiwi fruit, peeled and thinly sliced
1 cup fresh berries, rinsed and dried
shredded coconut

1. To make the crust, place the raw pecans, raw almonds, cinnamon, cardamom, and ginger in a food processor fitted with the "s" blade and process until finely ground. Add the pitted medjool dates and process until well combined. Place mixture into a deep dish 9-inch pie plate and press evenly onto the bottom and sides. Chill the crust while you are preparing the filling.

2. To make the filling, place the kudzu and water in a small pan and let stand for 2 to 4 minutes until the kudzu is completely dissolved. Place juice, blueberries, and maple syrup into a blender and blend on high until very smooth.

3. Pour berry juice mixture into pan with kudzu. Place the pan over medium heat stir continuously until thick and clear, about 5 to 10 minutes. Take off heat and pour into chilled pie crust. Return pie to the refrigerator to set. It will take about 1 to 2 hours for the filling to set.

4. Rinse out the blender and put the cashews, maple syrup, water, and vanilla in. Blend on high until smooth and creamy. Set aside and prepare the fruit.

5. Take the pie out of the refrigerator. Spread the cashew cream over the filling.

6. Now, place the sliced mango, peach, kiwi, and fresh berries into your own unique design over the cashew cream layer. Sprinkle with shredded coconut if desired. Return pie to the refrigerator until ready to serve. Pie will keep for up to 3 days in the refrigerator. Leftovers make a wonderful breakfast!

Variation: Use raspberries, strawberries, or cherries instead of blueberries for the filling.

Raw Stone Fruit Pie

This is a wonderful mid-summer pie when stone fruits are in season. Peaches, plums, nectarines, apricots, and cherries are all considered stone fruits because of their pit in the center of the fruit. Any combination of ripe stone fruit will do. The optional cashew topping below can be added to create an extra rich dessert. Pie will keep up to 3 days, covered, in the refrigerator.

MAKES ABOUT 8 SERVINGS

Crust:
2 cups raw pecans
1 tablespoon cinnamon
pinch ground nutmeg or cardamom
8 to 10 medjool dates, pitted
1 tablespoon virgin coconut oil

Filling:
2 ripe peaches, cut into slices
2 ripe plums, cut into slices
1 ripe nectarine, cut into slices
2 to 3 small apricots, cut into halves
1 cup cherries, pitted and cut into halves
1 ½ cups organic apple, peach, or apricot juice
2 tablespoons kudzu
1 to 2 tablespoons agave nectar

Optional Topping:
1 cup raw cashews
3 to 4 tablespoons agave nectar or maple syrup
2 to 4 tablespoons water
1 tablespoon vanilla

Garnish:
shredded coconut

1. To make the crust, place the pecans and spices in a food processor and process until pecans are finely ground. Add dates and coconut oil and process again until the mixture resembles a fine meal. Pour into a 9-inch deep dish glass pie plate and evenly press to the bottom and sides.

2. To make the filling, arrange the fruit in the crust in any pattern you like. Place into the refrigerator while preparing the next step.

3. Place the juice, kudzu, and agave nectar into a small saucepan. Let the kudzu dissolve in the cold liquid for about 5 minutes then place pan over medium heat.

4. Bring mixture to a simmer, stirring frequently. Turn heat down and cook until mixture is thick and clear, stirring frequently, for about 10 minutes.

5. Remove from heat and pour over fruit. Immediately place pie into the refrigerator to chill for at least 30 to 60 minutes.

6. To make the cashew topping, place all ingredients into a Vita-Mix and blend until smooth and creamy, adding additional water, a little at a time, to desired consistency. It should be fairly thick. Place cashew cream in dollops on top of the filling. Sprinkle with shredded coconut if desired. Continue to chill until ready to serve.

Lemon Teascake

This recipe makes for a delicious vegan and gluten-free dessert. The recipe is adapted from a dessert served at the former Café Ambrosia restaurant in Seattle, Washington.

SERVES 6 TO 8

Crust:
1 cup rolled oats, lightly ground
¼ cup brown rice flour
¼ cup arrowroot powder
½ cup walnuts, ground
½ teaspoon sea salt
1 teaspoon vanilla extract
3 tablespoons maple syrup
¼ cup melted virgin coconut oil

Filling:
½ cup uncooked millet
2 cups water
½ cup raw cashews
½ cup pure maple syrup
⅓ cup fresh lemon juice
2 teaspoons vanilla extract
1 teaspoon lemon flavoring

> ### Going Gluten-Free Tip
>
> If you are gluten sensitive then be sure to use Certified Gluten-Free Oats.

1. Rinse millet in a fine strainer under cold running water. Place millet and water in a small pot with a tight fitting lid. Bring to a boil then turn heat down to a low simmer and cook for 45 minutes.

2. While the millet is cooking, preheat the oven to 350 degrees F. In a small bowl, mix the ground oats, brown rice flour, arrowroot powder, ground walnuts, and sea salt.

3. In another small bowl, whisk together the vanilla, maple syrup, and coconut oil. Add the wet ingredients to the dry and mix together. Press into a 9-inch pie plate or a 9-inch spring form pan. Bake in the oven for 10 to 12 minutes. Let cool for at least 30 minutes.

4. Place the cashews, lemon juice, maple syrup, vanilla, and lemon extract into a blender fitted with a sharp blade. Blend on high for 1 to 2 minutes or until all ingredients are blended together and have a creamy consistency.

5. If you own a Vita-Mix, you can simply add the millet and continue to blend until smooth and creamy. Otherwise, transfer the cashew-lemon mixture to a food processor fitted with the "s" blade and add the cooked millet; process mixture for 1 to 2 minutes or until very creamy.

6. Pour filling into cooled crust. Let sit at room temperature for about an hour, then refrigerate until ready to serve.

7. Add sliced fresh fruit or fruit-sweetened berry jam on top of the teascake for added flavor and color. Kiwis and cherries are our favorite toppings.

Spiced Pumpkin Pie

This pie is a nutrient-packed dessert that is as delicious as it is healthy. Agar is a seaweed gel that will cause the filling, when cooked and cooled, to become firm. You will need one medium sugar pie pumpkin for this dessert. If you enjoy the buttery flavor of pie crust then you may want to opt for the Earth Balance or organic butter instead of the coconut oil in the crust recipe below.

MAKES ABOUT 8 SERVINGS

Pecan Crust:
¼ cup raw pecans, ground
½ cup arrowroot powder
¾ cup brown rice flour
½ teaspoon xanthan gum
½ teaspoon sea salt
5 to 6 tablespoons virgin coconut oil, Earth Balance margarine, or butter
3 to 4 tablespoons cold water

Pumpkin Filling:
¾ cup raw cashews
½ cup water
3 cups cooked sugar pie pumpkin flesh, still hot
¾ cup pure maple syrup
¼ cup arrowroot powder
2 teaspoons cinnamon
1 teaspoon ginger powder
¼ teaspoon nutmeg
¼ teaspoon cloves
½ cup water
4 teaspoons agar flakes

1. Preheat oven to 350 degrees F.

2. To bake the pumpkin, slice it in half then scoop out the seeds. Place it flesh side down in a large baking pan with ¼ to ½ inch of water in the bottom. Bake at 350 degrees F for 45 to 55 minutes, or until flesh is very soft.

3. To make the crust, grind pecans in a coffee grinder until fine. Place ground pecans, arrowroot powder, brown rice flour, xanthan gum, and sea salt into a medium bowl and mix together thoroughly. Add coconut oil, Earth Balance, or butter and work together with fingertips or a pastry cutter until it has a brown sugar consistency. Add water and form dough into a ball.

4. Place dough in between two pieces of waxed paper and roll out. Gently remove one of the sheets of waxed paper and place the rolled dough into a 9-inch deep dish pie plate then remove the top layer of waxed paper. Flute edges. Prick crust a few times with a fork. Bake crust in preheated oven for 10 minutes. Let cool.

5. To make the filling, place the cashews and ½ cup water in a blender and blend until smooth, 1 to 2 minutes. Place cashew cream into a food processor and add pumpkin, maple syrup, arrowroot powder, spices and process until smooth and creamy.

6. In a small pot, pour in the ½ cup water and bring to a boil. Add agar flakes, lower the temperature to a simmer. Gently stir the mixture until all of the flakes have dissolved, a few minutes.

7. Immediately put the hot agar mixture into the food processor with the pumpkin filling and process until thoroughly combined. The key to making the filling turn out correctly is to make sure that the pumpkin filling is still very hot when adding the dissolved agar to it; otherwise, the agar will gel up immediately.

8. Pour filling into baked crust. Bake in a preheated 350 degree oven for about 45 to 60 minutes or until cracking appears on the top of the filling. Let pie set at room temperature for 1 to 3 hours or until cool. Slice and serve. Store remaining pie, covered, in the refrigerator for up to a week.

Decadent Chocolate Bundt Cake

This cake is gluten, dairy, soy, and egg-free making it an excellent choice for those with multiple food sensitivities. The extra richness comes from the beets, which provide moisture, sweetness, and added minerals to the cake. Serve cake with fresh organic berries or Warm Berry Sauce, page 315.

MAKES ABOUT 8 SERVINGS

> 2 cups brown rice flour
> ½ cup tapioca flour
> ¾ cup unsweetened cocoa powder
> 1 ½ teaspoons baking soda
> 1 ½ teaspoons xanthan gum
> ½ teaspoon sea salt
> 1 cup grated cooked beets, about 1 large peeled beet
> ½ cup melted virgin coconut oil
> 1 cup maple syrup
> 1 cup water
> 2 tablespoons apple cider vinegar
> 1 tablespoon vanilla

1. Preheat oven to 375 degrees F. Oil a bundt pan with coconut oil.

2. In a medium sized bowl place the brown rice flour, tapioca flour, cocoa powder, baking soda, xanthan gum, and sea salt; mix together well with a fork.

3. For the 1 cup of grated cooked beets, first trim the ends off of the large beet then cut it into quarters. Place the quartered beet into a steamer basket in a pot filled with about 2 cups of water. Place a lid on the pot and steam for about 30 to 45 minutes or until beets are very tender. Let cool then remove the peel and grate. Measure out 1 heaping cup. The steamed beets can also be pulsed in a food processor fitted with the "s" blade to save time.

4. In a separate bowl, place the grated beets, melted coconut oil, maple syrup, water, apple cider vinegar, and vanilla. Mix well with a wire whisk. Pour the wet ingredients into the dry and mix well, though be careful not to over mix.

5. Immediately pour batter into oiled bundt pan and place into the preheated oven. Bake for 25 to 30 minutes for a metal pan; and 35 to 40 minutes for a stone pan. Remove from oven and let cool for about 10 minutes in the pan. Then flip it over onto a cake platter or plate. Serve each slice with some fresh berries.

Gingerbread Cake *with Maple Cashew Sauce*

This scrumptious dessert will delight gingerbread lovers of all kind. We like to make this cake for either Thanksgiving or Christmas as a special treat. Cake is delicious served by itself or with the cashew sauce.

MAKES ABOUT 8 SERVINGS

Cake:
2 cups brown rice flour
½ cup tapioca flour
2 teaspoons baking powder
1 ½ teaspoons xanthan gum
½ teaspoon baking soda
½ teaspoon sea salt
2 teaspoons ginger powder
2 teaspoons cinnamon
½ teaspoon ground cloves
½ cup melted virgin coconut oil or extra virgin olive oil
½ cup maple syrup
½ cup blackstrap molasses
½ cup water
1 tablespoon vanilla

Maple Cashew Sauce:
½ cup raw cashews
2 to 3 tablespoons maple syrup
1 teaspoon vanilla
2 to 3 tablespoons water

1. Preheat oven to 350 degrees F. Oil an 8 x 8-inch square baking pan.

2. Combine the dry ingredients in a medium bowl. In a separate bowl, combine the wet ingredients. Add the wet to the dry and mix well with a wire whisk. Pour the batter into the oiled baking pan and bake for about 25 minutes.

3. For the sauce, place all ingredients in a blender and blend until smooth and creamy. Let cake cool for about 10 minutes. When ready to serve, slice cake and drizzle each piece with maple cashew sauce.

Berry Peach Iced Nut Cream

This is a delightful alternative to ice cream, especially since dairy foods are one of the most common food sensitivities.

MAKES ABOUT 4 SERVINGS

½ cup raw cashews
1 large orange, juiced
1 teaspoon vanilla
½ ripe avocado
1 cup frozen raspberries
½ to 1 cup frozen strawberries
½ cup frozen peach slices

1. If you own a Vita-Mix you can blend all of the ingredients in it. Otherwise, use a blender to blend until creamy and smooth the cashews, orange juice, and vanilla.

2. Then transfer the cashew mixture to a food processor fitted with the "s" blade and add the avocado, frozen raspberries, frozen strawberries, and frozen peach slices then process until smooth, thick, and creamy.

3. Serve immediately, or freeze for later use. To serve frozen nut cream, let it stand at room temperature for about 5 to 10 minutes then place into the food processor and process until soft and creamy.

Chocolate Banana Iced Nut Cream

Here is another alternative to ice cream, a delicious chocolate version. If you are a chocolate lover, then try stirring in some organic chocolate chips to this.

Makes About 4 Servings

> ½ **cup raw cashews**
> **2 tablespoons water**
> ¼ **cup maple syrup or agave nectar**
> **3 large frozen bananas, broken into chunks**
> **2 to 4 tablespoons organic cocoa powder**

1. If you own a Vita-Mix, you can blend all of the ingredients in it. Otherwise, use a blender to blend until creamy and smooth the cashews, water, and maple syrup.

2. Then transfer the cashew mixture to a food processor and add the banana chunks and cocoa powder, and process until smooth, thick, and creamy.

3. Serve immediately, or freeze for later use. To serve frozen nut cream, let it stand at room temperature for about 5 to 10 minutes, then place into the food processor and process until soft and creamy.

Avocado Fig Fudgesicles

These amazing little treats were created by Tom and are perfect for an afternoon summer snack or evening dessert. You will need a set of plastic Popsicle molds for these. You can add more or less cocoa powder depending on how rich you would like these.

MAKES ABOUT 4 FUDGESICLES

> 1 ripe avocado
> 4 fresh black mission figs
> 4 medjool dates
> 2 to 4 tablespoons organic cocoa powder
> water sufficient for blending

1. Place all ingredients in a food processor or Vita Mix and blend on high, adding water as necessary, for 1 to 2 minutes or until very smooth and creamy.

2. Pour into Popsicle molds, insert sticks, and freeze for 6 to 8 hours or overnight.

Scrumptious Snacks

"The first wealth is health"

~Ralph Waldo Emerson

Snacking in between meals on wholesome food is a great way to keep blood sugar levels stable, energy levels high, and can even help you from overeating at a single meal. Snacking is also very important for children, pregnant and lactating women, and endurance athletes as their energy demand is very high.

This chapter provides a few nutritious snack recipes, most of which can be packaged to be taken with you during the day or packed in your child's lunchbox.

Quick Nutritious Snack Ideas:

- **Hummus** spread onto brown rice crackers or flax crackers such as Mary's Gone Crackers

- **Raw almond butter** spread onto brown rice cakes

- **Organic celery** dipped in almond butter

- **Organic Popcorn** (*page 355*) cooked in virgin coconut oil on the stove and seasoned with Herbamare and nutritional yeast

- **A handful of raw walnuts** and some sliced organic apple

- **Organic baked blue corn chips** and fresh organic salsa

- **Rice crackers**, such as, San-J brand Black Sesame Rice Crackers

- **Trail mix** made from raw nuts and dried fruit

- **Raw assorted organic vegetables** (cauliflower, carrots, red bell pepper) dipped in Lemon Tahini Sauce (*page 312*) or Hummus (*page 297*)

- **Fresh organic seasonal fruit**

- **Frozen fruit,** such as cherries, blueberries, raspberries, and peaches. This is a great snack for children to be eaten any time of day.

Collard Green and Hummus Roll-Ups

These nutritious little snacks are great to take with you to work, school, or on a hike. Any tender young green can be substituted for the collards. Try broccoli leaves from your garden or young black kale leaves. Generally, the younger the green, the more tender and sweet it will be. If you desire, try adding a slice of organic turkey on top of the hummus. Also, any fresh vegetable can be added for the filling...you decide!

MAKES 4 SERVINGS

> **4 raw collard greens**
> **½ cup hummus (or more)**
> **grated carrot**
> **chopped cucumber**
> **avocado slices**
> **organic turkey slices (optional)**

1. Rinse and pat dry the collard greens. Slice in half, lengthwise, removing the tough stems.

2. Next, spread a thin layer of hummus over the collard green half. At one end, place a thin row of carrot, cucumber and avocado. If using turkey, place it over the hummus before you add the vegetables.

3. Begin rolling from the filling end, keeping it very tight. Once it is rolled, insert a toothpick into the center to keep it together. Serve immediately or refrigerate for up to 2 days.

Variation: Instead of using hummus, try using the Raw Almond and Vegetable Pate on *page 302* for a delicious, raw alternative.

Hummus and Barbecued Onion Wrap

This tasty wrap sneaks in some shredded vegetables, is easy to prepare, and parts of it can be made up ahead of time. The wrap provides calories, protein, and essential vitamins and minerals needed for sustained energy and cognitive function during the day.

MAKES 2 WRAPS

Barbecued Onions:
2 large red onions
1 tablespoon extra virgin olive oil
pinch sea salt
2 to 3 tablespoons organic, gluten-free barbecue sauce

The Wrap:
2 brown rice tortillas, warmed *(see page 88)*
½ cup of hummus
½ cup barbecued onions
1 small carrot, grated
½ small zucchini, shredded
½ cup finely sliced romaine lettuce

1. To make the barbecued onions, remove the skins from the onion, cut in half, and then thinly slice into crescent moons. Heat a large stainless steel skillet over medium heat, add the olive oil, then add the sliced onions and pinch of sea salt.

2. Sauté the onions for about 7 to 10 minutes or until onions are very soft. Remove from heat and stir in barbecue sauce. Onions can be stored in an airtight container in the refrigerator for up to a week.

3. To assemble the wrap, place the tortilla onto a flat surface or a plate. Spread ½ of the hummus evenly over one side of the tortilla. Place ½ of the barbecued onions, shredded carrot, shredded zucchini, and thinly sliced romaine lettuce into a line in the middle of the wrap.

4. Tightly roll, and then cut in half. Serve immediately or wrap in waxed paper for later use.

Autumn Harvest Trail Mix

The walnuts and pumpkin seeds in this mix are rich in essential fatty acids. The figs are a great source of fiber and potassium. Raisins are one of the top sources of the trace mineral, boron, which helps to provide protection against osteoporosis.

MAKES ABOUT 5 CUPS

1 cup raw walnuts
1 cup raw pumpkin seeds
1 cup dried figs
1 cup raisins
2 cups dried apple slices

1. Place all ingredients into a large glass jar and gently shake to combine ingredients.

2. Store in a cool dry place.

Super Antioxidant Trail Mix

The antioxidants in this trail mix are indeed super. Antioxidants are chemicals that have been shown to fight cancer, heart disease, and aging. The almonds provide the antioxidant vitamin E. In fact, ¼ cup of almonds provides nearly half of your daily need for this vitamin. Scientific research has demonstrated that eating almonds daily can significantly lower your risk of heart disease. Dried apricots contain significant amounts of the powerful antioxidant vitamin A. This vitamin quenches free radical damage to cells and tissues. Dark chocolate is high in plant phenols, specifically called cacao phenols. These antioxidants work to reduce free radical damage in the body. In fact, dark chocolate has the highest ORAC (oxygen radical absorbance capacity) value per 100 grams compared to other foods such as raisins, kale, spinach, and broccoli. Blueberries famed antioxidant power comes from phytochemicals called anthocyanidins, which also gives them their dark bluish-purple color. These antioxidants neutralize free radical damage to the collagen matrix of cells and tissues. Remember to always purchase organic, unsulphured, dried fruit and organic dark chocolate. Our favorite brand of chocolate is Dagoba.

MAKES ABOUT 3 CUPS

> **1 cup raw almonds**
> **1 cup dried apricots**
> **one 2-ounce organic dark chocolate bar, cut into chunks**
> **½ cup dried blueberries**

1. Place all ingredients into a large glass jar and gently shake to combine ingredients.

2. Store in a cool dry place.

Brown Rice Crispy Treats

Serve these tasty and nutritious treats to children for an after school snack. They are also great to take with you on a camping or hiking trip. We like to use Erewhon's Gluten-Free Crispy Brown Rice Cereal which can be found at most health food stores. For the chocolate topping, we use Dagoba dark chocolate which is gluten-free.

MAKES ABOUT 15 SQUARES

2 to 3 tablespoons virgin coconut oil
1 cup brown rice syrup
¾ cup almond butter or unsalted peanut butter
1 teaspoon vanilla
6 cups Brown Rice Crispy Cereal

Optional Additions:
¼ cup sesame seeds
½ cup pumpkin or sunflower seeds
½ cup chopped nuts (cashew, almond, walnut)
½ to ¾ cup raisins or dried cranberries

Optional Topping:
organic dark chocolate

> *Ingredient Tip*
>
> If you are gluten-sensitive then be sure to use a rice crispy cereal that is gluten-free, as some brands do contain barley malt which contains gluten.

1. Put coconut oil into a medium-sized saucepan and heat over medium heat. Add brown rice syrup and almond or peanut butter. Heat until tiny bubbles form, stirring constantly with a wire whisk. Immediately take the pot off the heat and add the vanilla. Stir it again.

2. Place brown rice crispy cereal into a large bowl and add any of the optional additions. Pour the hot rice syrup mixture over it. Immediately mix together with a wooden spoon.

3. Pour mixture into a 9 x 13-inch pan and press mixture flat. You may need to place a little coconut oil or water on your hands so the mixture won't stick to them.

4. If you would like to add the chocolate topping, then take desired amount of dark chocolate and place into a heavy-bottomed saucepan over very low heat. Heat until completely melted, stirring occasionally. Then pour over top of crispy treats, spreading evenly with the back of a spoon. Sometimes I top half of the pan with chocolate and leave the other half plain. Cool completely before slicing into bars.

Raw Energy Balls

This is a great snack to take with you on a long hike or a long day at work. You can also add one to your child's lunchbox for a sweet, nutritious treat.

MAKES ABOUT 1 DOZEN BALLS

1 cup raw almonds or walnuts
1 cup medjool dates, pitted
¼ cup raisins
¼ teaspoon cinnamon
¼ teaspoon ground cardamom
¼ cup raw almond butter

shredded organic coconut

1. In a food processor fitted with the "s" blade grind the almonds until finely ground. Add the dates, raisins, and spices. Grind to a fine meal.

2. Add the almond butter, process again until thoroughly mixed.

3. Form into balls and roll in shredded coconut.

4. Store in a sealed container on the counter for up to 3 days, or refrigerate for up to a week.

Popcorn

Once you begin to make your own popcorn, you won't ever want to go back to eating microwave popcorn! Popcorn makers are another popular way of making popcorn, but unfortunately the combination of the heat and the plastic can cause highly toxic plastic compounds to leach into the popcorn. We prefer to use the age old method of cooking the kernels in a large pot over heat. Once cooked, the popcorn can be seasoned in a variety of ways. You can use plain sea salt, Herbamare, nutritional yeast, dried herbs, or even a combination of a little organic butter and maple syrup!

MAKES ABOUT 4 TO 6 SERVINGS

3 to 4 tablespoons virgin coconut oil
½ teaspoon sea salt
1 to 2 cups organic popcorn kernels

1. Heat a large 6 or 8-quart stainless steel pot over medium-high to high heat. Add coconut oil and sea salt.

2. Once the oil has melted, quickly add the popcorn kernels. Cover the pot with a lid, clear glass is preferable here. Shake the pot continuously to prevent burning.

3. The popcorn is done once you here very little popping sounds. Immediately remove pot from the heat source and pour popcorn into a large glass bowl. Season with your favorite seasonings.

Fresh Fruitsicles

This is a great way to use and store the fresh fruit of summer. I like to have many Popsicle molds on hand and make all sorts of different flavor combinations. Popsicle molds can be found at just about any kitchen or toy store in the summer. Using the whole fruit makes for a healthful snack alternative to the sugary popsicles you buy at the store. Below are a few different ideas. Try some, then create your own combinations.

MAKES ABOUT 6 POPSICLES

Strawberry Banana Coconut
    1 to 2 cups fresh strawberries, trimmed
    1 ripe banana, cut into chunks
    ½ cup coconut milk
    2 to 4 tablespoons maple syrup or agave nectar

Strawberry Peach Orange
    1 to 2 cups fresh strawberries, trimmed
    1 ripe peach or nectarine, cut into chunks
    ½ cup fresh squeezed orange juice
    2 to 4 tablespoons maple syrup or agave nectar

Blueberry Cherry Apple
    1 cup fresh blueberries
    1 cup fresh cherries, pitted
    ½ cup apple juice
    2 to 4 tablespoons maple syrup or agave nectar

1. Place all ingredients for popsicles into a blender and blend until smooth.

2. Pour into Popsicle molds. Insert stick, and freeze for 6 to 8 hours, or overnight.

3. To release Fruitsicle from mold simply run under hot water for about 30 seconds or so.

Delicious Drinks

"Age is an issue of mind over matter. If you don't mind,
it doesn't matter."

~Mark Twain

aving a few drink recipes on hand can be a delicious way to add extra
nutrients and phytochemicals to your diet. For example, beverages with
lemons and limes contain numerous anti-cancer compounds, flavonoids,
and a healthy dose of vitamin C. The herbal tea recipes in this chapter are cleansing,
stimulating to the digestive system, and provide a rich source of minerals.

Making your own nut milk is actually very easy and the milk recipes provided in this
chapter can be used in other recipes as well. Nut milks are so versatile and tasty
you'll find that preparing them becomes part of your weekly routine.

Kombucha
fungus japonicus
(Pronounced kum-BOO-sha)

Kombucha is a drink made from tea, sugar, and a special kombucha culture. A kombucha culture looks sort of like a large pancake, though it conforms to fit the shape of the container it is in. The culture itself is a living relationship of different beneficial bacteria and special yeast cultures. The sugar is a simple carbohydrate that provides food for the yeast and bacteria. The tea provides substances that aid in the brewing process: caffeine, oxygen, nitrogen, tannic acid, vitamins, and some minerals. The yeasts break down the sugar and the bacteria then digest the yeast byproducts which create your kombucha brew. After the fermentation process is complete you are left with: probiotics (beneficial bacteria), enzymes, acids (acetic, lactic, ascorbic, glucuronic), alcohol (0.5 %), carbon dioxide and carbonic acid, glucose and other simple sugars (about 5%, depending on how much sugar used), B vitamins, and amino acids. You can order a healthy kombucha culture from **www.culturesforhealth.com***. Though, if you ask around, you are sure to find someone who is willing to give you one.*

MAKES 8 CUPS

> **7 cups purified water**
> **¾ cup organic cane sugar**
> **3 to 4 organic black or green tea bags**
> **1 healthy kombucha culture**
> **1 cup kombucha brew as starter**

1. Start with a clean kitchen. Clean a large glass jar or bowl and set it on the counter. Boil 7 cups of purified water. Place the organic sugar into your jar or bowl. Then pour the boiling water over the sugar and add 2 to 4 organic black or green tea bags. Let steep 15 to 20 minutes. Cool to room temperature.

2. Add your kombucha culture and 1 cup starter brew. Cover jar with a clean cloth or paper towel secured with a rubber band.

3. Let sit in a dark place for 7 to 12 days.

4. Strain your brew into a clean container and store in the refrigerator, reserving 1 cup for your next batch. Start the process again with your kombucha culture.

5. Each time you brew, your culture will "birth" another culture. You can give these away, plant them in your garden for compost, or use them to have a few batches of kombucha brewing at once.

Super Immunity Cocktail

We make this cocktail from late fall through early spring when the cold and flu season is around. Ironically, this is also the same time when we can't get enough vitamin D from the sunshine (for those of you living above the 35th parallel). We will mix it up in a glass then pour it into little shot glasses.

SERVES 1 ADULT OR 2 CHILDREN

> **the juice of 2 Valencia oranges**
> **1 tablespoon pure cod liver oil**
> **two 1000 IU capsules vitamin D**
> **one 200 mcg capsule selenium picolinate**

1. Place all ingredients into a glass and whisk together using a fork.

2. Pour into shot glasses and serve immediately!

Almond Milk

Almond milk can be made raw by simply soaking almonds overnight in a little water which increases their digestibility. My favorite way to use raw almond milk is to pour it over a bowl of uncooked rolled oats and sliced bananas for a late night snack. You can also make smoothies with almond milk. Try blending up some frozen peaches, raspberries, and almond milk for a refreshing and nutritious smoothie.

MAKES ABOUT 3 CUPS

> ½ cup raw almonds
> 3 cups water
> 2 tablespoons maple syrup or 2 pitted medjool dates
> pinch sea salt

1. Place almonds into a small bowl and cover with purified water. Soak at room temperature for about 6 hours or overnight.

2. After the almonds have soaked, rinse them well under warm running water. Place them in a blender with the water, maple syrup or dates, and sea salt. Blend on high for 2 to 3 minutes or until you have a very smooth milk.

3. If you would like it even smoother you can pour the milk through some cheesecloth into a container and squeeze out any remaining liquid.

Cashew Milk

Cashews are a softer nut, and therefore do not need to be soaked overnight to blend well as almonds or hazelnuts do. Use fresh cashew milk to pour over a cooked whole grain cereal for breakfast such as the Warming Three Grain Morning Cereal on page 107 or use it to make fruit smoothies.

MAKES ABOUT 2 ½ CUPS

   ½ cup raw cashews
   2 cups water
   2 to 3 tablespoons maple syrup
   pinch sea salt

1.   Place all ingredients into a blender fitted with a sharp blade.

2.   Blend on high until very smooth. Taste and adjust sweetness if necessary.

Hazelnut Milk

I love the flavor of hazelnut milk; it has a distinctive nutty flavor. Try making smoothies with hazelnut milk. I like to blend up frozen wild blueberries or huckleberries with about 1 cup of hazelnut milk. This raw nut milk is also great drunk on its own.

MAKES ABOUT 3 CUPS

> **½ cup raw hazelnuts**
> **3 cups water**
> **2 tablespoons maple syrup or 2 pitted medjool dates**
> **pinch sea salt**

1. Place raw hazelnuts into a small bowl and cover with water. Soak at room temperature for about 6 hours or overnight.

2. After the hazelnuts have soaked, rinse them well under warm running water. Place them in a blender with the water, maple syrup or dates, and sea salt. Blend on high for 2 to 3 minutes or until you have a very smooth milk.

3. If you would like it even smoother you can pour the milk through some cheesecloth into a container and squeeze out any remaining liquid.

Agave Limeade *with Raspberry Ice Cubes*

This delicious and colorful drink is wonderful for a summer picnic. Children will love to drink the limeade and eat the raspberries from the melted ice cubes. Limes contain flavonoids called, flavonol glycosides, which have been shown to stop cancer cells from dividing. Limes are also an excellent source of vitamin C.

MAKES 4 ¾ CUPS

Limeade:
½ cup freshly squeezed lime juice
¼ cup agave nectar or honey
4 cups water

Ice Cubes:
1 ice cube tray
fresh raspberries
water

1. To make the limeade, place lime juice, agave nectar, and water into a large glass pitcher. Stir well, and adjust sweetness if desired.

2. To make the ice cubes, place one raspberry into each ice cube mold, pour water to cover and place into the freezer. Freeze for 6 hours or overnight.

3. To serve, place the raspberry ice cubes into t he pitcher with the limeade. Serve immediately.

Stevia Lemonade

I like to have a pitcher of this on hand to drink throughout the day. Our children love this drink also. Both lemons and limes contain potent anti-cancer compounds called limonoids, which stop cancer cells from proliferating. Lemons are also an excellent source of vitamin C.

MAKES 4 ½ CUPS

> ½ cup freshly squeezed lemon juice
> 4 cups water
> 1 to 2 teaspoons stevia powder, or to taste

1. Place all ingredients into a large glass pitcher and mix well.

2. Taste and adjust sweetness if necessary.

Hot Mulled Cider

We make this in the fall and winter when the chilly weather has set in. Our children love to drink it. Try and find a local organic apple orchard that sells cider and stock up in the fall when the cider has just been pressed. You can freeze it and use it throughout the season.

MAKES ABOUT 6 CUPS

> **6 cups organic apple cider**
> **2 large organic orange slices**
> **4 to 5 slices fresh ginger**
> **5 cinnamon sticks**
> **2 teaspoons whole cloves**

1. Place all ingredients in a large pot. Simmer, covered, over low to medium-low heat for about 1 hour.

2. Strain out spices by pouring contents through a fine mesh strainer into another pot.

3. You can keep the pot on the stove on warm if you would like to serve it over an extended period of time.

Cocoa Mole Smoothie

This scrumptious smoothie can be served as a drink with any Mexican style meal. Try freezing your peeled ripe banana into small chunks to make the blending easier. The cinnamon is the secret ingredient to this great tasting drink!

MAKES ABOUT 2 CUPS

½ cup raw cashews
1 cup water
1 large frozen banana
1 to 2 tablespoons organic cocoa powder
1 to 2 tablespoons agave nectar
½ to 1 teaspoon cinnamon
¼ teaspoon chili powder, or to taste

1. Place the cashews and water into a blender fitted with a sharp blade. Blend on high until smooth and creamy.

2. Then add the banana chunks, cocoa powder, agave nectar, cinnamon, and chili powder; blend well. Serve immediately.

Cooling Strawberry Orange Smoothie

Serve this simple smoothie in early summer when strawberries are in season. To freeze fresh picked strawberries, simply cut the tops off and place onto a cookie sheet and freeze. When frozen, you can transfer strawberries into a sealed container.

MAKES ABOUT 3 CUPS

> **2 cups frozen strawberries**
> **½ cup frozen peach slices**
> **1 cup freshly squeezed orange juice**
> **2 to 3 tablespoons agave nectar**

1. Place all ingredients into a blender and blend until smooth.

Summer Peach and Ginger Smoothie

This smoothie is a great way to use extra peaches from the summer harvest. The sweetness of the peaches and the spiciness of the ginger provide a wonderful combination.

MAKES ABOUT 2 CUPS

 2 ripe peaches, halved and pits removed
 1 ½-inch piece fresh ginger, peeled and chopped
 ½ cup coconut milk
 2 to 3 tablespoons agave nectar
 1 cup ice cubes

1. Place the peach halves, ginger, coconut milk, and agave nectar into the blender and blend on high until very smooth. Taste and add more agave if necessary.

2. Next, add the ice cubes and blend until desired consistency. Serve immediately.

Cleansing Root Tea

This tea is actually called a decoction because the roots are simmered in water rather than being steeped. Licorice root is an adrenal balancer which is very helpful in times of stress; burdock root helps to purify the blood and stimulate the liver; dandelion root also works to stimulate the liver and purify the blood; and the ginger acts as a powerful anti-inflammatory. I like to drink this tea before bed because your body's mechanisms of detoxification are most active during sleep. Sometimes we like to add a little dried nettles and oat straw after the roots have been simmered.

MAKES ABOUT 3 CUPS

>   1 tablespoon dried licorice root
>   2 tablespoons dried burdock root
>   2 tablespoons dried dandelion root
>   1 tablespoon fresh chopped ginger
>   3 to 4 cups water

1. Place all ingredients into a medium sized stainless steel or glass pot, cover and bring to a gentle boil.

2. Immediately reduce heat to low and simmer for 20 to 30 minutes.

3. Remove from heat and add any leafy herbs such as nettles, oat straw or red clover. Steep for 10 to 20 minutes more with the lid on if you added any extra herbs.

4. Strain through a fine mesh strainer into a wide mouth mason jar. Add agave nectar or honey if desired. Drink as desired; store any unused portions in the refrigerator in a covered jar.

Sweet Nettle Ginger Tea

Nettles are an amazing source of many different minerals. You can harvest nettles in the springtime when the shoots are small and the leaves are tender. Dry nettle leaves in a food dehydrator and store in a glass jar with a tight fitting lid. We like to make this delicious and nourishing tea often; our whole family loves it!

MAKES ABOUT 4 CUPS

1 tablespoon dried licorice root
5 slices fresh ginger
¼ cup dried nettles
4 cups water

1. Place licorice root and ginger into a medium sized stainless steel or glass pot, cover and bring to a gentle boil.

2. Immediately reduce heat to low and simmer for 20 to 30 minutes. Remove from heat and add dried nettles; steep for 10 to 20 minutes, or longer, with the lid on.

3. Strain through a fine mesh strainer into a wide mouth mason jar. Drink as desired; store any unused portions in the refrigerator in a covered jar.

Warming Raspberry Leaf Almond Drink

This drink is intended to nourish breastfeeding mothers, especially immediately following birth and in the early postpartum stage. The fennel seeds and raspberry leaves help to contract the uterus after childbirth and also promote the flow of breast milk. The almonds are very rich and nourishing, providing healthy protein and fats to the new mother. The ginger, cinnamon, and cloves are warming spices that help the digestive systems of both mother and baby.

MAKES ABOUT 6 CUPS

> 6 cups water, divided
> 1 cup raw almonds, ground to a fine powder
> one 2-inch piece fresh ginger, peeled and sliced
> 3 sticks cinnamon
> 4 whole cloves
> 2 teaspoons fennel seeds
> 3 tablespoons dried raspberry leaves
> ⅓ cup honey or to taste

1. Place 4 cups of the water in a pot with the ground almonds and simmer on low for 30 minutes, covered. Be very careful not to let the heat get too high, or the ground almonds and water will boil over, which can make quite a mess!

2. Place the other 2 cups of water in a smaller pot with the ginger, cinnamon sticks, cloves, and fennel seeds and simmer for 30 minutes, covered. Then take the pot off the stove and add the raspberry leaves, let steep for 10 to 20 minutes with the lid on.

3. Strain the herb mixture into a blender and discard the herbs, then add the almond milk mixture and blend at a high speed for a couple of minutes. Add the honey and blend for one more minute. Taste and adjust sweetness if necessary.

4. Strain drink through a fine mesh strainer if desired.

APPENDIX

Measurement Equivalents

1 tablespoon	=	3 teaspoons		
2 tablespoons	=	$\frac{1}{8}$ cup	=	1 ounce
4 tablespoons	=	$\frac{1}{4}$ cup	=	2 ounces
$\frac{1}{3}$ cup	=	5 tablespoons + 1 teaspoon		
$\frac{1}{2}$ cup	=	8 tablespoons	=	4 ounces
1 cup	=	16 tablespoons	=	8 ounces
1 pint	=	2 cups	=	16 ounces
1 quart	=	2 pints or 4 cups	=	32 ounces
1 gallon	=	4 quarts	=	128 ounces

Food Allergy Substitution Charts

Gluten

Ingredient:	Replace with:
Wheat Flour in baking (including spelt, kamut, rye)	Replace 1 cup wheat flour with ⅞ cup gluten-free flour + 2 tablespoons tapioca flour + ¼ teaspoon xanthan gum
Flour for dredging or as a thickener	Use equal amounts of arrowroot powder instead
Tortillas	Use brown rice or corn tortillas instead
Oats	Use certified gluten-free oats instead
Soy Sauce	Use wheat-free tamari instead

Dairy

Ingredient:	Replace with:
Cow's milk	Non-dairy milk (unsweetened works best)
Buttermilk	Use 1 cup soy milk or hemp milk mixed with 1 tablespoon lemon juice
Butter	Use virgin coconut oil or Earth Balance Margarine
Yogurt	Soy yogurt

Eggs

Ingredient:	Replace with:
2 Whole Eggs in baking	Grind 2 heaping tablespoons of flaxseeds in a coffee grinder, then whisk with 5 to 6 tablespoons very hot water. Add this mixture to the batter where you would add the eggs
Scrambled eggs	Sauté crumbled tofu in olive oil with turmeric, salt, and pepper

Soy

Ingredient:	Replace with:
Tamari	Replace ¼ cup tamari with about 1 to 2 teaspoons sea salt or Herbamare mixed with ¼ cup liquid (vegetable stock, citrus, water)
Tofu or Tempeh	Replace with beans, meat, fish, or vegetables
Soy Milk	Vegetable Stock, Hemp Milk, or other non-dairy milk

Hidden Food Sources of GLUTEN

*R*emoving gluten from your diet can be a very challenging experience. It is found in so many things, from stamp adhesives to cereal. By removing processed foods from your diet and replacing them with whole foods, you automatically eliminate many of the hidden food sources of gluten. Luckily these processed foods are not conducive to health, so when you eliminate them from your diet your overall health will likely improve significantly.

- **Baking Powder:** Some brands of baking powder contain gluten. Look for a brand that says "gluten-free" or make your own. Here is the recipe: ¼ cup baking soda + ½ cup cream of tartar + ½ cup arrowroot powder. Place ingredients into a glass jar with a lid and shake gently. Store jar in a cool, dry place.
- **Beer:** Beer and ale are fermented and contain gluten from the wheat and barley from which they are made. Distilled liquors do not contain gluten because the gluten peptides cannot survive the distillation process.
- **Bread:** Bread made with flours such as whole wheat flour, white flour, unbleached flour, all purpose flour, spelt flour, kamut flour, barley flour, and rye flour all contain gluten as well as any sprouted breads containing the sprouted grain flours of wheat, spelt, kamut, barley, and rye.
- **Brown Rice Syrup:** Some brands use barley although Lundberg Brown Rice syrup is gluten-free.
- **Candy:** Wheat flour or starch may be used to prevent sticking during the shaping and handling of candy. Gluten may also be an ingredient in candy.
- **Caramel Color:** In the United States caramel color is made from corn, although caramel color may contain gluten in the form of wheat starch or malt syrup if it was foreign made.
- **Cereal:** Breakfast cereals are often made from wheat, spelt, kamut, barley, and rye. Many cereals, commercial and natural brands, contain malt flavoring, malt syrup, or barley malt. Be sure to read labels.
- **Citric Acid:** Citric acid can be fermented from wheat, corn, molasses, or beets. While corn is the only source used by U.S. manufacturers, about 25% of the citric acid used in food and drinks in the U.S. is imported by from other countries which may use wheat.
- **Coffee:** Some flavored coffee drinks use wheat as a flavor carrier, though pure coffee is gluten-free.
- **Dairy Products:** Some dairy products contain modified food starch which may contain gluten. Products such as yogurt, cottage cheese, and sour cream may contain this starch. In addition malted milk, chocolate milk, and cheese spreads may contain gluten.
- **Dextrin:** In the U.S. dextrin is usually made from corn or tapioca, but it can be made from wheat.

- **Egg Substitutes:** These products are not entirely made of eggs and therefore can contain many additional ingredients, including wheat.
- **Emergen-C:** Some flavors of Alcer Emergen-C vitamin C drink mixes may contain wheat.
- **Flavorings:** Natural flavorings are usually gluten-free, though some flavorings for meat may contain wheat.
- **Flour:** Make sure all flours say Gluten-Free. Even rice flour can be cross-contaminated with gluten when produced in a mill that is not certified gluten-free.
- **Grains:** The cereal grains wheat, spelt, kamut, barley, bulgur wheat, and rye all contain gluten. Gluten-free grains include amaranth, buckwheat, corn, millet, teff, rice and quinoa.
- **Malt:** Malt may be made from barley and therefore could contain gluten.
- **Maltodextrin:** In the U.S. maltodextrin <u>cannot</u> contain gluten unless it is declared on the ingredient label. It is usually made from corn, rice, or potato in the U.S. Foreign-made food products containing maltodextrin may contain gluten.
- **Meat:** Fillers are used in many processed meats including sausages, luncheon meats, and hot dogs and need to be avoided on a gluten-free diet. Also be sure to avoid self-basting turkeys.
- **Miso:** Miso usually contains barley, although some varieties use brown rice. Miso made with brown rice can still contain gluten in the *koji*, which can contain be either barley or wheat. Look for a miso that uses rice koji and is labeled "gluten-free."
- **Modified Food Starch:** This is usually made from corn in the U.S. although it can be made from other ingredients, including wheat, if foreign-made. The contents of the starch should be declared on the label, though these rules do not apply to the pharmaceutical industry where gluten may be used.
- **Non-Dairy Milk:** Some non-dairy milk brands can contain a very small amount of barley malt to which the gluten-sensitive individual can react to. In addition, some brands may also contain wheat. Look for a brand that is labeled "gluten-free."
- **Oatmeal:** Oats are naturally gluten-free although most oats sold in the U.S. may be contaminated with gluten during harvesting, processing, or packaging. Look for Certified Gluten-Free Oats.
- **Packaged Dessert Mixes:** Pudding mixes, cake mixes, frosting mixes, and cake decorations all usually contain gluten. Look for the word gluten-free on the label.
- **Pastas:** Pasta is usually made from semolina flour, or wheat flour which contains gluten. Look for pastas that are made from rice, corn, or quinoa. In addition, look for any pasta labeled as "gluten-free."
- **Seasonings:** Packaged seasoning mixes made from a combination of spices and herbs usually contain wheat flour as a carrier and it may or may not be declared on the label.

- **Soups and Soup Mixes:** Many packaged or canned soups can contain gluten in the form of wheat as a thickener. Bouillon cubes usually contain gluten in the form of wheat being used as a binder.
- **Soy Sauce:** Soy sauce contains wheat. Look for wheat-free Tamari and use it to replace soy sauce.
- **Vegetable Starch:** Vegetable starch or vegetable protein on the ingredient label could mean corn, peanuts, rice, corn, soy, or wheat.
- **Vinegar:** Distilled vinegar made from grains is safe to eat because gluten cannot survive the distillation process, though malt vinegar contains gluten and is not safe to eat. Wine vinegars, brown rice vinegars, and apple cider vinegar are all gluten-free and are safe to consume.
- **Yeast:** Nutritional yeast or brewer's yeast is a by-product of the brewing industry and may or may not contain gluten. You may want to call the manufacturer. Baking yeast used to make bread rise is gluten-free. However, up to 75% of gluten-sensitive people may be yeast sensitive as well.

28 Day Elimination & Detoxification Diet

*E*limination diets have long been known to assist people in finding foods that trigger an immune reaction. Every person is biochemically unique. Some people eat certain foods and feel strong and healthy. Other people eat the same foods and feel weak and sick. If your body reacts poorly to a particular food, you are said to have a "food sensitivity." For decades, health conditions have been attributed to food sensitivities, however health care providers have not always acknowledged this. One of the reasons is that these sensitivities are not IgE-mediated and cannot be confirmed by standard laboratory skin prick tests. However, they can be identified using an elimination diet. The goal of this diet is to find out what foods might be irritating your body through a process of elimination.

When the immune system is over stimulated, many different health conditions can occur. Fibromyalgia, chronic fatigue, psoriasis, eczema, digestive problems, irritable bowel syndrome, chronic migraines, GERD (gastroesophageal reflux disease), anxiety, constipation, diarrhea, arthritis, asthma, sinus problems, and weight gain or weight loss can all be associated with a food-mediated immune reaction. When the food triggers are taken away, the immune system is able to calm down. This allows for normal cellular healing and detoxification to take place.

An elimination diet begins by detoxifying the body from foods that have been causing various health conditions. Providing the body with certain foods during this time can assist with the healing process. After ten days, certain foods are slowly added back in, one at a time, to detect an immune response. Any reactions then are noted.

The following 28-day diet is a strict plan designed to promote cellular healing and to allow for the identification of foods that cause an immune reaction. It is very important to adhere to the diet 100% to gain the desired results. The more you can eliminate the foods that may trigger an immune reaction, the more likely that you will be able to eliminate your symptoms. For example, research on gluten sensitivity has indicated that as little as 100 parts per million of a trigger food can launch an entire immune reaction. As you are trying to determine foods that cause an immune reaction, it will be important for you to question all foods you eat and the ingredients that make up those foods.

Dining out during an elimination diet would be very difficult as most restaurant grills have gluten on them and most restaurant foods have dairy, gluten, egg, corn, or soy contained in baking powders, sauces, spices, and salad dressings. The ideal approach would be to prepare all of your own food for the entire 28 days.

During the first week on this diet, it is possible that you might feel worse before you feel better. Some people have noted flu-like symptoms, lethargy, unusual bowel movements, headaches, joint discomfort, nausea, weakness, and fatigue. This will go away and is most often replaced with more energy, clarity, and a calm digestive system. Many people note that by day 12, they feel better then they have in years.

Tips for elimination diet success:

- Before beginning the diet, discuss it with your family. Sometimes it works best to have someone participate with you (spouse, friend, sister, etc…)

- Plan ahead of time when doing this program. Make sure that it does not fall over a vacation or holiday.

- Keep a journal of your symptoms throughout each phase of this diet. Common symptoms of a food sensitivity include fatigue, nasal congestion, headaches, muscle aches, abdominal pain, joint pain, vomiting, skin rashes, irritability, hyperactivity, and dark circles under the eyes. Symptoms may occur soon after eating, within a few hours, or even two days later.

- Nutritional supplements, over-the-counter medications, and chewing gum can all contain irritating proteins. It is best to closely examine the ingredients and decide if they need to be excluded during this diet.

- Exclude all alcohol, coffee, and cigarettes for the entire 28 days.

- Remember to use purified water for the smoothies and all other recipes.

Getting Started

The first 2 days of this diet begin with a green smoothie fast. That means drinking nothing but green smoothies, pages 97 to 99, and purified water for breakfast, lunch, dinner, and snacks. It is important to make sure the smoothies taste good to you. Therefore, you might want to vary the ingredients you use. Get creative because you are going to be having at least one of these a day for the next 27 days.

Days 1 and 2:

- Diet is initiated by a two day cleanse of pure water and green smoothies without bananas or citrus.

- Tom's Medicine Chest Smoothie, *page 99*. Leave out lemons until day 10. Try using collard greens and spinach in the smoothie until you are used to the flavor. Then you can add cabbage, romaine lettuce, parsley, or any other green that you desire. The greener the better! Adding tart apples and very ripe pears to this smoothie makes it very delicious. Many people will make a fresh blender full every morning to drink throughout the day.

Phase 1

Phase 1 of this diet is about consuming hypo-allergenic foods, such as fresh fruit (excluding strawberries, citrus, kiwis, bananas, and pineapple), steamed vegetables, raw salads with avocado, roasted yams (with olive oil) or steamed sweet potatoes, squash, lentils, adzuki beans, mung beans, quinoa, teff, and brown rice. The goal is to eat whenever you are hungry. All of these foods are nutrient-dense, but very light in calories. You might find that you need to eat quite frequently in order to keep hunger at bay. Continue with the green smoothies and plenty of purified water or mineral water. Snack on organic raw sunflower seeds, raw pumpkin seeds, dried figs, and currants if you need a "trail mix" to get you through.

Days 3 to 9:

- Slow cooked sweet brown rice with wakame seaweed. Use sweet brown rice and add ¼ cup extra water, wakame seaweed, and cook on low heat for over an hour or until a porridge consistency has been reached.

- Cooked teff, *page 106*, or quinoa, *page 217*, with a pinch of sea salt.

- ¼ cup Broccoli Sprouts and/or 2 Dandelion leaves eaten before grain meals.

- Vegetables and fruits eaten freely except potatoes, tomatoes, citrus, eggplant, strawberries, peppers, pineapples, kiwis, and bananas.

- Make sure to eat plenty of avocados, parsley, cabbage, kale, broccoli, cauliflower, collards, Brussels sprouts, pears, cherries, raspberries, and cilantro.

- Add in cooked lentils, mung beans, and adzuki beans which are prepared at home. Canned beans may be cross-contaminated with gluten grains.

- Continue with green smoothies and plenty of purified water and mineral water.

Phase 1 Menu Ideas:

- Tom's Medicine Chest Smoothie, *page 99* (without lemon)

- Bowl of fresh or frozen organic berries (except strawberries)

- Fresh or frozen organic cherries

- Fresh or dried figs

- Fresh Bok Choy, Green Salads, Celery, Carrots, Avocados
  Steamed Kale, Collards, Cabbage, Broccoli, Cauliflower, or Brussels Sprouts

- Basic Brown Rice, *page 214*

- Adzuki Beans, *pages 140 to 143*

- Mung Beans, *pages 140 to 143*

- Mung and Adzuki beans can also be sprouted for a real energy boost.

- Lentils, *pages 140 to 143*

- Luscious Lentil and Brown Rice Casserole (without the red wine vinegar), *page 260*

- Steamed yams and/or sweet potatoes rolled up in Napa cabbage leaves with adzuki beans and avocado

- Freshly cooked grains can be topped with steamed vegetables and avocado slices

Phase 2

Phase 2 is about adding a few potentially reactive foods back into your diet. Pay attention to the nuances of your body and your mind when adding these foods back in. If you notice any uncomfortable changes, then take that particular food out. Do the same with the rest of the foods that you re-introduce.

Days 10 to 15:
- Add in lemons and limes, or recipes containing these for the next 3 days. Ideally, you would consume the suspect food 3 times a day. Add lemons and limes to green smoothies, dressings, marinades, and purified water.

- Try the Lemon and Lentil Soup on *page 150.*

- Look for any adverse reactions like fatigue, headache, joint pain, vomiting, diarrhea, constipation, gas, bloating, eczema or other rashes, fever, foggy thinking, etc. Stop using lemons and limes if you have any reaction. Wait 24 hours, or until symptoms completely calm down before the next step.

- On day 13, if no reaction from lemons and limes, add in recipes with wheat-free tamari, and/or sprinkle the tamari on vegetables, gluten-free grains, and seeds. Look for reactions once again.

- If you have a reaction, stop all tamari and remove from diet. Wait 24 hours or until symptoms completely calm before starting Phase 3.

- If no reactions, then add in all recipes except those containing tofu and tempeh, meat, dairy, corn, eggs, yeast, and gluten.

- Continue with green smoothies and plenty of purified water or mineral water.

Phase 3

This is the time to add in nightshade vegetables, tree nuts, and all beans and soy foods. Start by adding back in nightshade vegetables. Then add in tree nuts. Then add all beans, including soy. If you do well with these, it might be time to try some salmon. Introduce each new food over a three day period.

Day 16 to 28:

- Add in nightshade vegetables (potatoes, tomatoes, peppers, eggplant) for three days.

- Add in tree nuts over a three day period (no peanuts).

- Add in tempeh and tofu recipes for three days. If no reaction, then follow all recipes in this book except those that contain oats, eggs, corn, yeast, and dairy.

- At anytime, if you add a recipe or food item that causes symptoms, remove that item from your diet.

Phase 3 Menu Ideas:

- Lemon Garlic Tempeh, *page 244*

- Tofu marinated in tamari and lemon or lime then sautéed in coconut oil

- Quinoa and Black Bean Salad, *page 234*

- White Bean and Vegetable Stew, *page 270*

- Pine Nut Studded Rice, *page 224*

- Indian Fried Rice, *page 222*

- Raw Energy Balls, *page 354*

- Creamy Cauliflower Soup, *page 162*

- Wild Salmon with Lemon, Garlic, and Thyme, *page 277*

- Indian Chicken Curry, *page 286*

- Cleansing Root Tea, *page 369*

Challenge Potentially Irritating Foods

By now you are probably feeling great. Many people will choose to continue without these foods. If you would like to add these foods back in to see how they react in your body, follow the directions below.

- Add in eggs, dairy, oats, gluten, corn, and yeast **one at a time**.

- Try gluten-free rice bread to test yeast; milk for dairy; certified gluten-free rolled oats for oats; sprouted rye bread for gluten; polenta for corn; and poached or scrambled eggs for eggs.

- Eat these foods three times a day for three days.

- With any reactions, stop immediately and wait for 24 hours or until symptoms subside before challenging the next food.

**For more information on the elimination diet plus new recipes, please visit www.WholeLifeNutrition.net.

Introducing Solid Foods to Infants

*W*hen and what to feed infants is a question many parents ask. Introducing or avoiding certain foods is a very important aspect of keeping an infant's digestive system strong and healthy. Potential allergic reactions may be avoided if proper care is given in this very sensitive period.

Exclusive breastfeeding for at least the first 6 months of life will give your baby's immune system lifelong protection. Breastfeeding keeps the infant's digestive system strong by providing nutrients for a healthy inner ecology. Cow's milk formula or soy-based formula introduced during the first 12 months can disrupt the immune system and increase the chances for allergies or food sensitivities. Sometimes a mother may find herself in an emergent situation where she is unable breastfeed for a period of time. We have known many women who have opted to supplement with breast milk from another breastfeeding mother during this time. This is an ideal arrangement that continues to protect the infant's developing immune system. Though if breast milk is not an option, please talk with your child's physician about a hypoallergenic formula.

Introducing nutritious, whole foods into your infant's diet builds a foundation for life-long healthy eating habits. During the first three years of life, and especially during the first two years, your child's taste buds are developing. This means that your child will get accustomed to the foods you offer. If freshly prepared, vibrant, whole foods are all that is given, your child will naturally be attracted to those types of foods as he grows older. But if highly refined baby cereals, processed, salted foods are offered, then those are the types of foods your child will most likely be attracted to as she grows older. It is much easier to set up the taste buds to desire healthy food, than to try and change later on.

When introducing first foods, freshly made baby food can be easily prepared from organic fruits and vegetables. Vegetables may be steamed, and then pureed with a small amount of purified water to desired consistency. Younger babies need their food fairly thin and watery, while older ones do fine with thicker food. Soft, in-season fruits, such as peaches, plums, pears, apricots, cherries, and melons, can be blended raw to provide useful digestive enzymes. Grains, which are more difficult to digest than vegetables or fruits, are best introduced after 8 or 9 months of age when pancreatic enzymes are more abundantly produced.

Below is an *informal* schedule for introducing solid foods. Keep in mind that each baby may vary in readiness to accept solid foods. The simple ability to sit unassisted, swallow foods, and the maturity of baby's digestive and immune systems are important determining factors. It appears to be very important that solid foods are completely avoided before 6 months of age, and it may be unnecessary to start solids even at this age. Exclusive breastfeeding may continue for 9 to 12 months. By this age, most babies will be quite eager and ready to eat.

When beginning with solid food, it is paramount to **introduce one new food at a time**, while observing for reactions such as sneezing, runny nose, eczema, skin rashes, rash around the mouth or diaper area, changes in stools, or changes in personality. If you notice any of these signs, wait to offer that particular food again for another month.

6 to 9 months:

Focus on hypo-allergenic foods such as steamed, pureed vegetables and pureed soft fruits. Start out with 1 to 2 tablespoons of food per day. Some babies do fine also with berries at this stage. Frozen berries can be placed into the mesh feeding bags for teething.

- **winter squash (including pumpkin)**
- **yam or sweet potato**
- **summer squash (zucchini, patty pan, crookneck)**
- **applesauce (I make my own by gently cooking peeled apple slices and then pureeing them in a blender into a smooth sauce)**
- **banana**
- **prunes**
- **broccoli**
- **Jerusalem artichoke**
- **cauliflower**
- **cherries**
- **apricots**
- **peaches & nectarines**
- **plums**
- **pears**
- **melons**
- **carrots**
- **beets**
- **parsnips**
- **green peas**

8 to 9 months:

Focus on hypo-allergenic, pureed foods. Increase quantities of foods as infant's appetite suggests. When introducing whole grains, it is best to soak them overnight in purified water to improve digestibility. The water can be drained off in the morning, and the grains can be then be cooked according to directions of page 212. Adding extra water and cooking for a longer period of time will further improve the digestibility of whole grains.

- quinoa (cooked and pureed)
- millet (cooked and pureed or Morning Millet Cereal, *page 103*)
- brown rice (cooked and pureed or Sweet Rice Cereal, *page 104*)
- avocado
- kiwi
- dulse flakes (added to foods for extra minerals)

9 to 12 months:

Focus on low allergen foods that help to develop chewing, swallowing, and the pincer grasp. Puffed brown rice is a fun snack that helps to develop the pincer grasp. Cut soft fruits, beans, or potatoes into small chunks or lightly mash. Freshly made fruit and green smoothies are particularly nutritious and easy to digest; these can be introduced at 9 months. Non-dairy and gluten-free hemp milk and rice milk can be introduced at this stage. They can be used in recipes where non-dairy milk is called for or sipped on in small amounts, though they are not a substitute for breast milk. Increase quantities of foods as infant's appetite suggests.

- oatmeal (from gluten-free oats)
- potato
- cabbage
- kale (pureed)
- collard greens (pureed)
- lettuce (pureed)
- Green Smoothies (made without lemon), *pages 97 through 99*
- string beans
- blueberries
- raspberries / blackberries
- cranberries (best to soak dried cranberries in water before feeding)
- papaya
- lima beans
- split pea soup (cooked without salt)
- Oatmeal Blueberry Banana Pancakes, *page 110*
- pumpkin seeds (ground to a powder and added to foods or pumpkin seed butter)
- sunflower seeds (soaked and pureed with food or ground to a powder)
- blackstrap molasses (added to foods in small amounts for extra iron)
- nori seaweed (eaten plain as a snack for extra minerals)
- hemp milk
- rice milk
- virgin coconut oil
- extra virgin olive oil
- kudzu (try Cherry Apple Pudding, *page 320*)

12 to 18 months:

Focus on foods higher in bulk and calories. Continue to watch for signs of food allergy/sensitivity reactions as stated above. Lemons and limes may be introduced in small amounts. Tofu is best introduced closer to 18 months. Keep in mind that some infants may react to these and to watch for signs.

- **grapes (cut up)**
- **Swiss chard**
- **spinach**
- **asparagus**
- **onions**
- **garlic**
- **tomatoes**
- **eggplant**
- **bell peppers**
- **strawberries**
- **Hummus,** *page 297*
- **cooked beans**
- **kombu seaweed**
- **lentils**
- **tofu (cut into little cubes and boiled in water or sautéed in olive oil with a dash of tamari)**
- **buckwheat**
- **lemon**
- **lime**
- **goat milk**

18 to 24 months:

Focus on foods high in protein and calories to support growth. Soak whole nuts overnight in purified water to aid in digestion and chewing. Meats are best slow cooked in soups or stews to aid in digestion.

- **soy foods**
- **turkey**
- **lamb**
- **chicken**
- **fish**
- **eggs**
- **almond butter**
- **cashew butter**
- **almonds**

- cashews
- pecans
- Brazil nuts
- walnuts
- oranges
- pineapple
- brewer's yeast

2 to 3 years:

Introduce allergenic foods one at a time and watch for a reaction. If a reaction occurs, remove the food from child's diet and wait at least one month before trying again.

- gluten (wheat, spelt, kamut, rye, barley)
- cow's milk and other dairy products
- corn
- beef
- clams and other shellfish
- peanuts and peanut butter

Useful Resources

*T*he following books and websites can further your knowledge on topics that we have discussed in this book. Though many of them focus on health and wellness, few are 100 % gluten-free.

Books on Cooking

Extraveganza: Original Recipes from Phoenix Organic Farm, Laura Matthias

Food Allergy Survival Guide: Delicious Recipes and Complete Nutrition, Vesanto Melina, MS, RD, Jo Stepaniak, MSEd, and Dina Aronson, MS, RD

Food to Live By: The Earthbound Farm Organic Cookbook, Myra Goodman

GRUB: ideas for an urban organic kitchen, Anna Lappé and Bryant Terry

The Chopra Center Cookbook: Nourishing Body and Soul, Deepak Chopra, MD, David Simon MD, and Leanne Backer

The Splendid Grain: Robust, Inspired Recipes for Grains with Vegetables, Fish, Poultry, Meat & Fruit, Rebecca Wood

The Stevia Cookbook: Cooking with Nature's Calorie-Free Sweetener, Donna Gates and Ray Sahelian, MD

Wild Fermentation: The Flavor, Nutrition, and Craft of Live-Culture Foods, Sandor Ellix Katz

Books on Health

Eat Fat, Lose Fat: The Healthy Alternative to Trans Fats, Dr. Mary Enig and Sally Fallon

Fast Food Nation: The Dark Side of the All-American Meal, Eric Schlosser

Food and Healing: How what you eat determines your health, your well-being, and the quality of your life, Annemarie Colbin

Green for Life, Victoria Boutenko

Healing with Whole Foods: Asian Traditions and Modern Nutrition, Paul Pitchford

Healthy at 100: The Scientifically Proven Secrets of the World's Healthiest and Longest-Lived Peoples, John Robbins

Hope's Edge: The Next Diet for a Small Planet, Frances Moore Lappé and Anna Lappé

Seeds of Deception: Exposing Industry and Government Lies about the Safety of Genetically Engineered Foods, Jeffery Smith

Textbook of Functional Medicine, Institute for Functional Medicine

The Body Ecology Diet: Recovering Your Health and Building Your Immunity, Donna Gates with Linda Schatz

The China Study: The Most Comprehensive Study of Nutrition Ever Conducted and the Startling Implications for Diet, Weight Loss and Long-term Health, T. Colin Campbell, PhD and Thomas M. Campbell II

The Coconut Oil Miracle, Bruce Fife, CN, ND

The Encyclopedia of Healing Foods: A User Friendly Guide to the Nutritional Benefits and Medicinal Properties of Foods, Michael Murray, N.D. and Joseph Pizzorno, N.D., with Lara Pizzorno, M.A., LMT

The New Whole Foods Encyclopedia: A Comprehensive Resource for Healthy Eating, Rebecca Wood

The Slow Down Diet: Eating for Pleasure, Energy, and Weight Loss, Marc David

Total Wellness: Improve Your Health by Understanding and Cooperating with Your Body's Natural Healing Systems, Joseph Pizzorno, N.D.

Ultra Metabolism: The Simple Plan for Automatic Weight Loss, Mark Hyman, MD

Web Resources

www.celiac.com - View this site for a list of "Safe and Forbidden Gluten-Free Foods and Ingredients" and other information related to celiac disease and gluten intolerance.

www.gluten.net -This is the website of the Gluten Intolerance Group. Check out this site to find a group in your area.

www.celiac.nih.gov - This is the official website of the US government on celiac disease and gluten sensitivity.

www.glutenfreemall.com - Shop for hundreds of gluten-free products here.

www.glutenfreeoats.com - Shop for Certified Gluten-free Oats here.

www.creamhillestates.com - Shop for Certified Gluten-Free Oats here.

www.vegsource.com - Get more information here on a plant-based diet. This site also contains excellent video footage of world renowned nutrition experts speaking on the benefits of a whole foods diet.

www.whfoods.com - The World's Healthiest Foods website offers the latest scientific information about the benefits of the World's Healthiest Foods and the specific nutrients they provide. They also offer practical, simple, and affordable ways to enjoy them and fit them into your individual lifestyle.

www.informedeating.org - The Center for Informed Food Choices (CIFC) advocates for a diet based on whole, unprocessed, local, organically grown plant foods. CIFC believes that placing these foods at the center of the plate is crucial for promoting public health, protecting the environment, and assuring the humane treatment of animals and food industry workers.

www.ewg.org - Environmental Working Group, or EWG is a nonprofit research organization based in Washington, D.C., that uses the power of information to protect human health and the environment.

www.organicconsumers.org - The Organic Consumers Association is a grassroots non-profit public interest organization campaigning for health, justice, and sustainability. The OCA deals with crucial issues of food safety, industrial agriculture, genetic engineering, children's health, corporate accountability, Fair Trade, environmental sustainability and other key topics.

www.pesticide.org - The Northwest Coalition for Alternatives to Pesticides protects the health of people and the environment by advancing alternatives to pesticides.

www.foodsecurity.org - The Community Food Security Coalition is a non-profit organization dedicated to building strong, sustainable, local and regional food systems that ensure access to affordable, nutritious, and culturally appropriate food for all people at all times.

www.wholefoodsmarket.com - The world's leading natural and organic foods supermarket. Check the site to find a store near you.

www.coopdirectory.org - To find a food co-op in your area, search this site.

www.localharvest.org - Providing a comprehensive list of local food sources, CSA's, food co-ops, and more across the country.

Quick Recipe Reference Guide

Breakfast

Fresh Breads & Muffins

Soups

Fresh Salads and Vegetables

Whole Grains

Vegetarian Main Dishes

Fish, Poultry, & Meat

Dressings, Dips, & Sauces

Nutritious Desserts

Index

Oven Fries, 205

Cook's Notes

Cook's Notes

_____

_____

_____

_____

_____

_____

_____

_____

_____

_____

_____

_____

Cook's Notes

Cook's Notes

Whole Life Nutrition is located in beautiful Bellingham, Washington and offers Nutritional Counseling, Cooking and Nutrition Classes, Health Food Store Tours, and Support Groups to supply the necessary life skills needed to make lasting, positive change a reality.

For more information on Whole Life Nutrition, including new recipes, nutrition information, updates, and upcoming events, please visit **www.wholelifenutrition.net**